LEXICOGRAPHICA Series Maior

LEXICOGRAPHICA

Series Maior

Supplementary Volumes to the International Annual for Lexicography
Suppléments à la Revue Internationale de Lexicographie
Supplementbände zum Internationalen Jahrbuch für Lexikographie

Edited by
Sture Allén, Pierre Corbin, Reinhard R. K. Hartmann,
Franz Josef Hausmann, Ulrich Heid, Oskar Reichmann,
Ladislav Zgusta

122

Published in cooperation with the Dictionary Society of North America (DSNA) and the European Association for Lexicography (EURALEX)

Marta Chromá

Legal Translation and the Dictionary

Max Niemeyer Verlag
Tübingen 2004

To Ladislav Zgusta

Bibliografische Information der Deutschen Bibliothek

Die Deutsche Bibliothek verzeichnet diese Publikation in der Deutschen Nationalbibliografie; detaillierte bibliografische Daten sind im Internet über *http://dnb.ddb.de* abrufbar.

ISBN 3-484-39122-7 ISSN 0175-9264

Gedruckt auf alterungsbeständigem Papier.
Druck: Laupp & Göbel GmbH, Nehren
Einband: Verlags- und Industriebuchbinderei Nädele, Nehren

Table of contents

Foreword VII

I. Introduction 1

II. Law dictionary and the language of the law 3

1. Objectives of the Dictionary 3
1.1. Defining target users 5

2. Legal framework 6
2.1. Validity of Czech legislative texts 7
2.2. Differences between legal systems 9
2.2.1. Quantitative comparison with other legal systems 10
2.3. Differences among English-speaking countries 11

3. Linguistic framework 13
3.1. LSP, LLP and Terminology 13
3.1.1. LSP and LLP 13
3.1.2. Terminology 15
3.1.2.1. Definition of the term 17
3.1.2.2. Functional subcategorization of terms 19
3.1.2.3. Grammatical subcategorization of terms 20
3.1.2.4. Terminological phrasemes 29
3.1.2.5. Synonymy in terminology 31
3.1.2.6. Homonymy *versus* polysemy in terminology 33
3.1.2.7. Jargon and terminology 34
3.2. Linguistics of Translation 37
3.2.1. Genre-based approach to translation of legal texts 41
3.2.1.1. The Czech language as the target language 42
3.2.1.2. The Czech language as the source language 45
3.2.2. Levels of translation 47
3.2.3. The issue of equivalence 50
3.2.3.1. Functional equivalence 54
3.2.3.2. Interference 57
3.2.3.3. Lacunas 58

4. Lexicographical framework 59
4.1. Theory of lexicography 59
4.2. Conceptual dictionary 63
4.3. Types of explanations 68
4.4. Collection of material and entry-processing 71
4.4.1. Headword 72
4.4.2. Exemplification 74
4.4.3. Formatting an entry 75
4.5. Software and Statistics 80

III. Conclusion 81
1. Summary of findings 81
2. Implications for future research 83
2.1. Applied linguistics 83
2.2. Lexicography 83

IV. Zusammenfassung 84

V. Résumé 99

VI. Bibliography 113

Foreword

The last decade of the 20th century saw an extensive reconstruction of the whole society after fifty years of totalitarian regimes in former Czechoslovakia. The law resumed its key role during the restoring of democratic stability in the country and it became open to inspiration and influence from abroad. Intensive international communication recommenced but only a few people were able to interact in legal foreign languages. Almost no bilingual law dictionaries were available that might serve the new needs of legal professionals, translators and general public. For teachers of foreign languages in law schools it was necessary to study the basics of law in the country or countries of their foreign language to satisfy their students' zeal for linguistic competence in foreign law. The first concrete product of my study was a students' preliminary edition of the *English-Czech Law Dictionary* in 1993, followed by its regular hardback and electronic versions in 1995. The next five years were devoted to the writing of the *Czech-English Law Dictionary with Explanations* published in 2001. Since the work on the dictionary was not only exciting but also inspiring and instructive with regard to the comparison of how the language and the law function in both systems I have decided to share my experience with others who may be contemplating doing similar work involving their native (not widely spoken) language and law on the one hand and English and Anglo-American systems of law on the other. This treatise outlines basic aspects and features of linguistics and law that were dealt with in the course of the dictionary-making as well as lexicographical approaches towards some more complex problems.

I would like to express my sincere gratitude and thanks to all those who contributed their comments, practical help, and – especially – moral support. To name but a few, I would like to begin by expressing my deep appreciation to Professor Zgusta for his valuable advice and comments. My thanks belong to Professor Šarčević for her inspiring email correspondence on the language of law and the role of legal translation, and to Professor Bhatia, Professor Candlin and Professor Gotti for their comments and support within the GILD project (Generic Integrity in Legal Discourse in Multilingual and Multicultural Contexts) which helped me to understand interlinking factors between research into genres and lexicography. Much thanks is also owed to Jana Dvořáková, Deborah Thackray and Renata Hrubá, my colleagues at the Department of Foreign Languages at the Charles University Law School in Prague, for their reading through of the whole text and providing insightful comments.

To my family I would like to express my sincerest thanks for their tolerance and support during all those years of life with dictionaries.

Finally, I would like to express my gratitude to Dr. Thomas Ehlen and Norbert Alvermann of Max Niemeyer Verlag in Tübingen for their supportive approach.

June 2004

Marta Chromá

I. Introduction

Although the modern history of Czech bilingual lexicography, where the Czech language serves as either the target language (TL) or the source language (SL), dates back to the first half of the 19th century (Josef Jungmann's "Czech-German Dictionary" in 5 volumes, 1834–1839)[1], substantial developments in comparative lexicology were made after World War I. As is well-known, the Czechoslovakia of that time became a centre of modern philology and linguistics, represented, in particular, by the Prague Linguistic Circle established in the 1920s. It was the inspirational atmosphere of the Prague School of (functional) Linguistics that encouraged some members of the Circle and linguists attached to it to engage in the branch of applied linguistics we today call 'languages for specific / special purposes' (LSP). The branch was termed 'hospodářská lingvistika' (linguistics for business purposes, Wirtschaftslinguistik), and the language was called 'hospodářský jazyk' (language for business purposes, or commercial language, Fachsprache).

The new linguistic branch developed particularly in relation to the establishment of a new type of post-secondary school, namely the commercial college (C. 'obchodní akademie')[2]. Soon it became obvious that just general purpose knowledge of foreign languages was insufficient for the envisaged future professional needs of commercial college graduates. Similar developments occurred in German-speaking countries and Holland (Picht and Draskau, 1985: 26). Attempts were made to describe and analyse specific features of the commercial language, particularly from a functional perspective (Kopeckij, 1935; Vančura, 1934).[3] It is sometimes said that those involved in this branch of applied linguistics created the Prague School of Terminology (Felber, 1982: 121).

World War II interrupted the promising developments and achievements of the Prague Linguistic Circle,[4] and, consequently, of languages for specific purposes. Although most pre-war initiatives and activities were condemned to bare survival or were totally prohibited under the communist regime after 1948, the tradition of the functional approach had become firmly rooted in language studies at Czech and Slovak universities.

In the early 1950s, the first departments of foreign languages were set up in the Czechoslovak universities in order to teach Russian as a compulsory subject, and, as optional subjects, other foreign languages for specific purposes to all students regardless of their field

---

1 Jungmann's main intention was to introduce the Czech language as a highly developed, stable and rich means of communication to the German-speaking population of the Habsburg empire. English-Czech lexicography is represented by "A complete pronouncing dictionary of the English and Bohemian languages, for general use" compiled by Karel Jonáš (Charles Jonas), and published in Prague in 1892. The "Bohemian-Czech Interpreter" by the same author was published in Chicago in 1865. Jonas also published the "Czech-English and English-Czech Dictionary" in the USA in 1889. In 1906 the "English-Czech Dictionary" by V. A. Jung was published in Prague.

2 "C." in the beginning of bracketed information stands for "in Czech"; similarly, "E." stands for "in English".

3 Lexicography of that time is represented by the "Czech-English Dictionary" written by H. T. Cheshire, V. A. Jung et al. and published in two volumes by J. Otto Publishers in 1933–1935. This dictionary was based on the "Czech-English Dictionary" written by V. A. Jung, which was never completed due to the sudden death of the author.

4 Nikolaj Trubeckoj died in Vienna in 1938, Vilém Mathesius in 1945, and Roman Jacobson left Prague at the beginning of World War II and settled in the USA in 1945.

of study. These departments were established primarily to teach non-linguist students (such as students of medicine, law or mechanical engineering) the foreign languages of their subject-area. They were independent of departments of language and literature (such as an English language and literature department) established at philological schools of Czech universities in the 19th century.[5] These departments of foreign languages became the main centres of research in languages for specific purposes and applied linguistics for both pedagogical purposes and specialist lexicography. Thus, since the 1960s, bilingual dictionaries of terminology relating to business and commerce, medicine, many spheres of engineering and technology, chemistry and numerous other disciplines have been published.

However, before 1990 little work had been done in the field of bilingual legal lexicography[6]. The Department of Foreign Languages of the Law School of Charles University in Prague undertook a research project between 1984–1989, aimed at producing bilingual lexicons featuring frequently used terminology, which were intended to assist law students during their legal foreign language courses. The lexicons, called "lexical minima", were divided into thirteen branches of law and contained the most frequently encountered terminology in each branch. Four variations of such lexicons were created: Russian-Czech, German-Czech, French-Czech and English-Czech.[7] After 1990, the Russian language ceased to be the only compulsory language for specific purposes to be studied by all students at Czech universities, and a new era commenced in both LSP research and bilingual lexicography.

---

5 The first department was constituted at Karl-Ferdinand University in Prague in 1872.

6 The Russian-Czech law dictionary was compiled by E. Hušková (Rusko-český terminologický slovník pro právníky, Praha: SPN 1957) as a regular bilingual dictionary for nation-wide use.

7 Kopecká, A., Linhartová, A.: Anglicko-česká tematická lexikální minima I, II (SPN, Praha 1987) (English-Czech Subject-Area Lexicon I, II)
Tomanová, J., Horálková, M.: Německo-česká tematická lexikální minima I, II (UK, Praha 1985) (German-Czech Subject-Area Lexicon I, II)
Olšovská, M., Pravda, M.: Francouzsko-česká tematická lexikální minima I, II (SPN, Praha 1986) (French-Czech Subject-Area Lexicon I, II)
Zimová, J. a kol.: Rusko-česká tematická lexikální minima I, II (SPN, Praha 1984) (Russian-Czech Subject-Area Lexicon I, II)
Zimová, J., Koníčková, N.: Příruční rusko-český slovník obecné, obecněvědní a obecněprávní slovní zásoby v právnických textech I, II (SPN, Praha 1989) (Concise Russian-Czech Dictionary of General, Formal and Legal Vocabulary in Legal Texts)

II. Law dictionary and the language of the law

1. Objectives of the Dictionary

The writing of the "Czech-English Law Dictionary with Explanations" (C. "Anglicko-český právnický slovník s vysvětlivkami", abbreviated as CELDE) is the outcome of several professional activities relating to law: teaching English for law to Czech law students and legal practitioners (judges, attorneys, legislators, notaries, and so on); teaching the basics of Czech law, legal Czech, Anglo-American law and legal English to Czech students of, as well as practitioners engaged in, translation and interpreting; our own translating and interpreting activities; and, finally, previous lexicographical experience in writing the English-Czech Law Dictionary. Hartmann (1989: 14) uses the term 'purpose-specificity' to denote a common feature of all these activities: language teaching for particular learner groups, translation for particular requirements, specialized dictionaries for particular needs; particular means focused on law, law-related and law-oriented.

The main objective of the comparative study which led to the creation of the "Czech-English Law Dictionary with Explanations" is to help all those trying to translate Czech legal texts into English so that such translations can be both linguistically and legally correct, precise and accurate. A translated text should be comprehensible to those lawyers who are native speakers of English and whose legal system is based on Common Law. In making this bilingual legal dictionary an attempt has been made to apply what Susan Šarčević (1989a: 290) terms conceptual analysis. The core of the analysis is to compare legal concepts in both the source and target languages in order to measure the degree of equivalence between potential equivalent terms. Šarčević's conclusions will be discussed later.

Another aim of the CELDE is to contribute to the unification of different approaches towards translating Czech legal texts into English. Standardization (or codification in the terminology of the Prague Circle) of English translation equivalents of Czech legal terminology (both linguistic and subject-matter) seems to be crucial particularly in view of the accession of the Czech Republic to the European Union, where even before the enlargement on 1st May 2004, the 15 legal systems of the 15 member states and their 12 official languages created a bewildering amount of day-to-day work for professional translators. However, as Barnhart (1980: 39) argues, the question that should be asked is "In what ways is this dictionary authoritative?", knowing that no dictionary can be authoritative in all respects. The user of the dictionary must evaluate in his own mind the areas of competence of the dictionary he is consulting.

Thirdly, we have tried to map basic characteristic features of the Czech legal language including "deviations" from the general Czech language norm / standard.[1] One example can be given here: the term *odvolání* (E. 'appeal') is combined with the preposition *proti* (E. 'against') in general Czech. Such a prepositional collocation is of a standard nature both in general and legal Czech and may be combined with any noun or nominal phrase denoting an

---

[1] Traditionally, there are two clearly defined varieties of the Czech language: (a) "literary", i.e. standardized or codified Czech (C. 'spisovná čeština') supposedly taught at schools and required to be used in regular written texts of any kind, with the exception of fiction, and as a spoken language of instruction or for any other official purpose, and (b) common Czech (C. 'nespisovná čeština', 'obecná čeština'), i.e. a primary and wide-spread spoken variety of the national language.

act or decision that may be appealed against (*odvolání proti rozsudku* – E. 'an appeal against the judgment', *odvolání proti zamítnutí stížnosti* – E. 'an appeal against the dismissal of complaint', etc.). However, in legal Czech, there are two other prepositions quite regularly linked with *odvolání*, i.e. *z* (E. 'from') and *do* (E. 'to') combined almost exclusively with the decision of court. The phrases *odvolání ‹z› rozsudku*[2] and *odvolání ‹do› rozsudku* denote exactly the same concept and have the same legal effect as *odvolání ‹proti› rozsudku*. We tend to contend that the former two collocations (*odvolání z rozsudku* and *odvolání do rozsudku*) belong to a legal jargon, which will be discussed later. In legal English we can find an equivalent preposition for the Czech *odvolání z rozsudku*, i.e. 'an appeal from judgment'; although the search in our corpus of various English legal texts, consisting of about 2 million words, suggests that the English collocation 'an appeal from' /a judgment, decision/ is far more frequent than the Czech 'odvolání z' /rozsudku/, it belongs to standard legal language (i.e. unlike in the Czech law, it is a part of statutory language, for example, the Criminal Alien Deportation Amendments of 1990, sec. 4(5)(a)(iii) in the USA, or the Criminal Appeal Act 1995, sec. 7(2)(b) in the UK), and in its usage it serves, along with the primary phrase 'appeal against', as a counterpart to the Czech *odvolání proti rozsudku*. The Czech preposition *do* in the phrase *odvolání do rozsudku* has no equivalent counterpart in English, however the whole phrase can be freely translated as 'an appeal against a judgment' without any shifts in the legal sense.

Finally, our objective has been to find authentic equivalents in the Anglo-American system of law for words and concepts which seem to have been previously poorly translated from Czech into English. A frequently used Czech phrase *právní subjekt* has often been mistakenly translated into English as 'legal subject', primarily because in both Czech and English the noun (E. 'subject', C. 'subjekt') is a polyseme, and interlanguage interference contributes to the incorrect choice of terminological equivalents. The Oxford English Dictionary provides 18 main meanings, of which only one is assigned to law. This legal meaning is divided into three sub-meanings:

(a) a thing over which a right is exercised;
(b) a piece of property (in Scottish law);
(c) considered as the object of an agreement.

None of the above corresponds to the legal meaning of the Czech *subjekt* nor may it be combined with the attribute 'legal' in the sense of the Czech phrase. The English word 'subject' in its legal meaning can only be translated by the Czech legal term *předmět*. The comprehensive dictionary of the Czech language[3] provides three meanings of the Czech word *subjekt*, one of which applies to law and denotes 'an individual'. Czech law defines *právní subjekt* as a person (termed 'natural person') or entity ('artificial person') capable of entering into a legal relationship and thus acquiring rights and undertaking duties recognized by law. Such a definition corresponds to the English term 'legal person', which is the only appropriate equivalent of the Czech binominal term considering both the linguistic and legal aspects of the translation. The English term 'legal subject' can only be understood as a subject-matter of a contract which is in accordance with a statute and can be translated into Czech as an explicative terminological phrase with a postmodifying attribute *předmět /smlouvy/ v souladu se zákonem*.

---

2 Symbols ‹ › are used to make problematic letters, endings or affixes optically distinct from the rest of a word.

3 Bohuslav Havránek a kol. (1989): *Slovník spisovného jazyka českého* (Praha: Academia)

1.1. Defining target users

The definition of the user group is widely recognized as one of the most influential factors of lexicographical decision-making at the pre-lexicographical stage (Atkins 1993: 12). Malkiel (1980: 55) sees the second major partner of a lexicographer to be "the society at large – the group of average citizens of widely, even wildly, varying degrees of formal education and sophistication". Although such an assertion would fully apply to the users of a monolingual dictionary, it should not be understood in its literal sense when we speak about a bilingual, or translational, dictionary for specific purposes. It may be admitted, however, that potential users of the dictionary would constitute an aggregate diversified in motivation (why to consult the dictionary), and heterogeneous in their previous experience (in the language and law). Finally, our experience supports the observation by Piotrowski (1990: 277) that, referring to the arrangement and labeling in a dictionary, the average user "usually does not want any changes in the dictionaries he has been accustomed to" and "generally hardly ever uses sophisticated codes and conventions." Such observation underlies our approach to the formatting of dictionary entries although we could reasonably expect that the users of the CELDE would be university graduates possessing some basic skills to work with dictionaries.

As emphasized above, the primary objective of the dictionary has been to assist those who deal with Czech legal texts in trying to understand and transfer them into (legal) English. Potential users can generally be subdivided into two major sets of individuals: those primarily educated as linguists and usually without any legal background (mainly translators and interpreters, but also Czech teachers of legal English), and graduates of, or students at, law schools, usually lacking formal linguistic education. In addition, there are numerous dictionary users who are neither linguists nor lawyers (such as journalists). For these users, their educational background may be unrelated to either law or to the English language but their professional careers have brought them to a field relating to, and dealing with, law. Our experience has suggested, however, that anyone who intends to indulge in the language of law, thus becoming a possible user of the dictionary, should possess at least a solid intermediate knowledge of English (as a native Czech), or a solid intermediate knowledge of Czech if he or she is a native speaker of English (or any other language using English as a means of communication).

The most frequent reason why a Czech lawyer might consult the dictionary would be his or her intention to explain the relevant particulars of Czech law to a client or colleague coming from another country who speaks English (either as a native or second language). Teachers of legal English would use the dictionary with the same motivation (i.e. explaining the Czech legal reality) but with a different audience (students of law). Translators and interpreters would use the dictionary when transferring a Czech legal text into English, trying to be as precise and accurate in their communication as possible. Journalists may search for specific information when they need to understand specific legal facts and comment on them. Whichever subgroup a user of the dictionary belongs to, he or she will look for more than mere law taxonomies. The specific contexts of individual branches of law, larger syntactical units, explanations of polysemic (or polysemous) terms and concepts, and so on, would be useful tools to assist their orientation in the language of law.

It should be noted, however, that translators and interpreters form a user group of a specific type and ultimate significance. They assist the process of transposing one legal system (or its elements) into another legal language and system thus facilitating international collaboration among individuals or entities. Many of them act upon the state license of a "court interpreter"[4] granted by the Ministry of Justice of the Czech Republic. The official round seal they attach to their products should guarantee that their translation is linguistically and legally correct and accurate. It should be admitted, however, that the expected guarantee is quite frequently unjustified and unreasonable. To eliminate uncertainty in translators' and interpreters' clients the emphasis should be placed on professional competence in relation to law and linguistic proficiency in the legal language of both the source language and the target language, in addition to a perfect knowledge of both general languages. As Picht and Draskau (1985: 20, 21) emphasize, the acquisition of the language for specific purposes is compulsory for those employed in the special field and mediators of texts with a professional content (e.g. translators). They extended Picht's earlier demand that translators should have been trained in terminology (Picht 1982: 172), which forms only a minor portion of a specialist language.

Moreover, as Varantola (1998: 189) argues, translators try to find non-dictionary type information in dictionaries because it is not readily and systematically available from other sources; they also need information relating to longer stretches of text than a single lexical item. Supporting such opinion, Rogers and Ahmad (1998: 195) maintain that "translators might justifiably expect specialised dictionaries to codify the conceptual, grammatical and pragmatic information which is observable in language use by experts, technicians, marketing specialists, and so on, and in some cases, to normalise their use". It can be added here that the expectations of legal translators with respect to bilingual dictionaries depend upon their previous experience in the field of law: those with a longer history of translating legal texts will look for larger syntactic units as they can recognize their semantic autonomy; beginners will still try to identify every single word and look for their TL equivalents.

2. Legal framework

There are many potential problems in the translation of legal texts from Czech into English and these problems, in summary, can be seen as resulting from the three issues explained below:

(a) Czech legal terminology, as well as the whole legal discourse, has been unstable, developing, expanding, exposed to substantial foreign law influence, and out of strict legal and linguistic control since 1990 when the totalitarian regime collapsed;

(b) systemic and conceptual differences between Continental Law, upon which Czech law is based, and Common Law, one of the main sources of the Anglo-American system of law, should induce translators to not only intersemiotic (translation) analysis but necessarily to intrasemiotic analysis (Tomášek 1991: 153), i.e. semantic and legal interpretation of the source text; and

(c) the Anglo-American system of law comprises five quantitatively major legal systems – those of the USA, the UK, Ireland, Canada and Australia – and dozens of others which employ English as the official language and whose legal systems have been based on Common Law (such as former and recent members of the Commonwealth, or Scotland), and thus an extensive synonymy of English legal terms may be reasonably expected.

---

[4] There are more designations of these licensed translators: sworn interpreter, certified translator or interpreter, forensic interpreter. All these names suggest that a certain official procedure must have been gone through, in order to be so appointed.

European Community and European Union law and the *acquis communautaire*[5] written in English have been another source of equivalents in law as well as language. However, due to the fluctuating quality of translations, this source has not always been reliable and trustworthy. Moreover, the terminology of European law (as the vocabulary of a specialised subject-field) has not been fully standardized yet within the system of Czech law. The standardization process, undertaken by a specialized department within the Office of the Government of the Czech Republic, has primarily aimed at fixing, reducing or expanding the existing meanings of Czech law terms and terminological phrases, or coining new legal terms corresponding to the reality of European law; Czech in that context serves as the target language. In contrast to the EU project, the main task of the "Czech-English Law Dictionary with Explanations" has been to find English equivalents of the existing Czech legal terminology, reflecting the national legal system; Czech has been the source language.

The three issues highlighted above will be briefly discussed below.

2.1. Validity of Czech legislative texts

The accelerating speed at which the Czech Republic has been approaching the moment of accession to the European Union on 1st May 2004 has materially determined the recent progress of Czech legislation. The process has been rather chaotic and beyond control due to the extreme amount of legislation to be made compatible with that of the European Union. Legislative drafts have been prepared not only by legislative specialists (as are government bills) but frequently by lay persons assisting individual Deputies in the Chamber of Deputies[6] of the Parliament of the Czech Republic (as has been the case of almost all private member's bills). Whereas in 1998, 45 bills were enacted, the number multiplied and amounted to 96 in 2001. The general understanding has been that extensive legislative activities have substantially distorted the quality of legislative texts, using, for example, the same or similar terms to denote different facts without any attempt to interpret the meaning of the newly employed terms in the law itself.

One factor partially affecting discourse research in Czech law, with a special emphasis on legal terminology, and upon which the making of the dictionary was based, is the question of the validity of legislative acts, such as the concept of so-called "hidden derogation". Hidden derogation occurs when a new law is passed without express derogatory provisions relating to all the affected pieces of existing legislation. The absence of such a provision is due either to certain "legislative neglect" or to the ignorance of drafters or simply due to the lack of time that legislators (both members of Parliaments and employees in charge of drafting new laws in governmental ministries or the Houses) have to cope with. According to Kořenský, Cvrček & Novák (1999: 32–33) almost nothing has been done since 1918 to purify our legislation and make it transparent in this respect. Among the 30,000 texts published in the Collection of Laws[7] since 1918, one sixth are not legislative acts (e.g. various editorial announcements and

---

5 *Acquis communautaire* is a French term widely used in all EU languages in its original French form. It means all written documents, whether legally binding or not, issued by the EU institutions.

6 The Parliament of the Czech Republic consists of two houses: the Chamber of Deputies as the lower house, and the Senate.

7 Czech laws come into force on the day of their promulgation in the Collection of Laws of the Czech Republic (C. 'Sbírka zákonů České republiky'); the Collection is published and sponsored by the State (the Ministry of the Interior) and in addition to its printed version, there is a version available

comments, resolutions etc.). About 10,000 acts have been expressly repealed. The remaining 15,000 can be subdivided with respect to their validity as follows:

(1) one third goes on account of a "legislative muddle"[8] (i.e. during the years, some parts of laws have been repealed, some amended, and no accounts of such changes have been kept); in contrast, for example, any new or amended law passed by Australian Parliament is accompanied by an exhaustive list of all laws or regulations adopted earlier which have been affected by the newly passed law, and the changes in respective provisions are included in the list (e.g. the Corporations Act 2001);
(2) the second third consists of laws still in force but not in use, i.e. obsolete (such as the State Budget Acts where a new statute is passed every year but the previous one is not expressly repealed because it automatically ceases to apply at the end of the year for which it was passed);
(3) the remaining 5,000 legislative acts create the core of our legislation (more or less) which is in force.

Generally, the first ("muddled") group is tending to expand. Since 1990, despite a few affirmative resolutions of the Czech Government, no attempts have been made to free the valid legislation of all provisions affected by hidden derogation, therefore the legislative muddle has become more solid and somehow standardized. Czech statutes, with some recent exceptions, are still lacking an interpretation and definition parts where terms used in the respective law are explained or defined in the new context of the act in question.

As Kořenský, Cvrček & Novák (1999: 38) point out in their research, there is a strong tendency towards amendments to laws in the Czech Republic. In 1990, there were 159 new laws passed, of which 70 were amended laws; in 1994, 69 new laws of which 52 amended laws were passed; in 1997, 57 new laws of which 46 amended laws were passed. Our research has showed that the total of 96 items of adopted legislation in 2001 is subdivided into 36 new statutes and 60 amended laws; the Collection of Laws in 2002 contains 123 passed laws, of which 94 were amendments. Although the most recent process is sometimes referred to as a "legislative fury" by members of Parliament (compared with the "legislative flurry" of a couple of years ago), the significant problem is in the number of bills proposed to the Parliament rather than the number of laws passed: there were 237 bills proposed to Parliament in 2003, 86 of which were passed and became effective in 2003. The period between 1st January and 30th April 2004 immediately preceding the accession of the Czech Republic to the European Union on 1st May represented the most hectic legislative activity in the last 85 years: during those four months 68 laws were passed, of which 46 were amendments.

Naturally, every amendment represents a shift or a change in the scope and quality of employed terminology. Moreover, amendments have not been evenly spread over the whole range of legislation; they apply primarily to already amended laws, a process which is termed "self-destruction" by Kořenský, Cvrček & Novák (1999: 39). Five major Czech codes, creating the basis of the whole legal system, have been materially affected by that process, namely, the Civil Code, the Civil Procedure Code, the Criminal Code, the Criminal Procedure Code, and

---

on the Internet free of charge, thus serving two fundamental principles of legal regulation, namely the public nature of legislation and the principle of its availability to the public. The only official text of a law is that which is printed in the Collection.

8 The authors use the Czech designation "legislativní nepořádek".

the Commercial Code.[9] Changes after 1990 (the collapse of the communist regime) and 1993 (the split of former Czechoslovakia into the Czech Republic and the Slovak Republic) have been unique within Czech modern history with respect to the quantity of adopted legislation. We can reasonably assume that the changes have been one of major factors causing quite a chaotic situation not only within the legal system itself but also in the sphere of legal terminology and language, which is our main concern.

2.2. Differences between legal systems

Existing material differences between Czech law as a Continental Law derivative on the one hand, and the Anglo-American systems of law based on Common Law on the other, create a large area of potential discrepancies in finding Czech-English equivalents. Looking for a suitable equivalent requires both an extensive knowledge of Czech law and an inquiry into the system of Anglo-American law in order to find an identical, similar, or closest in meaning legal institution, rather than following the pure semantic meaning regardless of any context.

The absence (or apparent absence) of an equivalent concept and term in the Anglo-American system of law requires a certain degree of explanation, and the creation of what Arntz (1993: 16) calls an "equivalent paraphrase". The explanatory paraphrasing of a source language term denoting a concept previously unknown in the target language may be evidenced, for example, in translating the Czech legal term *přestupek* into English. The Czech term has two interconnected meanings:

(a) To a layperson it means in general Czech any violation of a rule, morals, law or discipline;

(b) In Czech law, it denotes a specific transgression of administrative law committed by a natural person (an individual), since the system of Czech law does not consider such acts to be of sufficient gravity to constitute a criminal offence.

The Anglo-American system of law, however, classifies unlawful acts based on identical facts as the Czech *přestupek* in its legal sense as crimes, for example traffic offences or breaches of the peace. Therefore, the Czech *dopravní přestupek*, which is the most common and best-known type of this unlawful act may not be translated as 'traffic offence', because, under Czech law, it is not an offence which would be reflected in criminal or police records (whereas offences are so reflected); it is a violation of administrative law where a person can be punished with a pecuniary penalty based on a ticket, with no consequences for his or her criminal history. Nor can it be translated as a 'traffic violation', because this term is used in English law as a terminological synonym for a 'traffic offence', and as such, implies and assumes the criminal nature of the act, which in the case of the Czech *přestupek* does not reflect reality. Moreover, *přestupek*, in its legal meaning, is quite extensive, and covers a wide range of breaches of law, the consequences of which are not, according to Czech law, serious enough to constitute a crime. To make the Czech term quite explicit in English, we have to add an attribute to explain the meaning and create an explicative term 'administrative infraction' (or 'administrative delict') to expressly denote the substance of the wrongful act.

---

[9] For example, the Civil Procedure Code, adopted in 1963, was amended 5 times before 1990 and 43 times between 1990 and 2004; the Commercial Code, adopted in 1991, was amended 27 times; and the Trade Act, adopted in 1991 as essential legislation in business licensing, was amended 71 times by 2004.

2.2.1. Quantitative comparison with other legal systems

As Kořenský, Cvrček & Novák (1999: 36) suggest, no material differences can be seen in the quantity of passed legislation in continental law countries. There are variations due to the different systems of division of legislative responsibilities between the central legislative authority and law-making bodies of regions, and different traditions in official publication. They found out that it can be proved statistically that countries such as France, Spain or Italy continuously produce a larger bulk of legislation than those in the North – Sweden, Finland or Norway. If we consider the quantity of adopted legislation, the experience of the Czech Republic resembles the development in Austria, including a certain legislative "boom" after World War II and, similarly, a "depression" in the late 1950s, although reasons for the latter were different in both countries.

A comparison of the production of primary legislation (i.e. laws) in major English-speaking countries with the situation in the Czech Republic in 2001 and 2003 respectively can be seen in the following table:

2001 / 2003	UK	USA	Canada	Ireland	Australia	Czech Republic
passed laws	30 / 50	137 / 198	45 / 29	55 / 47	170 / 150	97 / 87
of which amendments	0 / 9	14 / 25	21 / 14	13 / 8	116 / 112	60 / 63
%	0 / 20	10 / 13	46 / 48	24 / 17	68 / 75	62 / 72

(Data sources: the Internet websites of the parliaments of the above mentioned countries)

The table shows no significant differences among the UK, Ireland and Canada with respect to the number of laws passed during two calendar years not necessarily corresponding with regular sessions of parliament.[10] The USA and Australia passed a similarly high number of laws, which was admittedly due to their federal status. The Czech Republic stood in between the two margins: a relatively high amount of adopted legislation was the visible result of the so-called "legislative flurry"[11] declared by the recent social democratic Government in 1998. Australia and the Czech Republic can be compared with regard to the percentage of amended laws; however, as noted earlier, unlike the Czech legislators their Australian colleagues have been extremely diligent in maintaining detailed records of all statutes and individual provisions affected by newly passed or amended laws.

There are many factors influencing the number of enacted laws – the legislative tradition and the system of law (continental law v. common law) being only two of them. On the other hand, none of the above mentioned and listed countries has ever allowed "legislative muddle" to sneak into the system. For example, a digest of Australian laws for 1999 consists of 145 pages

---

[10] For example, the British Parliamentary session is usually from November to the October of the following year.

[11] Although this terminological metaphor has been used to denote a sudden burst of activity even in the US Congress, it says nothing about the quality of the process. In the Czech context, the whole process led to a substantial deterioration of the quality of legislation passed by the Parliament, simply because the houses were objectively unable to pay sufficient attention to every single bill.

listing not only 202 laws newly enacted or amended, but also hundreds of valid statutes affected by the new enactments (by means of derogation or amendment).

One more point should be made in this context, namely the work of legislative drafters in the Czech Republic. As pointed out by Chromá (2003b: 67) the only official manual regulating legislative drafting is known as "The Law-Making Guidelines", a document issued by the Government which serves as recommendation only and is not legally binding. Since there is no centralized training of legislative drafters they acquire their skills only through direct experience in drafting new bills or amendments of existing legislation in legislative departments of individual ministries. The turnover of employees in these departments has been quite high since 1990; as a consequence, the quality of proposed legislation is generally worsening from the point of view of drafting techniques. The second problem arises in Parliament: no matter how perfect a draft law may be at the moment of its being submitted to Parliament, it normally suffers substantial "damage" with respect to legislative technicalities as a result of many inconsistent amendments passed by both Houses.[12] In proposing changes to the bill under consideration, Deputies and Senators typically do not respect the opinions of professional legislative drafters and experts; their primary objective is to ensure the interests of their own political parties.[13]

2.3. Differences among English-speaking countries

Differences within Anglo-American legal terminology among individual English speaking countries constitute another problem for translation. It should be noted, however, that different sets of difficulties apply to translation into English and from English respectively. For example, the British legal term 'company', as defined in the Companies Act 1985, is identical in its legal meaning and effect to the US 'corporation' defined by the Revised Model Business Corporation Act 1984;[14] thus, considering their linguistic features one may assume they are synonyms. However, the two terms should be used interchangeably neither within the British or US law system nor in translation into English, since the term 'company' in US law usually denotes an unincorporated entity,[15] whereas 'corporation' in original British legal texts regularly means an entity established not primarily for profit-making (e.g. 'public corporation') to be registered with the Companies House.[16]

Similarly, the British 'frustration' (as a kind of the discharge of contract) has its US counterpart 'impossibility', which is surprisingly a literal translation of the Czech term

---

[12] The latest example may be Act N. 14/2002 Coll. to amend the Ownership of Flats Act: the proposed bill contained one amending provision which was, according to the Government, sufficient to alleviate the existing problems; it consisted of 27 provisions at the end of the legislative process, 23 of which were of no effect in relation to the original intent and, moreover, led to some hidden amendments of other laws.

[13] This conclusion is based on the author's collaboration with the Legislative Department of the Senate over a period of three years.

[14] It should be noted that corporate law falls within the jurisdiction of individual states of the United States, therefore there is no uniform business organizations statute applicable to the whole of the country.

[15] The latest edition of Black's Law Dictionary states the term *company* to be synonymous with corporation; the latter, however, remains the statutory term.

[16] Companies House is an official governmental agency in charge of the official register of companies in the UK.

nemožnost used in identical contexts; the British 'theft' (defined by statute – The Theft Act 1967 – to be a proper legal term) is termed 'larceny' in US legislation; the British word 'jail' is a popular name for a prison whereas 'jail' in American English[17] denotes a place for pre-trial temporary confinement, synonymous with a police cell or holding cell; and there are dozens of other examples such as these. Consequently, several questions arise: which of two or even three terms (for example, British 'statutory instrument', American '/executive/ regulation', or Australian 'legislative instrument' for Czech *podzákonný právní předpis*) should be suggested as a better equivalent for a respective Czech term in a Czech-English law dictionary? Should there be any preference at all? Should there be instructions on how to translate legal texts as a part of the dictionary? Answers would be fully dependent on the linguistic, subject-field and social contexts as well as the publisher's policy. Where the origin of a particular term is certain, and its distribution invariable, a gloss or any other comment with respect to this may be made in the dictionary. However, the author of a dictionary should keep in mind that any such comment may restrict a potential user of the dictionary in his or her choice when seeking an appropriate equivalent. We tend to claim that no specialist bilingual dictionary may precisely instruct users in such or a similar situation: the choice of equivalents will depend on the purpose for which the dictionary is consulted (e.g. translating a legal text, informing a client, teaching legal languages), the linguistic and legal competence of the user himself or herself, the addressees, or recipients of the target text, the genre of the legal text in the source language and its counterpart in the target language, etc. It would be rather impractical to produce instructions or guidelines due to the wide range of legal topics, genres and contexts, the large scope of legal texts to be translated, and the extensive coverage of functions to be met by the translated legal texts.

Steiner (1989: 255) recommends that a bilingual dictionary of a general language should include "related portions of the dictionary of meanings, related data from encyclopaedias, a look into a thesaurus, appropriate diagrams, pictures and illustrations as well as charts and tables, and of course, a detailed grammar", along with the translation equivalents in order to avoid a bilingual dictionary being a stockpile of equivalencies divorced from real texts. The same requirement should apply to a bilingual law dictionary although the feasibility of such a lexicographic project will always be confined to the author's competence and energy, the publisher's policy and the potential of the relevant market. Obviously, the easiest way is to produce an electronic version of a dictionary that is carefully programmed in a multimedia format. Such an approach would allow users to examine and consult legal resources both in the source and target languages, citations and precise meanings of potential equivalents, references to relevant legislation and cases in both languages, and so on. Users would be better prepared and equipped to decide which of the suggested equivalent should be preferred.

---

[17] The term *jail* in the USA denotes a confinement established and run by a local authority, such as a county; prison is a penitentiary institution established and operated by a State or the federal government.

3. Linguistic framework

Generally, law is expressed through language and the language is a medium of legal thoughts.[18] Communication among all actors in public or private legal relations can only be pursued through the language common to all participants in the respective legal act. The first step towards understanding law is to understand the language through which the law is expressed; as Knapp points out (1995: 120), academic lawyers usually subdivide the language into three major areas according to the prescriptive or descriptive nature of speech acts, namely the language of legislation (being highly prescriptive), the language of judgments (both prescriptive and descriptive), and the language of legal representation (descriptive).

The linguistic framework of the writing of the "Czech-English Law Dictionary" consists of two major areas that will now be discussed:

(1) the language for specific purposes (LSP), the language for legal purposes (LLP) and their main component – terminology as the vocabulary of a specialised subject-field, and

(2) translation strategies used for the interlanguage transfer of a legal text.

3.1. LSP, LLP and Terminology

3.1.1. LSP and LLP

Depending on the branch of linguistics in which one is involved, one will speak of either a language for special or specific purposes, or of a sublanguage, scientific language, or specialized language (Pearson 1998: 28). Widdowson (1979a: 24) proposes a slightly modified understanding: "The way English is used in science and in other specialist subjects, [...] may be more satisfactorily described not as formally defined varieties of English, but as realizations of universal sets of concepts and methods or procedures which define disciplines or areas of enquiry independently of any particular language." Such a view seems to be very close to what John Sinclair, in his keynote speech entitled "The articulation of meaning"[19], called *local grammar*. We use the term language for specific purposes (LSP) to denote a subsystem of the general language system which consists of (describing and analysing) the selection, combination and use of existing morphological, lexical and syntactic units, structures and patterns that would best serve the specific stylistic, discourse and generic functions of a text in a concrete subject area and specific social context. Specificity of the subsystem seems to be primarily a pragmatic category reflecting the communicative purpose and needs of the users – professionals in the respective subject field. Although Picht and Draskau (1985: 3) define LSP as a "formalized and codified variety of language used for special purposes and in a legitimate context", we would argue that such a definition may apply only to what they call an LSP variety, i.e. a language for a specific subject field, such as a language for legal purposes, a language for business purposes, or a language for mechanical engineering. Empirically, we can assume that there are connections and junctures among individual subject-field varieties. We are unaware, however, of any comprehensive linguistic research analysing a wide range

---

[18] Exceptionally, legal regulation can be expressed by non-linguistic means, such as traffic signs; however, for the purposes of dictionary making this means can be disregarded.

[19] 14th European Symposium for Special Purposes, University of Surrey, Guildford, UK, 18th–22nd August 2003.

of different subject-field varieties of either the Czech language or of English in order to establish the common core, thus "materializing" LSP. When we speak about a concrete subject-area language used as a means of communication, the term LSP variety will be used although we recognise the inaccuracy of the term.

Referring to Lehrberger (1986: 22), Pearson (1998: 31) lists six features which help to characterize an LSP variety:

(1) limited subject matter (such as law);

(2) lexical, semantic and syntactic restrictions (such as the use of terminology);

(3) "deviant" rules of grammar (such as the English legal term 'an information' preserving in all its procedural meanings a countable status, which is considered obsolete and rare in general language; see, for example, OED CD ed.);

(4) high frequency of certain constructions (such as highly formalized sentence patterns in statutory texts);

(5) text structure (such as legislation or contracts); and

(6) the use of special symbols.

The first three features as applied to the language for legal purposes will be mentioned later; structural and textual linguistics, i.e. items (4) and (5), are beyond our present purpose. The last aspect, although limited in its appearance, is very important when citations of various legislative sources or laws are to be translated from or to the Czech language.

A material difference between Czech law and Anglo-American law exists in the use of the symbol "§". Whereas Czech statutes are subdivided into "sections",[20] each of which starts with the symbol "§" and the respective Arabic numeral, British legislation is fully free of the symbol although they subdivide their statutes into "sections", too. Visual discrimination in British statutes is made through a bold type of the respective Arabic numeral followed by a dot. Sections in both systems are further subdivided into *subsections* (C. 'odstavec'), *paragraphs* (C. 'písmeno'), and *subparagraphs* (C. 'věta').[21] Thus, a citation of a provision in a Czech statute may be: "§12, odst. 3, písm. a, věta třetí". The same citation of a British statute would be: "s. 12 (3) (a) (iii)". The situation will become more complicated for an English-Czech translator or any other person who is unaware of the differences in designation of parts of English and Czech legislative texts and who is expected to translate them into the other language. While a literal translation of the whole of the Czech citation into English would be odd but, in principle, comprehensible to an English lawyer, our experience suggests that a literal transposition of the English citation into Czech would be hardly understandable even to a lawyer provided he or she has no previous knowledge of the British legal system.

---

20 Larger subdivisions of a statute are *title* (C. 'hlava'), *chapter* (C. 'část'), *part* (C. 'díl'), and *subpart* (C. 'oddíl'), however, there are no strict rules applicable to their designation. It should be noted that the term *chapter* has two different meanings in the Anglo-American legislative contexts: (a) the number under which the law in question was passed by parliament during the particular parliamentary session; and (b) a subdivision of a statute.

21 The English *subparagraph* is visually structured and preceded by small Roman numerals. The Czech *věta* is placed in a simple order of individual sentences making a complex statement without any visual structuring or numbering.

3.1.2. Terminology

The word 'terminology' is usually assigned three different concepts (Sager 1990: 3):

(1) the set of practices and methods used for the collection, description and presentation of terms;

(2) a theory, i.e. the set of premises, arguments and conclusions required for explaining the relationship between concepts and terms which are fundamental for a coherent activity outlined in preceding item;

(3) a vocabulary of a special subject-field.

We will use this word in its obviously most frequent meaning (i.e. that of (3)), as a collection of terms which represents the system of concepts of an individual subject-field.
Traditionally the lexical and semantic restrictions of an LSP variety have been represented by the vocabulary of the respective subject field. Research has confirmed (Poštolková 1984: 16–17) that the language of a Czech LSP variety encompasses a wide range of lexical units subdivided into three groups: (a) subject-area terminology, (b) vocabulary of scholarly research, and (c) lexical units of general language. Applying this trichotomy to the language of law, both Czech and Anglo-American, each category should be made precise. As Zimová, Koníčková (1989) showed in their "Concise Russian-Czech Dictionary of General, Formal and Legal Vocabulary in Legal Texts" as well as Riley (1995: 73–79) in her study of the vocabulary of English law, there are three types of lexical units in the legal language:

(1) *"Pure" law terminology:* Czech *cese* (E. 'assignment') or *extradice* (E. 'extradition'), and English *estoppel* (C. 'překážka uplatnění žalobního nároku') or *detinue* (C. 'zabrání cizí věci') fall into this category. It is a relatively scarce group of words or phrases (such as legal maxims) that are not used outside the branch of law unless stylistically marked. A limited repertoire of legal Latin both in Czech and English may be assigned to this group as well.[22]

(2) *Law terminology found in everyday speech:* these are words with related legal meaning, such as Czech *pozemek*, *nedbalost* and their English counterparts 'land' and 'negligence' translated respectively (their semantic quality and distribution is identical in both Czech and English). Next, there are a few words with different legal and general meanings, such as Czech *titul* and its English counterpart 'title' (again the semantic quality and distribution of the word is the same in both languages). Some words would have more than one meaning in both languages, such as Czech *právo* (translated into English as either 'law' or 'right' depending on the context of its use) and English *law*, denoting either the system as such or a piece of legislation depending on its grammatical quality, namely the category of countability.

(3) *Everyday words which are assigned a special connotation in a given legal context;* this often happens when a word or phrase regularly and primarily used in common speech

---

[22] The set of Latin terms and phrases used in legal Czech does not correspond to the repertoire of legal Latin used in English law. The most frequent Latin attributive terminological phrases used by Czech lawyers, namely *de lege lata* (according to valid law) and *de lege ferenda* (according to proposed or intended legislation) are unknown to Anglo-American lawyers; similarly, the descriptive terms *ratio decidendi* and *obiter dicta* designating two different components of a judicial decision issued by courts in English-speaking countries are not used in legal Czech since the law of precedents is not pertinent to the continental system of law, judgments issued by Czech courts are structured in a different manner and generally are not binding on lower courts.

> become a part of the subject-matter of a statute thus acquiring new semantic dimensions either expanding or narrowing their original meaning. For example, a British law called the "Welfare of Pigs Act 1998" provides a definition of a pig for the purposes of that law: "'pig' means an animal of the porcine species of any age, kept for breeding or fattening". If a pig fails to fulfil either of the two qualifying conditions, i.e. "kept for (a) breeding or (b) fattening", his or her owner or breeder stays outside the scope of that law and no punishment applies to him or her should they fail to observe any of the provisions of the law.

Terminology is apparently the most visible part of vocabulary for specific purposes. It has been profoundly described, analysed and standardized (ISO R 1087 1990) primarily in the areas of exact and natural sciences and in technology. Legal terminology has not been a subject of standardization by the International Organization for Standardization (ISO), established in Paris in 1947; however both academic and practising lawyers in many countries have assisted the codification of their legal terminology through the publishing of monolingual law dictionaries explaining essential legal institutions and concepts pertinent to the respective legal system. Our experience has suggested that most lawyers without a sufficient linguistic background use the concepts 'terminology' and 'LSP variety' indiscriminately, thus reducing the language of law to a mere set of legal terms.

Newmark (1988: 160) suggests that terminology makes up perhaps 5–10% of a text; our recent survey (Chromá, in print c) showed that the percentage of terms appearing in legal texts is higher. We studied five different pieces of legislation dealing with arbitration, four of them written in English (two produced in "original" English by British and US legislature respectively; the other two written in "international" English of international organizations) and one in the Czech language passed by Czech legislators: the Arbitration Act 1996 (United Kingdom) contains about 22% of terms; terminology in the Federal Arbitration Act 1925, as amended (USA), makes up about 20% of the whole text. The lexis of the UNCITRAL Model Law on International Arbitration encompasses 21% of terminology; and terms in the European Convention on International Commercial Arbitration form 26% of the text. The difference in proportions of terms and non-terms in the Czech Act N.216/1994 Sb. (Act providing for Arbitration Proceedings and Enforcement of Arbitral Awards) is even larger: 29% of the text is made up of terminology.[23] We can reasonably assume that relatively high percentages of terms contained within legislative texts may result from two major factors: (a) a high degree of repetitiveness of terms in legislative provisions; and (b) most terms are binominal and/or multiverbal phrases and not mononymous expressions. In order to provide reliable data confirming or refuting Newmark's estimate it will be necessary to extend the calculation to different genres of arbitration texts, such as explanatory memoranda with respect to the legislation in question as well as to textbooks dealing with the arbitration topic published both in English and Czech.

---

[23] For the purposes of simple counting, only nominal terms were considered (including gerund); no terminological verbal constructions typical of the legal language of legislation were taken into account.

3.1.2.1. Definition of the term

The International Organization for Standardization has played a crucial role in developing the theory of terminology and safeguarding the practice of term-formation. As mentioned earlier, their attention has focused on the terminology of science and technology rather than on humanities or law. A similar situation exists within the Czech Institute for Normalization and Standardization (ČSNI) and its Technical Normalization Committee (TNK) responsible for Czech terminology for technology and science as a part of Czech technical standards. Legal terminology is outside the scope of their responsibilities as it is not included in technical standards.

ISO (R 1087, 1990), however, assisted linguistics in describing and analysing terminological concepts, and finding their adequate designations thus enriching onomasiological processes. It has been generally agreed that terms should be accurate, concise, easy to spell and pronounce; they should allow the formation of derivatives and be linguistically correct (Felber 1984: 181–2). Thomas (1993: 46) suggests that, preferably, a term should also be monosemous (having one meaning) and at the same time mononymous (consisting of one word), and a member of a term system. Superanskaja, Podolskaja and Vasileva (1989: 14) emphasize a pragmatic aspect of a term involving users in establishing the characteristics a term. They give a three-dimensional definition: a term is

(1) a special word (or phrase) accepted in a professional activity and used under specific circumstances;

(2) an expression denoting a concept as a part of the system of concepts of a specific subject-field; and

(3) a basic conceptual element of a language for specific purposes.

Čechová et al. (1997: 157) circumscribe a term by contrasting it with other parts of the lexicon as follows:

> Termínem z hlediska lexikologie rozumíme takové pojmenování, které je v rámci disciplíny jednoznačným pojmenováním oboru. Jde o pojmenování nocionální, neexpresívní, má funkci nominativní a kognitivní. Termín je v rámci oboru ustálený a je buď definován, nebo fixován konvencí oboru, jeho význam je ostřeji ohraničený než u jiných vrstev slovní zásoby a bývá někdy identifikovatelný nezávisle na kontextu.
>
> (Within the system of lexicology, the term shall be understood as a designation that is unequivocal within the respective subject-area. It is a notional, non-emphatic designation fulfilling its onomasiological and cognitive functions. The term is firmly established within the subject-area, and may be either defined or fixed by conventions of that subject-area; its meaning is more precisely delimited than those in other layers of lexicon, and sometimes it may be identifiable regardless of context. (*Translated by author*)

We can easily apply Felber's definition to a legal term: it should be accurate, concise, linguistically correct and allow for derivative-formation. There are monosemous and mononymous legal terms both in Czech civil procedure (such as *petit*) and its equivalent counterpart 'prayer' in English judicial petitions and complaints. However, most Czech legal terms are multi-word expressions and phrases, and polysemy, although unwanted and unintended, can be traced in different branches of law. A rough estimate of entries contained in the Blacks's Law Dictionary (7th ed.) suggests that the proportions of one-word terms and multi-word terms in Anglo-American law is 33 and 67% respectively; the ratio in the most extensive Czech Law Dictionary[24] is 26% of one-word terms and 74% of multi-word terms[25]. Polysemy is even more widely spread within English legal terminology than in Czech law.

There are few legal terms that one may recognize as legal terms without any given context. Czech criminal procedure term *obžaloba* clearly denotes its legal rootedness and meaning outside any linguistic or social context. Its English conceptual counterpart and equivalent *indictment* possesses almost the same characteristics. However, as Nida (1975: 104) points out, in most discourses the intended meanings of terms are clearly marked by the context both linguistic and non-linguistic. The English word *complaint* may serve as a legal term in a specific context of civil or criminal proceedings. In the context of civil procedure, it would be a written statement of the plaintiff's case ('návrh' or 'žaloba' in Czech); in a criminal prosecution, it would stand for the formal accusation or charge of the defendant and the Czech equivalent would be 'obžaloba'.[26] Pearson (1998: 36) goes further: "Terms can only be considered as terms when they are used in certain contexts and that all of the discussion about whether or not a term is really a term is irrelevant if the discussion is not rooted in reality". Such an assertion bears ultimate truth where the interlingual transfer of terms is considered. A non-lawyer would hardly expect the Czech verbal phrase *zlehčovat podnik* to be part of a statutory provision (sec. 50a(1)(e) of the Commercial Code). The phrase should be transferred to legal English so that the words of law may be employed. Therefore, the English phrase 'disparage the business' should be used in translation since the verb *disparage* (and *disparagement* as its derivative) is used in Anglo-American law in the same situation (but not its synonyms *undervalue* or *vilify*).

Although we speak about the language of law it does not necessarily mean that all terms used in legal texts are of legal origin. For example, accountancy terms are an important component of a certain part of business law. Thus the Czech term *pohledávka*, serving indiscriminately as one expression for both law and accounting, can be translated into English either as a legal term 'claim', or an accounting term 'receivable'. What is decisive in the translation is the context. An immediate linguistic context may suggest that the plural of the Czech term is likely to denote the book-keeping concept, however, a larger non-linguistic context of a concrete branch of law would help make the selection of an equivalent more precise: the Czech term *pohledávka* in its legal sense would be primarily found in procedural law such as bankruptcy or civil proceedings. In deciding whether the Czech *pohledávka* denoting an accounting concept still may be categorized as a term in a legal text we would maintain Pearson's argument (Pearson 1998: 13) that "all words or phrases that have special reference, regardless of the subject-field to which they belong, and which may also form a part of the lexicon of another subject-field must be considered to be a part of terminology of that subject field".

---

24 Madar, Zdeněk: Slovník českého práva, (Praha, Linde 1995)

25 The percentage is achieved by simple counting of one-word and multi-word terms as contained in the two letter sections: letter C in Black's Law Dictionary, pp. 202–388, i.e. 186 pages – 1239 one-word terms and 2531 multi-word terms; and letter P in the Czech dictionary, pp. 924–1157, i.e. 233 pages – 565 one-word terms and 1596 multi-word terms. The two letter sections are the largest in the respective dictionaries.

26 The choice between 'indictment' and 'complaint' as a translational equivalent for Czech *obžaloba* will depend primarily on the gravity of the crime prosecuted ('indictment' being for a more serious offence) and on the jurisdiction of the ultimate recipient of the translation since 'complaint' is used primarily (but not exclusively) to commence the prosecution of offences of medium gravity in the US.

3.1.2.2. Functional subcategorization of terms

It is obvious that terms are of a different quality and type and have different functions. The terms can be classified according to various criteria. Bečka (1992: 73) subdivides terms into three functional groups according to their quality:

(1) *specialist terms* or *terms of art* (C. 'odborné termíny') designating scientifically determined, i.e. defined or definable, concepts;
(2) *descriptive terms* (C. 'popisné termíny') designating objects scientifically classified and described, i.e. nomenclature or taxonomy; and
(3) *technological terms* (C. 'technologické termíny') designating phenomena of practical application of technological research and science.

The language of law primarily encompasses the first two categories, and as Fillmore (1978: 168) points out it is filled with taxonomies. Looking at legal taxonomies from a comparative Czech law and Anglo-American law perspectives, we should note that taxonomies are inherent in the whole system of a specific subject-field, therefore, it would be unlikely to find corresponding classification in the other legal system unless international law were in question. Fillmore gives an example of the English term *homicide* (C. 'usmrcení') as a high-level taxon having three subparts called *excusable homicide* (C. 'usmrcení vylučující protiprávnost'), *justifiable homicide* (C. 'usmrcení z právního důvodu'), and *felonious homicide* (C. 'úmyslné zločinné usmrcení'). *Felonious homicide* is further subdivided into *murder* (C. 'vražda'), *manslaughter* (C. 'zabití', although it is a simple translational equivalent and not a statutory term as there is no crime of such a nature in the Czech Criminal Code), and *infanticide* (the Czech explicative legal equivalent is 'vražda novorozeného dítěte matkou'; the first three words create the semantic equivalent of the English term, but the Czech legal equivalent is complemented with the perpetrator of the crime, namely *matkou* 'by mother', which is only implied in the English term). *Murder* is further subcategorized according to degrees of seriousness into the first or second degree murder. Such subclassification of homicide will be easily translatable into the Czech language but not transferable into the taxonomy of Czech criminal law. The Czech Criminal Code recognizes three crimes resulting in the death of a person collectively designated as "crimes against life and limb": *murder* (free of any subcategorization; it occurs when intent to kill can be proved); *deadly injury* (or *bodily injury resulting in death*; this is the killing of a person where felonious intent cannot be proved), and *infanticide* as explained above. Only *infanticide* is a crime defined identically in both legal systems as far as the facts of an act are concerned (killing of a child by mother as a result of her post-natal depression); what differs is the duration after the birth of a child when *infanticide* can be committed (within the first six weeks of a child's life under Czech law and twelve months in the UK).

Considering the normativity of terminology Galinski (1982: 189) recognizes "descriptive terminology", representing a descriptive norm of terms, i.e. their present usage, and "prescriptive terminology" representing a prescriptive norm, i.e. that is standardized and recommended for application by an authority. Applying this dichotomy to the language of law the latter would encompass terms as defined by and contained in statutes. Terms developed through case law and conventions would also fall into this category in common law countries (Tiersma 1999: 109). Descriptive terminology would, in addition to statutorily defined terms used in everyday legal practice, also contain professionalisms as a part of legal jargon. Although jargon will be discussed later, we will give one example of this dichotomy. The

Czech Criminal Procedure Code provides for bail to be granted under certain circumstances. The statutory term for this is *peněžitá záruka* (E. 'pecuniary security'). In Galinski's understanding it is a prescriptive term declared as such by the law. In legal practice, however, the term *kauce* (E. 'bail') is widely used. Whereas the Anglo-American legal system employs the term *bail* in both legislation and everyday legal practice, Czech law practitioners use the two terms discriminately according to the "formality" of the situation (such as an attorney approaching the judge in a courtroom asking the court for *peněžitá záruka* for his client, and the attorney talking to his client explaining what *kauce* is). Obviously, the prescriptive (statutory) and descriptive (pertaining to everyday legal usage) nature of legal vocabulary should be taken into consideration and indicated when providing potential equivalents in a bilingual law dictionary.

3.1.2.3. Grammatical subcategorization of terms

Grammatical characteristics of terms and terminological phrases may either serve as a distinctive feature with respect to their meaning, or may help identify the meaning. Hoffmann (1982: 399) distinguishes four levels that can be differentiated in relation to terms, namely morphemic, categorial, lexemic and syntagmatic. This area is very wide and rich in material, however we will concentrate only on basic features at each level that are relevant for the making of a bilingual law dictionary, and provide a few examples to serve as illustration.

A. Terminology and morphemes

Prefixes and suffixes as inflectional formatives facilitating the creation of new derivatives in term-formation, their transfer from the source language and problems in their transposition to the target legal language, fall within this category.

(1) The Czech derivative verbs *‹od›mítnout* a *‹za›mítnout* (as well as their nominal derivatives *odmítnutí* and *zamítnutí*) may be (mistakenly) understood to be interchangeable synonyms in common Czech. For a lay person, for example, there would be no difference in the meaning of the Czech phrases *odmítnout odvolání* and *zamítnout odvolání*. The two verbs, however, represent two significantly diverse (but not antagonistic) approaches of the appellate court: the former suggests that the court would not deal with the application at all (usually on the grounds of some technical mistake or lack of formalities), the latter denotes that the court has considered the appeal but has found no grounds for reversing the first-instance judgment. A similar distinction applies to phrases relating to the legislative process: the Senate (as the Upper House) may *odmítnout návrh (zákona)* or *zamítnout návrh*. The former suggests that the Senate would not deal with the bill at all but directly send it for presidential assent. The latter phrase is used when the bill has been considered by the Senate, who decide to return the bill to the Lower House as being inadequate for further proceeding. Translational equivalents of the two verbs (and their nominal derivatives), formally distinguished only by their prefixes, should be found accordingly. To 'reject' or 'refuse' (*reject an appeal, refuse a bill*) would be functional equivalents of the Czech *odmítnout*, whilst 'dismiss' would be the only equivalent for the Czech *zamítnout* in all contexts (*dismiss an appeal, dismiss a bill*).

The Czech verbs *‹o›dcizit* and *‹z›cizit* (as well as their nominal derivatives *odcizení* and *zcizení*) are used indiscriminately in popular speech, but they represent two substantially different terms in legal Czech. The former belongs to criminal law and constitutes one material element of theft, whereas the latter is part of property law and may be described as the disposing of property, for example, by sale or bestowal. *Odcizit* and *odcizení* should be translated as 'misappropriate' and 'misappropriation' respectively (unlike the Czech prefix *od-*, the English prefix *mis-* suggests a certain degree of unlawfulness); *zcizit* and *zcizení* have their respective equivalents 'alienate' and 'alienation' in legal English.

(2) The Czech combined suffixes *-telný*, *-telnost*, suggesting that something may be done or pursued, have their English counterparts *-able* (*-ible*), *-ability* (*-ibility*). The Czech phrase *vykonatelný rozsudek* may be comprehensibly translated into English as 'enforceable judgment'. A different type of modality may be preferred in an original English legal text, namely 'judgment to be enforced'. Our understanding of such a choice has been that, unlike the adjective 'enforceable' serving only as an attribute of judgment and saying nothing about the consequences of such a decision, the latter phrase seems to express almost no other possibility than the suggestion that the judgment is final and conclusive and will be enforced, thus implying a logical consequence of the closed judicial procedure. On the other hand, the Czech *vykonatelnost rozsudku* should be translated into English as 'enforcement of judgment' since English law dictionaries generally define the phrase as the processes through which the orders of a court may be enforced. A semantic equivalent "enforceability" is almost unused in original legal English but is however sometimes found in international varieties of English, namely English developed within the European Union or United Nations.

(3) The Czech legal terms *výmaz* and *přezkum* (derived from perfective verbs *vymazat* /'expunge, erase, delete'/, and *přezkoumat* /'review'/) were created with a zero suffix in order to emphasize their official one-off nature (unlike their common Czech synonyms *vymazání*, *přezkoumání*). Their English equivalents, however, are 'expungement, erasure, deletion' and 'review' respectively, which may serve either as legal terms or common language, depending on the context.

(4) The English agent-noun suffix *-or* in legal terms denoting the person acting, as opposed to the person acted upon denoted by words suffixed with *-ee*.[27] Tiersma (1999: 98–99) considers the creation of nouns with the *-ee* suffix very functional in legal English. The suffix *-ee* has primarily a dative sense, in which it acts as a passive agent noun for the indirect object. In most cases the suffix is appended to a verb-stem (except for *legatee* where the noun-stem legacy may be traced and which has no *-or* counterpart). Unlike *-er*, the legal suffix *-or* is always a stressed syllable. The suffix *-or* imparts a kind of technical or professional character to the ending, explaining the differentiation of the following variants; the following list is a compilation of examples provided by OED (CD ed.) and DMLU:[28]

appellor (C. 'informátor', but the exact equivalent would depend on the context) is a historical legal term denoting a person who has accused someone of a crime or informed against an accomplice, whilst *appealer* is an obsolete variant of *appellant* (C. 'odvolatel'), lodging an appeal with the court; *appellee* (Czech functional equivalent is

[27] For more information see Bauer, Laurie: *English Word-formation*, Cambridge Textbooks in Linguistics, CUP 1993, pp. 243-250.

[28] Garner, Bryan (1995): *A Dictionary of Modern Legal Usage*, 2nd ed. – Oxford: Oxford University Press.

an attributive terminological phrase 'osoba, proti níž směřuje odvolání') is a person appealed against (recently replaced by the term *respondent*);

assignor (C. 'převodce' or 'postupitel') is a person making over property rights; *assigner* (C. 'rozdělovatel' or 'přidělovatel' depending on the context) is one who allots, apportions or assigns in a general sense; *assignee* (C. 'postupník' or 'nástupce /na základě právního úkonu/') is a person to whom a right or property is legally transferred; *assignee* has a shorter variant *assign* used primarily in doublets such as *successors and assigns* (C. 'nástupci a nabyvatelé'), and almost always appears in plural; where singular is to be expressed, or only the latter term is to be used, *assignee* will be preferred;

bailor (C. 'úschovce') is a person delivering goods to another person for specific purpose, usually custody, and a *bailer* (C. 'odčerpávač' or 'čerpák') is a man or utensil used for bailing out a ship; *bailee* (C. 'schovatel') is one to whom goods are committed in trust for a specific purpose;

bargainor (C. 'prodávající') is a person making a legal agreement of bargain; it has its common English variant *bargainer* (C. 'prodavač') denoting a dealer or trafficker; *bargainee* (C. 'kupující') is a person to whom an agreement of bargain and sale is addressed;

creditor (C. 'věřitel') is a person lending money and his or her counterpart in the relationship is *debtor* (C. 'dlužník') as a person borrowing money; neither term has an *-er* variant; *debtee* may sometimes be found in the meaning of *creditor*; the word *creditee* denotes a person to whom something is sold on credit, thus becoming *debtor*; *debtee* is an obsolete term unused in recent legal English;

grantor (C. 'postupitel' or 'cedent') is one who makes a grant or conveyance in legal form, and *granter* (C. 'dárce') is a person who makes a simple grant, such as a gift; *grantee* (C. 'postupník') is a person to whom a grant or conveyance is made;

indorser (also spelled *endorser*) (C. 'indosant' or an explicative phrase 'převodce rubopisem') can also be spelled *indorsor* without any shift in meaning but the latter spelling variant is quite rare; *indorsee* (also *endorsee*) (C. 'indosát' or 'indosatář') is a person in whose favour a bill or note is indorsed (or endorsed);

lessor (C. 'pronajímatel') is a person granting a lease and has no *-er* nominal variant; *lessee* (C. 'nájemce') is a person to whom the lease has been granted;

mortgagor (C. 'zástavce' or 'zástavní dlužník') pronounced as [mɔːgɪ'dʒɔː(r)] is a person who makes over property as a security for debt, and *mortgager* is an obsolete spelling variant; *mortgagee* (C. 'zástavní věřitel') is a person to whom property is mortgaged (i.e. he lends money on mortgage);

obligor (the Czech language uses attributive phrase 'povinný ze závazku') as one who binds himself to another by contractual obligation, is pronounced as ['ɒblɪ,gɔː(r)], and *obliger* [ə'blaɪdʒə(r)] is an obsolete word but with the same meaning; *obligee* [ɒblɪ'dʒiː] (C. 'oprávněný ze závazku') is a person to whom another is bound by contractual obligation;

offeror (C. 'navrhovatel') is one who makes an offer to contract and *offerer* (C. 'nabízející' or 'nabízitel') may be anyone making an offer generally; *offeree* (C. 'osoba, jíž je návrh určen'); the Czech functional equivalent in the brackets is an explicative attributive phrase literally translated into English as 'a person to whom an offer has been made' which is a regular legal definition of an *offeree*;

payor (C. 'plátce' or 'poplatník') denoting a person making payment, can be seen primarily in law and American English, and *payer* is used in British English and general language; Czech law distinguishes between 'plátce', i.e. an individual or an entity paying taxes or social security contributions for others, such as an employer for his employees, or a shop-owner levying VAT collected on goods sold; or 'poplatník', designating an individual or entity paying their own taxes and other charges directly to the state; Anglo-American law employs only one term in either context); *payee* (C. 'adresát platby') is one to whom payment is made;

pledger (for a pawner) (C. 'zástavce', or 'zástavní dlužník') is entered in the OED as the only form of this word, however, ***pledgor*** pronounced as ['plɛdʒɔː(r)] has been widely used in American English and the Anglo-American system of law; *pledgee* (C. 'zástavní věřitel') is a person with whom a pledge is deposited;

promisor (C. 'povinný ze slibu') is a legal term for a person making a promise in law and *promiser* is used in general language; *promis(s)ee* (C. 'oprávněný ze slibu') is a legal term and denotes a person to whom a promise has been made;

transferor (C. 'převodce' or 'postupitel' or 'cedent') is a person making a legal transfer of property and *transfer(r)er* is one making any other transfer; *transferee* (C. 'postupník' or 'cesionář') is one to whom a legal transfer is made;

vendor (C. 'prodávající') is a legal term for a person disposing of property by sale used primarily in American law, and *vender* (C. 'prodavač'; colloguially 'stánkař') serves in a restricted sense of a street-seller; *vendee* (C. 'kupující') is a synonym of a *buyer*.

As can be seen from the brief list above, both suffixes are quite common in designating parties to various legal relations, however their use may be ambiguous. The following warning made by Garner (1995: 305) seems to be of importance when looking for adequate equivalents in a Czech-English law dictionary:

> The endings *-or* and *-ee* can be easily transposed by mistake. As a general matter, therefore, good (legal) drafters prefer *buyer* and *seller* over *vendee* and *vendor*; *buyer* and *seller* over *bargainee* and *bargainor*; and, in appropriate circumstances, *borrower* and *lender* over *mortgagor* and *mortgagee*. The stakes are often so high that it makes little sense to use forms that increase the possibility of errors.

Moreover, the suffix *-ee* seems to be more productive than *-or*. The use of *-ee* in law terms has been frequently imitated in the formation of various nonce-words (originally humorous but slowly sneaking into the general usage), such as *discriminatee* (who is discriminated against), *educatee*, *amputee* (a person whose limb has been removed), *abortee* (a woman upon whom an abortion is performed), *cheatee* (one who is cheated), etc., denoting the personal object of the verbs from which they are formed. We should admit, however, that such word-formation has been seen more in American than in British English.

B. Terminology and grammatical categories

Grammatical categories play a significant role in the translation of legal terminology, in particular, uncountable and countable varieties of one word distinguishing their legal meaning. The following examples should briefly illustrate problems that may occur with respect to translation.

(1) Countable v. uncountable nouns:

i. The Czech countable term *škoda*, or its plural *škody*, has its English equivalent 'damage' as a singular and invariable noun. The English term 'damages' denotes only the compensation that may be sought in and awarded by a court and is grammatically classified as pluralia tantum.

ii. The English uncountable term *liability* denotes legal responsibility ('právní odpovědnost' in Czech); the plural form *liabilities* means primarily the debts or pecuniary obligations of a person or company (in Czech 'závazky' or 'pasíva' depending on the context). Thus, the singular *a liability* may be used, however rather rarely, as a synonym for someone's duty.

iii. *Legal personality* is a binominal uncountable term referring to "the status of a human being or an artificial entity regarded by law as a person to whom it ascribes certain powers and capacities"[29] ('právní subjektivita' in Czech). The countable variable term *legal person* should be translated as 'právní subjekt' into the Czech language. However, some English legal texts use the countable singular *a legal personality* serving as a synonym for *a legal person*.

iv. The countable word *an information* denotes charges or the formal accusation against a suspect laid by the police or prosecuting attorney (the Czech equivalent 'obžaloba' seems to be the only functional equivalent although some formal elements of *an information* correspond to the Czech 'návrh na potrestání'). This seems to be the only situation in contemporary English when the word *information* serves as a countable variable noun.

v. The uncountable invariable noun *security* (for st.) denotes collateral pledged to guarantee the fulfillment of an obligation (C. 'zajištění'); the countable variable noun *a security* is an instrument evidencing a holder's ownership rights in a company ('cenný papír' in Czech).

(2) Parts of speech: conversion

A tendency to use adjectives or verbs as nouns can be seen in both legal Czech and English. De-adjectival conversion to nouns can usually be explained in terms of a well established adjective + noun phrase from which the noun has been ellipted (Quirk et al. 1995: 1561). However, the processes differ in legal Czech and English and what is created by conversion in Czech does not necessarily possess the same characteristics in English. The following examples illustrate the process:

Czech			English		
phrase	noun	type of conversion	phrase	noun	type of conversion
nevinná osoba	nevinný	A → N	innocent person	the innocent	A → N
obviněná osoba	obviněný	A → N	accused person	the accused	V → N
nezletilá osoba	nezletilý	A → N	minor person	a minor[30]	A → N
nemajetná osoba	nemajetný	A → N	indigent person	an indigent	A → N
odsouzená osoba	odsouzený	A → N	convicted person	a convict	V → N
podezřelá osoba	podezřelý	A → N	suspected person	a suspect	V → N

---

[29] Black's Law Dictionary, 7th edition, Westlaw Publishing, 1999.

[30] However, *a major* will never occur in the meaning of an adult.

Czech			English		
zadržená osoba	zadržený	A → N	detained person	a detainee	0
obžalovaná osoba	obžalovaný	A → N	person charged with	a defendant	0
oprávněná osoba	oprávněný	A → N	eligible / entitled person	obligee / promisee / creditor	0
povinná osoba	povinný	A → N	obliged person	obligor / debtor	0
zavázaná osoba	zavázaný	A → N	obligated person	obligor	0
obmyšlená osoba	obmyšlený	A → N	one benefitting from an insurance contract	beneficiary	0

As can be seen, legal Czech unlike legal English is quite consistent in converting attributive phrases into nominal designations, which are much frequent in occurrence than their unellipted counterparts (due to obvious speech economy applied by law practitioners).

There are some other examples of conversion in legal English (although not confined only to law) which have no counterparts in Czech:

to want (to be in need)	→ the want (of care)	V→N
the breach (of contract)	→ to breach (a contract)	N→V
the commission of a judge	→ to commission (judges)	N→V
the void election	→ to void an election	A→V

(3) Lexical negation

Another problem should be mentioned in this section, namely lexical negation as it is frequently used in legal English. The verb *fail + infinitive*, and its nominal derivative *failure+ infinitive*, have a semi-auxiliary meaning and, in this sense, the verb *fail* belongs to a group of catenative verbs (Quirk et al., 1995: 146). To extend Quirk's assertions, it should be noted that *fail (to)* is used in both active and passive constructions in legal English: clauses such as "the courts of common law failed to give redress" and "remedy fails to have been given by the court" may be found in English legal texts. The only syntactical function of the verb *fail to* is to suggest the negative form of the following infinitive suggesting the omission of an expected action, occurrence or performace, thus replacing the auxiliary *not* constructions. Legal Czech equivalents consistently use grammatical negation, for example: *fail to provide* (not to provide, C. 'neposkytnout'), *fail to decide* (not to decide, C. 'nerozhodnout'), *fail to submit* (not to submit, C. 'nepředložit'), etc. It should be admitted that an aspect of subjective fault may be perceived in such a construction (but is not prevailing). In the translation of such phrases into Czech, the noun *failure* turns the following infinitive into a negative form of the respective noun: *failure to provide* (C. 'neposkytnutí'; literally translated back into English as 'non-provision'), *failure to fulfil* (C. 'nesplnění'; literally in English 'non-fulfilment'), *failure to submit* (C. 'nepředložení' literally in English 'non-submission').

(4) Conjunct *rather than*

Finally, the contrastive replacive conjunct *rather than* should be mentioned. Its meaning in legal contexts is always adversative and can only be translated as the Czech adversative conjunction ‘nikoliv’. The following authentic clauses may illustrate the point:

“A rule made in the course of deciding cases, *rather than* legislation, is called a rule of common law.” (C. ‘Pravidlo vytvořené v průběhu rozhodování případů, *nikoliv* zákonem, se nazývá pravidlo obyčejového práva’)
“The aim of most public law provisions is the promotion of social objectives and the protection of collective *rather than* individual interests.” (C. ‘[...] ochrany kolektivních, *nikoliv* individuálních zájmů.’)
“The purpose of the case is to enforce the public duties of a state agency *rather than* to enforce the private rights of a citizen.” (C. ‘[...] vynutit veřejnoprávní povinnosti stáního úřadu, *nikoliv* osobní práva občana.’)
“Since trespass is a wrong done to the possessor only he *rather than* the owner can sue.” (C. ‘Poněvadž zásah do /užívacího/ práva je protiprávním činem namířeným proti držiteli, pouze držitel, *nikoliv* vlastník, může podat žalobu.’)
“Some actions are commenced by a petition *rather than* a writ, for example a divorce or a company liquidation.” (C. ‘Některá řízení jsou zahájena na návrh, *nikoliv* na základě oznámení o zahájení řízení, například žaloba o rozvod nebo prohlášení konkursu.’)
“Its purpose is to compensate the plaintiff *rather than* punish the defendant.” (C. ‘Jeho cílem je odškodnit žalobce, *nikoliv* potrestat žalovaného.’)

It is extremely important for a legal translator to be aware of this semantic “deviation” of the conjunct *rather than* in legal contexts. Its common meaning “with more propriety or advantage; with better reason or ground; more properly or justly”, as stated in the OED, if translated literally, will be legally inaccurate and may be misleading.

C. Terminology and lexemes

Lexemes consist of either one member (usually word), or of many members. The former are classified as mononymous, the latter as polynomial or polyonymous. The latter are sometimes also called phrasemes (Filipec & Čermák, 1985: 28) (cf. 3.2.3. below).

Traditional understanding of terminology (cf. Felber in 3.1.2.1. above) has been based on the assumption that terms should be mononymous, i.e. they should consist of one word, and at the same time they should be monosemous, i.e. bearing one meaning. Such a rule may generally apply to taxonomies, for example in criminal law, although not all crimes are denoted by a one-word term (e.g. *sexual assault* or *forcible entry* in English, or *vražda novorozeného dítěte matkou* in Czech law literally translated as ‘murder of a newly born child by his mother’; the occurrence of multi-word terms denoting crimes is significantly more frequent in Czech law than in the Anglo-American system of law). Monosemous, and at the same time mononymous, words would belong to the category of so-called terms of arts, or technical terms, that may be recognized as legal terms without any given context. In addition to the examples given under 3.1.2.1. above, there are a few procedural terms complying with the traditional understanding, namely *rozsudek* in the Czech language and its counterpart *judgment* in English (ordinarily with the deviation from regular spelling *judgement*).

A limited number of mononymous Czech terms have been formed as a result of the process called "univerbization" (Filipec and Čermák, 1985: 106). Univerbization is the transformation of a phraseme into one word as a result of language economy. The Czech *zpětvzetí* (literally translated as 'taking back') is one and the most significant example. This Czech noun has been formed in two steps: simple derivation of the verbo-adverbial phrase *vzít zpět* (E. 'take back') to its nominal form of *vzetí zpět* (N+Adv), and the creation of a one-word term by inversion (Adv+N) and joining into one noun so that the combination of the term with other lexemes into larger syntactic units is practicable. The English equivalent is *withdrawal*. It consists of the prefix *with-* (meaning 'away, back'), verbal root *-draw-* and nominal suffix *-al* as a formative of nouns of action common in legal English (cf. *removal, acquittal, committal, recital, dismissal, trial, denial*).

Other words which may be assigned to univerbization processes in Czech[31] are *proti*+N/Adj terms such as *protinávrh, protipohledávka* (or *protinárok*), *protisměnka*, etc. Their English equivalents would be formed with prefix *counter*+N (such as *counteroffer, counterclaim, counterbill*), or *cross*+N (such as *cross-action* or *cross-claim*). It should be noted, however, that there is a significant difference between *counterclaim* and *cross-claim* in that the former suggests "a claim for relief asserted against an opposing party after an original claim has been made" (Black's Law Dictionary 1999: 353), and the latter denotes "a claim asserted between co-defendants or co-plaintiffs in a case and that relates to the subject of the original claim" (Black's Law Dictionary 1999: 383). As there is only one possibility as to how to translate either one into Czech, namely *protinávrh*, the distinguishing features should be explained by a translator in extension of the equivalent: *counterclaim* as 'protinávrh protistrany', and *cross-claim* as 'protinávrh proti spolužalobci / spolužalovanému'. It should also be noted that *cross-claim* does not exist as a legal institution under Czech law; translating this term means introducing legal realia typical of the Anglo-American system of law into legal Czech, which usually requires some explanations to be provided by a translator either directly in the translated text or as a translator's note in a footnote.

Some Czech terms resulting from the process of univerbization and containing the prefix *proti-* have English equivalents without the corresponding *cross-* or *counter-* prefixes. The term *protiplnění* has its legal equivalent *consideration*[32] whose designation is differently motivated. The Czech adjective *protiprávní* is formed on a different principle compared to its English counterparts: the prefix *proti-* means 'against, contrary to', and fails to explicitly denote the negative substance of the English prefixes *un-* and *il-*. In this sense, the word-formational process of *protiprávní* is closer to that of *wrongful* (originally, 'full of wrong or injustice' did not mean that an act was openly illegal). *Protiprávní* without any particular context has more than one English equivalent: *unlawful, wrongful, illegal, illicit, illegitimate*. Each of them may be used in a different legal context and in combination with different determinants: *unlawful* is the most universal attribute in its usage denoting that an act is authorized neither by civil nor by criminal law; *wrongful* primarily suggests that the act is contrary to civil law (such as 'wrongful conduct' as a cause of an action for damages); *illegal* means "forbidden by law",

---

31 The adverb *proti* (E. 'against') transforms into a nominal prefix ('jmenná předpona') and combines only with nouns or adjectives.

32 The OED provides the following explanation of its semantic development: "At the first appearance (in about 16th century) it is hardly a technical term, or distinguishable from *motive;* it gradually acquired its precise technical meaning in the course of the 17th – 18th century. Natural affection was formerly called *good consideration*, as contrasted with *valuable consideration*, or that which is deemed to have value in a pecuniary sense: the distinction is now only of historical interest."

thus implying the criminal nature of an act (such as 'illegal search' or 'illegal entry', suggesting a crime has been committed); *illicit* is also used in criminal law in the same meaning, however, it can be found, in particular, as a part of the names of concrete crimes, such as 'illicit drug use', 'illicit drug trafficking', 'illicit distillation of liquors', or 'illicit manufacturing of goods'. Garner (1995: 416) assigns moral overtones to *illicit* in addition to the basic sense "not in accordance with, or sanctioned by law". The legal use of the last adjective *illegitimate* is confined to family law and denotes that a child was not born in lawful wedlock and, therefore, may be disregarded by law as a lawful offspring (in succession claims, for example).

D. Terminology and syntactical units

Generally speaking, a syntagma is composed of at least two units in sequence, creating a word-group reflecting certain syntactic relations of the sentence to which it belongs. There are two aspects of translating legal language where syntactic units should be considered:

(1) Nominalization: the language of law (both English and Czech) tends towards multi-verbization; the concentration of information in terms and other substantives or nominal groups diminishes the meaning of verbs, reducing their function to a syntactical one. Čechová et al. (1997: 160) assign the feature to the general category of nominalization; Dušková (1988: 418 – 419) points out that the syntactical nominalization (i.e. verbo-nominal predication) may only exist if there is a verb from which the verbo-nominal construction can be derived. In the absence of such a verb, lexical nominalization would occur.

Syntactical nominalization may be represented by the following examples: the phrase *porušovat zákon* may often be found in English texts as an adverbialized verbo-nominal construction 'to be in breach / violation of the law' expressing an instantaneous act (although 'to break / breach / violate the law' could also be used); the Czech phrase *požádat soud o co* would be 'to make an application to the court for st.', emphasizing again the instantaneous act.

Lexical nominalization should be used when translating the frequent Czech term *podnikat*, one of the key terms in business law. There is no verbal equivalent in English. Nominal constructions should be used instead; 'undertake business' or 'carry on business' would be the most suitable for all contexts where the Czech verb may occur; 'to run / operate the business' and 'pursue the business' may serve in some contexts. In all the phrases, however, the autosemantic function of the verbs has been reduced to an auxiliary verbalizing the construction the meaning of which consists in the noun.

(2) Prepositions determining the meaning of a term followed by a prepositional complement: there is a small number of terms the precise meaning of which may only be specified in collocation with a preposition connecting the noun with its prepositional complement: *an interest ‹in› property* means a share in property (or the right or title to property), whilst *interest ‹on› the principal* (or any other amount of money) means the money paid for the use of money lent. The term *liability* may be followed by two prepositional phrases each of which would denote a different meaning: *liability ‹for› st.* is legal responsibility for an act the breach of which would lead to a legal sanction ('liability for damage' means that a person caused the damage and will be sued for it; the Czech equivalent terminological phrase is 'odpovědnost za škodu'); *liability ‹to› st.* suggests that there is a duty to do something (for example, 'the liability to damages' means that the court ordered that the person would have to pay the compensation; the Czech equivalent terminological phrase is 'povinnost k náhradě škody'). The Czech

transitive verb free of an obligatory preposition *diskriminovat /koho/* must be translated as 'discriminate ‹against› someone' to accurately select one meaning of the polysemous English verb. The Czech noun *doručení/předvolání/ komu* in the context of judicial proceedings should be translated as 'service /of process/ ‹on/upon› someone' to denote the specific meaning of the polysemous English noun (or verb in a corresponding verbal phrase 'to serve the process ‹on/upon› someone').

3.1.2.4. Terminological phrasemes

Phrasemes are usually defined as constituents which function as elements of clause structure (Quirk et al., 1995: 60, 992n). Terminological phrasemes are syntactic units acquiring a stable and regular meaning typical for a certain specialist context. Fillmore (1978: 170) admits that "legal vocabulary, more than anything else I know of, forces us to recognize phrases as lexical items". For example, *maliciously damaging the property of another* is a terminological phraseme denoting a misdemeanour under U.S. law. Grammatically, it is a noun phrase consisting of the premodifier *maliciously*, the phrase head *damaging*, followed by the postmodifier *the property* and attributively complemented with *of another*.

Thomas (1993: 57–58) extends the definition of phraseological units; she assumes that terminological phrasemes should:

(1) include at least one linguistic/syntactic element;

(2) have a minimum of two elements, one with object characteristics, the other with verb characteristics;

(3) be no longer than a sentence;

(4) contain at least one concept represented by a term (also known as terminological phraseology);

(5) contain collocations which (i) may be in current usage for only a certain period of time and which (ii) may depend for their particular meaning on the text in which they appear.

The above mentioned terminological phraseme *maliciously damaging the property of another* meets all five requirements although most phrasemes would correspond to only some of them. The clause *I owe you*, better known as the acronym *IOU*, is a terminological phraseme denoting an informed memorandum acknowledging a debt. It fails to fulfil Thomas' last requirement under (5) above as the unit preserves its meaning independently of any specific context and has been used for quite a long time. However, we can still consider *I owe you* to be a terminological phraseme rather than a simple clause since its main function is to provide a title for a written statement of private debt, and not to really predicate the relationship between the parties.

Sager et al. (1980: 233) recognize the problems of identifying 'extended terminological units' which the special lexicographer faces when "making his decision about the unity of a term with reference to the knowledge structure of a discipline". The problem, however, subsists in deciding under which lemma (or headword, entry) the terminological phraseme should be placed, rather than in identifying the phraseme itself (which is usually determined by law dictionaries or statutes).

Basically, there are three types of terminological units in Czech law requiring three different approaches for their translation into English:

(1) Phrasemes *důkaz výslechem obžalovaného* (literally translated as 'evidence by testimony of the defendant'), and *zákonná domněnka svědčící manželu matky* (literally translated as 'statutory assumption indicating the husband of the mother') are multi-word terms of criminal

procedure and family law respectively. They were formed by elliptical nominalization (*důkaz* »je proveden« *výslechem obžalovaného*; *zákonná domněnka* »otcovství« *svědčící* »ve prospěch« *manžela matky* »dítěte«). Formally, these Czech phrasemes usually consist of (premodifier +) head + attributive postmodifier + complement (+ postmodifying attribute).[33] Functionally, they have no terminological counterparts in legal English and therefore translation should be done in such a way that the basic characteristics of the Czech term may be preserved: 'evidence by examination of the defendant' and 'statutory presumption of paternity of the mother's husband' respectively. Each autosemantic member of these composite phrasemes serves as a separate term in the Anglo-American law. In addition, 'presumption of paternity' serves as an English binominal term. However, the whole English phrases can hardly be called terminological phrasemes in the strict sense described above.

(2) The second type encompasses repeatedly used stipulating clauses, such as [1] *pokud zákon nestanoví jinak* (literally translated as 'unless the law provides otherwise'), [2] *pokud není stanoveno jinak* ('unless it is provided otherwise'), [3] *aniž jsou dotčena jiná práva* ('without other rights being affected'). Similarly, the complementing adjective phraseme [4] *ve znění pozdějších předpisů* ('in the wording of later regulations') is appended to the citation of a particular law. Quite often, there are phrases in English law similar in function although not necessarily accurate in the sense of literal translation. They are usually called functional equivalents (see Newmark 1988: 83, below) which can be extended to syntactic units larger than one-word terms. Thus, [1] can be transferred into English as either (a) *unless the Act provides otherwise* which is both a semantic and a functional equivalent; or (b) *except when otherwise provided by statute* being a functional equivalent having a different type of elliptical predication; [2] the English counterpart *in the absence of a provision to the contrary* is a functional equivalent nominalized in its syntactic form; [3] the English phraseme *without prejudice to any other rights* is a noun phraseme whereas its Czech counterpart is a stipulating clause of a complex sentence; and [4] *as amended* is an elliptical adverb phraseme (standing for "as it has been amended"), performing the same function as its Czech composite counterpart.

(3) The third type includes clauses containing the Czech verb *mít* (E. 'have') in its modal function, quite limited in occurrence but problematic in translation. These are not regular terminological phrasemes, but are confined to legal contexts, thus acquiring a certain amount of terminological characteristics, and their form is more or less stable. The following clauses can be found in Czech law:

[1a] *má-li soudce za to, že / soudce má za to, že* ...(literally translated as 'if the judge thinks that' / 'the judge thinks that'); or its reflexive variant

[1b] *není-li dohodnuta doba, má se za to, že...* (literally translated as 'if no time has been agreed it is thought that').

The Czech idiomatic phraseme *mít za to, že* in its meaning of 'to assume, presume, think' has traditionally been used in general Czech. The legal usage has shifted its function from a simple assumption without significant implications to the determination of circumstances that would create legal consequences. English catenative constructions (Quirk et al., 1995: 146–147) are used in legal English in the same contexts and meanings. Therefore, [1a] would read *where it appears to the judge that*, and [1b] *where time has not been agreed it appears that....* As the authors point out, such constructions have meanings related to the aspect of modality, but are nearer to main verb constructions than are semi-auxiliaries; however, like

---

33 Linguistic terminology as used by Quirk et al. (1995).

some semi-auxiliaries, they are closely related to constructions with the anticipatory *it*; our experience suggests that the *it* form prevails in legal English in such contexts.

[2a] *pachatel se měl dopustit trestného činu krádeže* (literally translated as 'the offender is said to have committed the crime'); or

[2b] *žalovaný měl způsobit škodu* (literally translated as 'the defendant is said to have caused damage').

Daneš, Grepl and Hlavsa (1987: 293) speak about the modal category of the expected occurrence or non-occurrence of a certain action in similar contexts of the construction *mít* + infinitive (usually of a transitive verb). In Czech procedural law, where similar clauses are to be found, the examples would denote that the defendant is more likely than not to have done something unlawful, thus committing a crime (criminal proceedings) or causing damage (civil proceedings). The clauses suggest, however, that the court has not decided the case and that the guilt or liability of the defendant has not been established at the time of speech; the clauses would be found in initial procedural documents such as complaints (both criminal or civil), prosecutor's statements, transcripts of those parts of a trial where evidence was produced, etc. An equivalent verb phrase with the same function in legal English is the passive construction of *to be alleged to have done st* (always with the past infinitive). Thus, [2a] would read *the offender is alleged to have committed a theft*, and [2b] *the defendant is alleged to have caused damage*. Although the passive verb phrase *to be alleged to have done st.* is not explicitly listed by Quirk et al. (1995: 147) as a catenative verb, we tend to assign it to that group since *allege* loses its primary function and serves as a modal verb preserving some semantic features of its primary meaning.

3.1.2.5. Synonymy in terminology

Generally, synonyms are two or more words (in the same language) having the same general sense, but each of them possessing meanings which are not shared by the other or others, or having different shades of meaning or implications appropriate to different contexts (OED, 2002). In a stricter sense, a synonym is a word having the same meaning as another, which Burton (1998: viii) calls an 'exact' synonym, and which almost does not exist in the languages of either Czech or English law.

As Filipec and Čermák (1985: 133) emphasize, two aspects should be considered: (a) the intension (as the internal content of a notion or the sum of the attributes contained in it) which can be identical or variant, and (b) the distribution of synonyms. Where the synonyms are identical with respect to both intension and distribution, full (or 'exact') synonymy occurs; there will be partial synonyms in all other cases, which prevail in occurrence. Even if we find legal terms that have identical meaning (i.e. the intension), their distribution would differ, e. g. they will be used in different branches of law. One example can be given here: *fault* (OED: something wrongly done, culpability) and *blame* (OED: responsibility for anything wrong, culpability) may be used interchangeably in most contexts of general English. In law, however, *fault* is precisely defined as "any deviation from prudence or duty resulting from inattention, incapacity, perversity, bad faith or mismanagement" and reference is made to the entry of *liability* as "legal responsibility enforceable by civil remedy or criminal punishment" (Black's

Law Dictionary, 1999: 623);[34] *blame* is explained as "responsibility for something wrong" (Black's Law Dictionary, 1999: 163) without any specification or reference. Various legal contexts we have worked with would suggest that *fault* is a "genuine" legal term defined by law and giving rise to liability (i.e. legal responsibility), whereas *blame* may serve as its synonym only in a wider legal context outside the scope of statutory or judicial writings.

Picht and Draskau (1985: 103) consider the problems of linguistic terminology operating in this area. They point out that "synonymy" and "equivalence" denote very similar phenomena. The only difference lies in the fact that "synonymy" refers to identity of a concept designated by different terms in the same language, while "equivalence" refers to the same phenomenon expressed in two or more languages. Non-linguists tend to confuse the two terms (see Burton's Legal Thesaurus 1998: 212). Lewandowska-Tomaszczyk (1990: 183) extends the problem to dictionary-making. She distinguishes between (a) the relation between a single linguistic unit and a sum of features or parts possibly defining its sense, as between the definiendum and the definiens; and (b) the relation between two or more single linguistic units, considered identical or near-identical in meaning in different languages, as in cross-language equivalents. The former refers to synonymy and its implications in lexicography (primarily monolingual dictionaries), the latter refers to equivalence as a major component of bilingual lexicography.

Some Czech linguists examining synonymy in terminology use the term "onomasiological doublets" to denote the origin of terminological synonyms in the Czech language. Poštolková (1984: 19) understands the process as denoting different conceptual elements of one term – concept. Generally, there are couples consisting of one member of Czech origin, the other being of foreign origin or a loan-word (e.g. *zákonný* (E. 'statutory'/ and *legální* /E. 'legal'), or a one-word term and its multi-word synonym (*civilista* /E. 'civilian'/ and a quasi-term *znalec občanského práva* (E. 'expert in civil law'). Filipec & Čermák (1985: 94) are even stricter: in their conception, terminological synonyms are only onomasiological doublets; synonymy of terms occurs, in particular, where (natural) attempts are made to find or coin a domestic term to replace that of foreign origin (such as calques or loan-translation). Such assertion, however, applies only to full terminological synonyms (see above), partial synonyms are not of such uniform origin. For example, *soudní jednání* and *hlavní líčení* are synonyms since they denote the same stage of procedure, namely the hearing before court in a courtroom, i.e. their intension is almost identical. However, the distribution of the terms differs: the former belongs to civil procedure and the latter to criminal procedure. Symptomatically, the English term *trial* is the only equivalent for both Czech terms.

Terminological doublets or triplets and synonym-strings in legal English and their translation into Czech create a separate area that would deserve special attention, however this would be beyond our present purpose of focusing on a Czech-into-English direction of comparison. As Garner (1995: 293–294) summarizes, scholars have not been able to agree on the explanation of origins of doubling, whether due to pairing "Old English" and "Old French" terms (such as *terms and conditions*), due to rhetorical mannerism, or simply due to the general disposition of lawyers to seek safety in verbosity rather than in discrimination in language. Garner provides a list of doublets and triplets and longer strings and comments on the desirability of their usage in legal English nowadays, essentially denying their necessity.

---

[34] Louisiana Civil Code, 1996 edition, in its article 3506 further subdivides the term *fault* into three degrees: *gross fault* (which proceeds from inexcusable negligence or ignorance; it is considered as nearly equal to fraud); *slight fault* (the want of care which a prudent man usually takes of his business); and *very slight fault* (which is excusable and for which no liability is incurred).

One Czech legal term may have several equivalents in Anglo-American law which are synonyms with different distribution in various contexts. The Czech *zákon* may be translated as 'act', 'law', 'statute' or even 'legislation'. The countable noun 'a law' would be a universal equivalent which may be used both in law ('the law in force') and other branches ('the laws of nature'). A 'statute' is a written law or a law passed by a legislative body denoting the written documents as such. This term would never occur in the title of a particular law; such function would be performed by the term 'act' (e.g. the Family Act, 1995). Finally, speaking about laws generally, the uncountable 'legislation' may be used. As Foxley and Gwei (1989: 113) argue, a pair of words may be synonymous in one context but not in another. The above-given explanation of the four equivalents of the Czech *zákon* would serve as an example. Although they are synonyms their distribution would differ contextually: 'statute' and countable 'law' could be used interchangeably if a written law is discussed (not mentioning its title); 'act' is the only one from the selection that may occur in the title; and 'statutes', 'laws' or 'legislation' may be used indiscriminately if a legal regulation reflected in its written form is under consideration.

Finally, two points should be mentioned here. First, the use of terminological synonyms in general language (particularly in mass media) leads to the loosening and, possibly, to dissolution of the original meaning as terms, which consequently leads to the indiscriminate use of various synonyms by non-lawyer translators. Naturally, this problem occurs in translations from English into Czech if they are produced by native Czechs (not distinguishing, for example, the above mentioned *soudní jednání* and *hlavní líčení* as possible equivalents of the English *trial*), or from Czech into English if done by English speakers of an origin other than Czech (not distinguishing among *legacy*, *devise* and *bequest* as possible equivalents for the Czech *odkaz*). Second, translating legal texts should be free from (excessive) creativity on the part of a translator. It is suggested that one term be used for one concept although synonyms may exist. As Šarčević (2001: 87) notes, the use of different terms to express the same legal concept may be misleading as it implies that reference is being made to a different concept.

3.1.2.6. Homonymy *versus* polysemy in terminology

Both homonymy and polysemy represent quite a difficult problem in legal translation since the effect of polysemy is in principle the same as that of homonymy – the representation of two or more meanings by a single form thus requiring different equivalents in the target language. Etymological relations seem to be crucial in dictionary-making as the two types should be distinguished as different headwords (homonyms) or various equivalents of one headword (polysemes). Traditional understanding of homonymy, as opposed to polysemy, is that homonyms have no common etymological roots or basis whereas polysemes have developed from one common form and acquired different or modified meanings through their devolution.

We would maintain Poštolková's assumption (1983: 24, 27) that terminological homonyms, are the same kind of terms used in different branches of science (for example, *líčení* /'trial'/ in criminal proceedings and *líčení* /'make-up'/ in the art of visagistes). Therefore, we argue that pure homonymy within one legal system exists in neither legal Czech nor legal English. The problem that lawyers as well as translators dealing with Czech and Anglo-American law face is rather extensive polysemy resulting from a general tendency in the languages to assign new meanings to the existing vocabulary.

As Riggs (1982: 160), (1993: 207) points out when explaining the substance of polysemy that valence denotes the type of term-to-concept relationship: when a word has one and only one meaning, it may be called univalent (or monosemic), and when it has two or more meanings it is multivalent (polysemic or polysemous); a multivalent (polysemous) term that has only one meaning within a given discourse community can be called unequivocal, whereas when it has several meanings in such a community, it is properly called equivocal. For example, the Czech term *likvidace* is an unequivocal polyseme, it may be used in many fields of science; however, the legal term *likvidace* is confined to company law (*likvidace společnosti*) and succession law (*likvidace dědictví*), with one equivalent in legal English, i.e. 'liquidation' ('liquidation of company' and 'liquidation of inheritance' respectively). Similarly, the Czech term *náprava* is an equivocal polyseme since it serves as a term in many areas (e.g. in car technology *náprava vozidla*, E. 'axle'), and it has more than one meaning in Czech law, reflected in its English equivalents *remedy* (in the meaning of legal redress) and *correction* (speaking about the rehabilitation of offenders). Descriptive terminology recognizes that a polyseme can be used unambiguously in context. Authors can use an equivocal term unambiguously if they supply contextual clues to show which of its possible meanings is intended (Riggs, 1989: 96). Prescriptive terms (such as those used in statutes) are either defined by the respective statute or their precise meaning is implied in a wider legal context because they have been defined in earlier laws and have become a part of the terminology.

Two examples of Czech polysemous terms may illustrate the above assumptions, namely *právo* and *věc*:

(1) *Právo* can be translated either as uncountable *law* if the system is meant, or a *right* where a justifiable claim is in question. The two meanings may be suggested by an immediate attributive context *objektivní právo* and *subjektivní právo* respectively. However, the distinguishing attributes are not a regular part of the terms; they would be used primarily in texts relating to the theory of law, or where the correct meaning is not suggested by a wider (textual) context or should be made more precise or accurate.

(2) *Věc* should be translated according to the branch of law involved: the context of procedural law (both civil and criminal) determines the English equivalent of *case* or *dispute*. Thus, the Czech phrase *nápad věcí* will be transposed into legal English as a *case load*. In property law, the Czech *věc* will be transferred as *a thing* or uncountable *property*; its attributive derivative *věcný* in a binominal term *věcná práva* would be translated as the *rights in things* or *property / proprietary rights*.

3.1.2.7. Jargon and terminology

There is no uniform definition of jargon as a variety according to the field of discourse, however there are many words, phrases and structures, primarily in legal English, but also in legal Czech, that should be considered with more care and attention, and always with a certain suspicion, particularly where they are to be translated into another language. A significant difference between English and Czech understanding of jargon as it is contained in textbooks and dictionaries may be traced.

A. Jargon and the English language

The problematics of jargon in the Anglo-American system of law is of such complexity that it goes beyond the purpose of this study. However, our rough estimate suggests that what is described as jargon below creates about 50% of all expressions and phrases in Black's Law Dictionary, one of the most respected works in monolingual legal lexicography. Therefore, we will provide a brief summary of opinions.

Quirk et al. (1995: 23) is quite rigorous, saying that when learned or technical language is used too obtrusively or to all appearances unnecessarily, it is often pejoratively referred to as "jargon". The expression "jargon" in all eight senses as defined in the OED is applied contemptuously to a language by one who does not understand it. The OED indiscriminately assigns the expression to the terminology of a science or art, or the cant of a class, sect, trade, or profession. Longman Dictionary (1992: 702) delineates "jargon" as (often derogative) difficult or strange language which uses words known only to the members of a certain group; Collins Cobuild (1995: 899) defines "jargon" as words and expressions that are used in special or technical ways by particular groups of people, often making the language difficult to understand. Webster's Dictionary (1981: 513) gives its first definition of "jargon" as a speech that makes no sense because it is confused or meaningless; only the last of its four definitions admits "jargon" to be specialized vocabulary and idioms of those in profession and refers to slang which is described with the same words.

Tiersma (1999: 107) provides quite a wide definition of jargon: "[...] any words or phrases that are commonly and fairly exclusively used by a profession or trade – even if relatively vague – can be labelled 'jargon' ". He also clarifies Mellinkoff's[35] understanding of 'argot' which would be called jargon today, i.e. the vocabulary of a trade, occupation or profession. Tiersma adds that "talking like a lawyer" seems to be the only function of legalese, i.e. legal jargon, thus suggesting that the speaker is a member of the legal fraternity.

Garner, as a major advocate of plain English in law, provides an extensive definition of jargon (1995: 476):

> Jargon refers to the language, spoken and written, that members of any social, occupational, or professional group use to communicate to each other. The term refers to the full range of specialized vocabulary, devised by lawyers to save themselves time and space in communicating with each other, and sometimes even to conceal meaning from those uninitiated into the law.

However, he is rather rigorous in saying that jargon is unacceptable when the purpose of using it is to demonstrate how much more the speaker or writer knows as a specialist than do ordinary listeners and readers, and shows that "jargonmongering" is unnecessary although rather widespread. Garner goes even further (1991: 184, 1995: 872) arguing that most 'lawyerly-words' are mere 'legaldegook', not irreducible terms of art that carry a meaning not otherwise to be precisely conveyed. In his analysis of the language of law, Garner (1991: 182) agrees that the main feature of jargon, as contained in the dictionaries above, is its difficulty to be understood. He recommends that lawyers should "avoid jargon and beware terms of art". Jargon in law in its narrower sense consists mostly of stilted words and phrases (such as *aforesaid, hereinafter, before-mentioned*) as distinguished from the terms of art which Garner defines as legal terms with a specific legal meaning. He calls "foreignisms" Latin phrases and French words such as *ex contractu* or *ab initio*, but others are considered to be natural, e.g. *ex parte, habeas corpus, voir dire*; some foreignisms are used even in the broader language, such as *bona fide* or *alibi*; however, they all account for much of the obscure lawyerly tongue (p. 186). Garner suggests that doublets and triplets as a part of jargon should also be avoided (such

---

[35] Mellinkoff , David: Language of the Law (Boston: Little, Brown & Co., 1963: 18).

as *possession, custody and control*, where the sole *possession* is a broad enough term to consume the other two members of the string).

In his latest book, Garner (2001: 34) specifies the position of legal jargon or legalese within the language of law: "Lawyers have to labor to acquire it since they must understand it, and then they should labor to give it up in their own speech and writing to be understood." Garner coins the word "legalism" referring to legal jargon that has an everyday English equivalent, such as *motion for vacatur* versus *motion to vacate*. He claims that many legalisms belong to adverbial or prepositional phrases such as *inasmuch as* (because), *instant case* (here), *in the event that* (if), etc. and are fully replaceable by expressions of general English.

B. Jargon and the Czech language

Czech linguists have traditionally provided more precise and consistent definitions of individual registers of the Czech language focussing primarily on two varieties, namely standardized Czech (SC) "spisovná čeština" and common Czech (CC) "obecná čeština". Daneš (1999: 292) speaks about diglossia in Fergusson's understanding of the term,[36] however, with some reservations since the common language is not uniform within the whole country and has its local modifications. Regularly, three groups of vocabulary are distinguished in a specialist language, namely "terminology", "professionalisms" and "slang". Terminology clearly belongs to the SC, whereas slang is a substandard register not to be seen in written texts for specific purposes. Professionalisms, or jargon, stand between the two margins and oscillate in their nature as well as usage.

Bečka (1992: 12) defines *jargon* as professional speech mixed with extraneous elements; he strictly separates cant as the special phraseology of a particular class of persons, or belonging to a particular subject, which is always depreciative or contemptuous. Čermák (1997: 57, 404), however, regards jargon as a set of expressions and ways of its use by a certain group of persons, and subdivides it into *slang* (professional groups) or *argot* (usually marginal social groups), thus clearly assigning jargon to the non-codified CC.

Čechová et al. (1997: 45) regards professional speech to be a "semi-variety" ('poloútvar' in Czech) of the Czech language, thus belonging to the SC, and she seems to be quite persistent in avoiding the term "jargon", traditionally classified as a part of the CC (or standing somewhere between). Professional speech and slang differ primarily in motivation of designation and in quite a stable vocabulary of the former. She points out however (p. 158), that there are no firm borders between terms of art, professionalisms and slang words, as professionalisms may gradually become terms of art and slang may evolve to become professionalisms.

Poštolková (1983: 31–32) describes how professionalisms come into existence: along with a codified term or terminological phrase, a derivative, composite expression or nominalized adjective may occur, or an abbreviation, acronym, metaphoric or loan word or phrase may appear. The main purpose seems to be condensation of appellation and economy of expression.

Daneš (1999: 295) notes that although technical terminology has been successfully codified (this unfortunately does not fully apply to legal terminology), the practical language communication tends to gradually turn to professionalisms or even slang; he supports Poštolková's assumptions that many new terms originate in these unofficial circumstances;

---

[36] Fergusson, C. A.: Diglossia. Word XV (1959, pp. 325–340)

they may be loaded with irregular mechanical adoption of foreign elements (primarily of English origin) or their improper imitation.

In conclusion, we would argue that jargon may not be confined only to the lexicon of a subject-field; as a subvariety of language, it also covers morphology and syntax (see examples below). A rough distinction can be made between Czech legal terminology and Czech legal jargon. There are no doubts with respect to prescriptive terms as used in legislation (see Galinski above) – they belong to terms of art, and as such to the SC. Descriptive terminology would also belong to the codified language (such as *kauce* or *petit*). However, the elliptical language in everyday legal and judicial practice would be jargon tending to condense and economize legal speech (and unofficial writings). For example, the clause *budeme žalovat vyklizení* (literally translated as 'we will sue eviction') means that an action to evict a tenant from his or her flat will be brought before the court; reflexive constructions of regularly irreflexive verbs may also be assigned to jargon, such as the phrase *rozhodnutí se rozkladuje* (literally translated as 'the decision protests itself'): it means that an administrative decision is to be challenged by the aggrieved party; the reflexive verb *rozkladovat se* is a pure legalism used instead of a standard verbo-nominal phrase *podat rozklad* (E. 'to subject to protest'); moreover, it has been derived (by law practitioners) from the noun *rozklad* '(E. 'protest' in administrative law) simply to condense the information using one performative verb in lieu of a verbo-nominal phrase requiring a more complex syntactical government. Thus, jargon in legal Czech would apply primarily to larger units than words, i.e. to syntactical units. Vocabulary would be marginally relevant although a few examples were given in our dictionary, such as *vytěžený svědek* i.e. witness interrogated by the police which surprisingly has its counterpart in English jargon: 'debriefed witness'.

3.2. Linguistics of Translation

Although much scepticism has been expressed with respect to its potential (see, for example, White, 1990: 257: "Translation, as I am now defining it is thus the art of facing the impossible, of confronting unbridgeable discontinuities between texts, between languages, and between people."), translation is a process and activity people cannot dispense with. Both literary translation and translation for specific purposes have played an irreplaceable role in the advancement of mankind, the former mediating aesthetic emotions, the latter assisting the rational progress of the world. As Sager notes (1997: 29), translators act as information mediators. Particularly, recent unifying processes in Europe would not have existed or functioned without translation. Since their beginning in 1957, the European Communities have maintained and promoted the idea of multilingualism.[37] With more than 1300 translators and 400 secretaries, the Translation Service of the European Commission (SDT), located in both

[37] The Treaty establishing the European Coal and Steel Community (ECSC) and the Treaty establishing the European Economic Community were signed by six states: Germany, France, Italy, Belgium, Luxemburg and the Netherlands. The four languages, German, French, Italian and Dutch were recognized as equally authentic. New countries accessing the Communities had to translate all primary Community legislation into their national (official) languages; subsequently, secondary legislation has been translated into national languages. The process continues with new member states and the number of official languages amounts to 20 allowing for hundreds of permutations of language combinations for translation purposes (it was 110 combinations of 11 official languages in 2003 before the EU enlargement on 1st May 2004).

Brussels and Luxembourg, is the largest translation agency in the world and their total production is more than 1,000,000 pages a year (Lavigne, 2001: 36). In addition, the separate translating service, called the Translation Directorate, shared between the Court of Justice and the Court of First Instance is staffed by 420 employees, of whom 295 are lawyer-linguists and 110 are assistants and secretaries. The Translation Directorate is one of a few agencies in the world which require that a translator of judicial documents should possess combined legal and linguistic qualifications of a very high standard.

The title of this subchapter is used in Newmark's (1981: 114) and Knittlová's (1989: 179) understanding of the term, referring back to Catford (1965). The main purpose of the linguistics of translation is to describe processes that may occur, and what steps should be taken in the course of translation, rather than to constitute a body of rules by means of which a perfect translation may be achieved. We consider translation to be an interlingual transposition to a target text (TT) of the information contained in a source text (ST), respecting its generic (i.e. the type of text) and discourse characteristics, and adapting them to the function of the target text and the presumed expectations of the target recipient. The rootedness of both the source language and the target language is manifested by their linkage to the cultural heritage of their speech communities: language is often felt to be one of the "dearest creations of the society" (Gallardo,1980: 62). The translator should carefully analyse the environment (linguistic, historical, social, political etc.) in which the source text originated, and transmute its significant and distinctive features into the target text considering the purpose of the translation. As Tognini-Bonelli (1996: 198) points out the translator has the task of 'reproducing', or 're-creating', the original interaction for a different audience; Bhatia (1997: 204) specifies that translation is not simply a matter of linguistic transference alone, but a genuine act of communication in its own right, perhaps more complex than communication in a singular semiotic system.

Naturally, the purpose of the target text may differ from that of the original; whilst the main aim of a literary translation is generally to mediate the aesthetics of the source text and communicate it to a speaker of another language, the objective of legal translation, as a special-purpose text translation, may differ according to the type of legal text: the Czech translation of any British normative text, such as a statute or statutory instrument, would never appear with the same normative function in Czech law; it may serve, for example, as a source of legal information for Czech lawyers, or an inspiration for Czech legislators, and so on. On the other hand, the Czech translation of one type of European secondary legislation, namely the Regulation, will become a component part of Czech law immediately after the accession of the Czech Republic to the European Union, so both the original[38] and the translation will serve the same purpose having the same force and effect.[39] Consequently we cannot maintain Sager's (1997: 37) assumption that the core knowledge contained in the derived TL document cannot in essence exceed the knowledge contained in the SL document. It would depend on the

---

38 It should be noted, however, that speaking about "the original" of any piece of European legislation is rather misleading. There should be more than one source text, i.e. different language versions, particularly English, French and German. Thus the translation is based on a comparative study of the three "originals" in order to accurately and precisely transpose the provisions into Czech law.

39 All Czech statutes come into force upon their publication in the Collection of Laws of the Czech Republic. The same force of law of EU legislation will be achieved by publishing in the Czech language the Community "collection of laws", called the Official Journal, which will become the third collection in the Czech system of law (the Collection of Laws, the Collection of International Treaties, the Official Journal).

purpose of the translated text and expected previous knowledge of the target text recipient: it may easily happen that the translator has to "frame" his or her translation with explanatory notes and comments, thus providing information in the target text going far beyond that contained in the source text. Obviously, the final product of his or her endeavours would be a rather specific type of explicative translation, combining traditional translation methods with a certain volume of original information inserted in the target text so that the core knowledge of the source text can be effectively communicated to and comprehended by the recipient (see Bhatia's comment above). Translation, therefore, presupposes what Tognini-Bonelli (1996: 198) calls 'displaced situationality' in two respects. The purely linguistic context (or co-text) is displaced because it will inevitably differ in the source language and in the target language. The extra-linguistic, situational features will also be changed, as the context is bound to refer to, and reflect a different culture, a different situation, and a different participant and his or her expectations. The change in context will, unless compensated for, lead to a misleading interpretation of the text, however faithfully it has been translated.

Essentially, there are two main schools of translation studies. Trosborg (1997b: 153), summarizing their principles, distinguishes between translations based on a linguistic approach, which hinges on the concept of equivalence, and those established on a functional (pragmatic) approach, whose main emphasis is on the function of the target text. She points out that the pragmatic model takes into account the situational conditions of communicative interaction and, accordingly, of the needs and expectations of the addressees or (prospective) recipients of the target text. In practice, however, a good translation[40] should be a combination of the two approaches: it should preserve a certain degree of equivalence (at the level of vocabulary, syntax, genre (text) and discourse (style)), and the process of transmission should be framed to the function of the target text, thus considering its potential recipients and purpose. An informal interview with a famous American jazz musician would be translated in a significantly different manner, for example, depending on if it were to be published in a nation-wide newspaper, or in a specialized journal for jazzophiles; the latter translation would try to preserve a substantial portion of jazz slang and cant as well as the aura of the jazz musician and the atmosphere of his or her utterances, whereas the newspaper translation would focus on facts revealed in the interview communicated in a language comprehensible to a wider non-specialist public.

Almost forty years ago, Nida (1964: 241–245), a distinguished representative of the traditional translation theory based on the linguistic approach, emphasized analytical study of both source and target languages,[41] and an analysis of the source text covering the lexico-grammatical features of the immediate unit, as well as the discourse, communicative and cultural contexts of the source language. Nida realized, however, that the cultural context of the target text should also be considered, which would necessarily include some thinking about the function of the target text.[42] A thorough linguistic analysis in the widest sense of the term

---

40 A "good translation" is a rather vague category if we speak about translation in general: a good literary translation should instigate similar aesthetic effects as did the original for the benefit of its readers; a good translation of a special-purpose text should mediate the information contained in the source text as precisely, accurately and fully as possible, reflecting the purpose of the target text.

41 In Nida's terminology, the target language is called the *receptor* language.

42 Eleven years later, Nida maintained the same approach but modified his terminology: "Essentially, the translation process is one in which a person who knows both the source language and the receptor language decodes the message of the source language and encodes it into an appropriate equivalent form of the receptor language."

will always remain a substantial part of a translator's work but not the sole component of the whole process. As Newmark (1988: 45) points out there are different translation methods, the division of which would depend on whether focusing on either the source language and text or the target language and text.[43] If we concede that a focus on the target text may prevail in the process of translation it would allow us to think widely about the functions and consequences of the translation, thus analyzing the stylistics and pragmatics of the translation. Knittlová (1991: 213) speaks about four degrees of translation:[44] the highest two degrees, i.e. modulation and adaptation, would be preferred if a focus on the target text applies. Modulation will require that the source text should be formulated anew (not simply reproduced) reflecting the potential of the target language, and adaptation would be used where substantial socio-cultural differences occur between the source and target language communities thus accommodating a different purpose or audience or both. Returning to the above example of the interview with the jazz musician, adaptation would be the approach applied in both cases mentioned there; however, the degree, type and focus of modification would obviously differ.

Placing an emphasis on the function of the target text (not its perception by the recipient), which predetermines the translation strategy (i.e. approaches, methods and procedures), has prevailed in recent sources. Trosborg (1997b: 151) refers to Nord's extended "skopos" theory[45] applied to translation (Nord, 1991: 8). Nord claims that translation is determined by its purpose (*skopos* for 'aim' or 'target' in Greek), i.e. a translation must fulfill certain requirements, which are defined by translation "instructions" (assignments) in order to be suitable for a certain purpose. These assignments, which should consist of more or less explicit description of the prospective target situation, are referred to as "skopos", i.e. the text function of the target text. Nord (1997: 46), explaining her functional model of translation, argues that it is no longer the source text which sets the standards for the translator's decisions in the translation process, but the intended recipient of the translation, whose reception will be entirely guided by target culture, expectations, conventions, norms, models, real-world knowledge, perspective, etc. Such an approach may apply, for example, to situations where a translator is asked to produce a so-called "executive memorandum": he or she is instructed by the recipient of the translated text to select and translate the main ideas of the source text for the recipient's information. However, the different function of the target text as compared with that of the source text is not confined only to the translation of special-purpose texts. The "Eight Digests of World Authors" ('Osm digestů světových autorů') were published in the Czech language by the publishing house Adonai in 2001, offering an "abridged" version of eight classical novels.[46]

---

[43] Where the source language is emphasized, Newmark speaks about a word-for-word translation, literal translation, faithful translation or semantic translation; in the case of the TL emphasis there are methods such as adaptation, free translation, idiomatic translation or communicative translation.

[44] The terms were originally used by J. P. Vinay and J. Darbelnet in their *Stylistique compare du francais et de l'anglais* published in Paris in 1958.

[45] The skopos theory was introduced by Hans J. Vermeer in 1978; the title of his article is *Ein Rahmen für eine allgemeine Translationstheorie,* and it is available in *Aufsätze zur Translationstheorie,* published in Heidelberg 1983.

[46] The "Digests" were awarded an anti-prize "Skřipec" (E. 'Rack') for the worst translation published in the Czech Republic in 2002. The worst-achievement prize was established by the Translators' Guild, the Czech association of translators, to help counter pressures created by unscrupulous publishing business practices combined with dilettantism.

3.2.1. Genre-based approach to translation of legal texts

The main objective of the "Czech-English Law Dictionary with Explanations" has been, as emphasized above, to help all those who have to translate Czech legal texts into English. We will concentrate on the Czech language as the source language, however, a few comments should be made on legal translation in general.

Legal texts are usually included within a wide group of so-called special-purpose texts (cf. Šarčević, 2000: 6). Sometimes, the term "non-literary texts" is used to denote all other texts but artistic works. In his speech on the linguistic aspects of translating non-literary texts almost thirty years ago, Jedlička (1977: 29–34) emphasized the contrastive approach to the analysis of the three levels constituting the preparatory stage of translation: the analysis of communicative situations where the source text and target text are used (Jedlička's term *stylová/komunikativní sféra*; i e. 'discourse analysis' in the recent linguistic terminology), the description of types of the source text and the target text regularly used in certain communicative situations (*stylový typ*; today's 'genre analysis'), and the analysis of registers of the source text and the target text (*stylová vrstva* as the choice of linguistic means).

Discourse analysis has been the focus of many publications in linguistics since the 1970s (for example, Sinclair and Coulthard 1975, Widdowson 1979a and 1979b, Candlin 1981, Brown and Yule 1983, etc.). Genre analysis proved to be of significant importance when non-literary genres (specialist communication events) were considered (e. g. Swales 1990, Bhatia 1993).

Legal discourse within the Anglo-American system of law has been studied primarily by law researchers and teachers in order to provide an extensive picture of how the law functions, as well as to produce guidelines, so that novices in law could have some standards for acting in a "lawyerly" manner (cf. recent works of, for example, Solan 1993, Garner 1991, 2001, Tiersma 1999, Krieger et al. 1999). Genre analysis of various English legal texts has also been dealt with, for example, in Bhatia 1987, 1994b, Trosborg 1997a, and others. However, no broad comparative genre analysis, reflecting systemic differences of legal systems and languages, has yet been pursued for the purposes of translation (so far as we are aware); bilingual countries such as Canada or Hong Kong have elaborated strategies for issuing bilingual legislation and other legal documents, nonetheless, there is one system of law applied within the whole country although composed of common law and continental French law, and common law and Chinese law respectively.

Legal translation should be based, among other things, on comparative genre analysis in order to make the transfer of legal information as precise, accurate and comprehensible as possible, and to shape the target text in a manner adequate to its purpose. As Bhatia (1997: 206–7) emphasizes, translators should "develop the understanding of the two codes, the acquisition of genre knowledge associated with the specialist cultures, sensitivity to cognitive structuring of specialist genres in the two specialist areas and then, and only then, they can hope to exploit generic knowledge of a repertoire of specialist genres by becoming effective translators of specialist discourse in a particular chosen field." However, conceptual differences between different languages have played an important, sometimes a crucial role, and as Arntz (1993: 6) notes, the differences are especially stark in legal terminologies. The legal language is always associated with a particular legal system which has developed by means of a historical process and which differs from other legal systems. Law can only be expressed through the respective language. Therefore, terminological work in the legal field is always connected with an exact study of the field in question and the concepts used.

3.2.1.1. The Czech language as the target language

There are many ways to divide the whole body of law. The division between public law and private law would best serve our purpose to describe the different approaches of the Czech Government to supervising the processes and contributing to the standardization of legal Czech.

The area of the language of private law has been free of any intervention by the State, except for passing relevant legislation to create the legal framework for establishing private legal relations and providing prescriptive terminology. It is fully within the responsibility of the final recipient of the translated text whether or not he or she accepts it as sufficient and adequate. The translator can generally be held professionally responsible for the result of their work; their legal liability may be claimed only where material damage has been caused due to a bad translation; damage must be proven before, and damages ordered by, a court. There is one exception to this common rule according to the latest amendment of the Criminal Procedure Code (s. 175a, the crime of "perjured interpreting"): where the translator or interpreter (as a sworn interpreter or ad hoc appointed by the police or court) intentionally performs badly before court, a government body or any other state agency, he or she may be sentenced to the maximum of eight years of imprisonment. One may argue that an officially licensed sworn interpreter[47] should always complete a perfect job. The following example to be used is one of dozens proving the opposite.

A. An English certificate proving the registration of a company was issued in 1940. The first part reads as follows:

> **Certificate of Incorporation**
> I hereby certify, that A. H. Parker & Sons (Gt. Britain) Limited is this day incorporated under the Companies Act, 1929, and that the Company is Limited.
> [...]

B. The certificate was officially translated by a sworn interpreter who had been licensed to translate from and to seven languages (Czech, English, French, German, Spanish, Italian and Latin). Moreover, the translator had a law degree and the title of JUDr (Ius utriusque doctor). The following translation of the above part of the certificate was attested and signed by that translator in 1992:

> **Osvědčení o založení akciové společnosti**
> Já tímto stvrzuji, že A. H. Parker & Synové (V. Británie) spol. s r. o. se tímto dnem stává akciovou společností dle Zákona o společnostech z r. 1929 a je to společnost s ručením obmezeným. [...]

[47] Sworn (or court or forensic) interpreters are licensed by the Minister of Justice of the Czech Republic upon nomination by the Presidents of Regional Courts to act in both translating and interpreting for courts and other official bodies, as well as for private persons who wish to submit a translated document to a government body or local authority, including all types of official registers or foreign institutions. However, there have been no uniform qualification requirements set centrally by the Ministry of Justice, therefore the quality of individual interpreters varies.

C. Translation errors, according to their nature, can be subdivided into legal and linguistic mistakes:

(i) Legal mistakes:

[1] the *certificate of incorporation* is the name of a general and uniform document proving that the company named in it has been officially registered in the Register of Companies. Therefore, it should be translated as *osvědčení o registraci společnosti* or *osvědčení o zapsání společnosti do rejstříku společností.* No attribute suggesting the type of company ('akciové') should be added.

[2] the name of company "A. H. Parker & Sons (Gt. Britain) Limited" should never be translated into Czech in such legal documents and certificates. It is the so-called 'corporate name' which is transferable neither as a whole nor in part into another language and should always remain in the original. Moreover, the abbreviation *spol. s r.o.* standing for *Limited* is a statutory abbreviation for a Czech type of company established under Czech law, which type the British company apparently was not. The translator may, if necessary, append an explicative note or comment.

[3] the confusion of two types of company, namely *akciová společnost* (E. 'stock company' and *společnost s ručením omezeným* (E. 'limited liability company'), is an essential mistake; at the time of issuance of the certified translation in 1992, the Czech Commercial Code, regulating registered companies, had been effective for two years. It should have been clear to the translator (particularly because he was a lawyer) that the *společnost s ručením omezeným* and *akciová společnost* were qualitatively two different companies and no hybrid might exist in Czech or British law, nor would it be legally comprehensible should the translator have created one. The translator should have consulted the Act of 1929 (or any other later statute relating to companies in the United Kingdom) to clarify the type of company mentioned in the Certificate. He would have found that the status of a British limited company is very close to the status of the Czech *společnost s ručením omezeným*, therefore the phrase *akciová společnost* should never have been used in this context.

(ii) Linguistic mistakes:

Compared to the above legal errors, linguistic imperfections are only minor and, unlike legal mistakes, do not interfere with the informational accuracy of the translation. The initial phrase *Já tímto stvrzuji* may easily dispense with the personal pronoun, which is preferably omitted in such clauses in Czech; the final phrase *s ručením o‹b›mezeným* instead of *s ručením omezeným* has rather an archaic form of the classifying attribute dating back to the 15th century;[48] another explanation might be that the translator has "adapted" the recent Slovak adjective 'o‹b›me‹d›zený'.

In public law, traditionally, international treaties binding on the Czech Republic have been the only legal texts to be translated into Czech. Translations have been the responsibility of the Ministry of Foreign Affairs and the quality of translated texts, published in the Collection of International Treaties, has varied. One reason for the insufficient attention paid to the quality of translation may have been that, in the case of a dispute over a treaty, the governing language would be the language of the original, which has never been Czech.

---

[48] Bělič, J., Kamiš, A., Kučera, K., Malý staročeský slovník (Praha: SPN, 1978, p. 232)

In 1999 a new unit was established within the Office of the Government of the Czech Republic, namely the Compatibility Department. It consists of three sections: (a) the section responsible for all Government bills being compatible with EU legislation; (b) the section responsible for revising translations of EU legislation in the Czech language; (c) the analytical section in charge of reviewing Czech positive law in the light of the EU acquis communautaire. The Revision Section was intended to play an extremely important and decisive role in the codification of new Czech terminology as transposed into Czech law from the EU legislation. The team is composed of both lawyers and linguists; the main outcome of their work is the Guidelines for Translation of EU Legislation (1995). This manual should be used by all those translating Community laws into Czech and the Revision Section has permanently augmented its volume with new terminology, or revised and modified older terms and phrases. The procedure of revising the translated texts, however, has been rather complicated and the final decision with respect to Czech equivalents of the European Community and European Union law terms, as well as sentence patterns, is left with the respective ministries where officials in charge are not always competent in both law and linguistics. As a result, the Guidelines contain a lot of imperfections and mistakes, and, as a material binding on translators, they contribute to the insufficient quality of Czech translations. Further, the translations serve as a basis for amendments to the existing Czech legislation, or new laws, required to be passed in the process of approximation of Czech law with that of the European Union. Thus, complex multi-clause sentences with unconsolidated Czech terminology from the translated European laws sneak into Czech legislation, making it even more unclear, incomprehensible and difficult to interpret and apply.

One brief example may be given here. The binding Guidelines provide on p. 29 that the following English, French or German statements should be translated into Czech as is given in the last box:

The opinion shall be recorded in the minutes; in addition, each Member State shall have the right to ask to have its position recorded in the minutes.
L'avis est inscrit au procès-verbal; en outré, chaque Etat membre a le droit de demander que sa position figure à ce procès-verbal.
Die Stellungnahme wird in das Protokoll aufgenommen; darüber hinaus hat jeder Mitgliedstaat das Recht zu verlangen, dass sein Standpunkt im Protokoll festgehalten wird.
Stanovisko je uvedeno do zápisu; kromě toho má každý členský stát právo požádat, aby byl v tomto zápisu uveden jeho postoj.

The first clause in the Czech translation *Stanovisko je uvedeno do zápisu* is syntactically incorrect. We are speaking about "contamination", i.e. the process by which two valences (or verbal complementations) are crossed to produce a single new form (Čermák, 1997: 222). It may be assumed that two Czech phrases were mixed: *uvést v zápise* and *dát do zápisu*. One semantic imperfection may be noted: the Czech word *postoj* has obviously been used here to avoid the repetition of *stanovisko* in the first part of the statement. The English *position*, French *position* and German *Stadtpunkt* may freely be translated as *názor*, which would be appropriate here. *Postoj* means a more general attitude whilst *názor* is an explicit demonstration of the attitude that can be expressly entered in the minutes.

3.2.1.2. The Czech language as the source language

There has been no official body responsible for standardizing translations of Czech legislation and other binding documents into foreign languages. Should any foreign partner (whether a partner of the State or a private individual or entity) require a Czech law to be translated and made more comprehensible this is done only as an unofficial translation without any legal force or effect. Even translations of the Czech Constitution and the Charter of Fundamental Rights and Freedoms placed on the official website of the Czech Parliament[49] are unofficial translations and may not be relied upon in the event of any conflict or dispute relating to their legal interpretation. Where contracts or other private documents are in question the English translation of the Czech original may serve as an equal counterpart only when it is explicitly so provided in the text of the contract. Documents relating to court proceedings (e.g. judgments, requests for international legal assistance from foreign courts, etc.) are translated by the licensed court interpreters mentioned earlier.

Two aspects of the translation of Czech legal documents ought to be considered: the linguistic and legal quality of Czech texts themselves and the quality of translation. Foreigners translating Czech legal texts into their mother tongue have always complained of the lack of clarity in the language, and had to face, and deal with, situations similar to those succinctly described by Brown (1995: 71) when she was talking about the translation of Russian legal texts:

> Sometimes a translator of Russian legal documents can feel that terminology is the least of her worries. Russian legal documents appear rife with ambiguity and vagueness, and possible errors. Compared to Western practice, Soviet legal drafting may have favored vagueness and ambiguity. These compositional habits vest more power in totalitarian state, by leaving it free to author its laws and then construe them. The relatively large number of apparent mistakes in Russian legal documents may result from the hurry and decentralization of legal drafting, increasing during perestroika and again after the 1991 coup. A clean translation, without footnotes, could either "correct" such passages or carefully reproduce them for a reader to notice and then wonder whether to fault the translation or the original document. Commentary in the context of a possible error has the advantages of protecting the translator, finessing the decision as to whether a given looseness is a mistake and, most important for Western investors, flagging trouble spots that potentially influence the interpretation of a law.

Although Czech legislation suffers from the same diseases, we would argue that the vagueness and ambiguity of laws have not fostered a greater power of the Czech state; on the contrary, this problem has opened channels for various quasi-legal practices primarily in business, and controversial and diverse interpretation by different courts has led to substantial legal uncertainty in the society.

Unlike English, Czech for specific purposes generally, and for law in particular, has had to face significant negative influences since 1989. Many language-destabilizing factors might be on account of precipitant changes in the society, some of them occur due to our generally declining knowledge of our mother tongue, whereas some may be put down to a neglectful use of Czech by Czech native speakers. Kraus (1995: 196) describes:

> V odborném stylu [...] se výrazně projevují procesy unifikace, tj. prolínání prvků odborného vyjadřování do publicistiky, do běžné mluvy, do umělecké literatury, a procesy diferenciace, tj.

---

[49] Http://www.psp.cz

vydělování okruhů stále více specializovaných. [...] Praktické důsledky má nejasnost tohoto vztahu zejména pro formulaci textů právních a obecněji žánrů normativní povahy, jako jsou smlouvy, nařízení, předpisy a vyhlášky. Dochází tu totiž často k rozporu mezi požadavky věcné přesnosti, úplnosti na straně jedné a obecné srozumitelnosti na straně druhé. [...] Vinu za výklad, který není ve shodě se záměrem zákonodárce, nemusí vždy nést čtenář, ať už poučený, nebo nepoučený. Víceznačné věty, rozsáhlé a nesourodé řetězce genitivních přívlastků, vyšinutí z vazby, to vše cestu k smyslu věty nejen zatemňuje, ale přímo znemožňuje.
(In the special-purpose variety of language, the process of unification can be seen, i.e. elements of the specialist language diffusing into the language of journalism, general language, literary language; and the process of differentiation, i.e. separating fields becoming more and more specialized [...] Practical consequences of the unclear relationship of the two processes can be seen in formulating legal texts and other genres of a normative nature, such as contracts, orders, guidelines and regulations. Discrepancies often arise between the requirement of subject-matter accuracy and completeness on one part, and general comprehensibility of the text on the other. [...] A reader should not necessarily be blamed, whether knowledgeable or ignorant, for an interpretation incompatible with the intent of the legislator. Ambiguous sentences, equivocal and disparate chains of genitive attributes, anacoluthons, all these make discovering the meaning of a sentence rather obscure or even impossible.) *(Translated by author)*

Žemlička (1995: 201) adds that Czech for specific purposes often contains "phrases, loan expressions, pseudo-neologisms and stylistic crudeness proving the unqualified, perfunctory approach of the author or translator." The main reasons are ascribed to the influence and "deleterious effect of the English language in the Czech speaking environment" as well as to significant gaps in the knowledge of the Czech language as shown by native Czech speakers. Apparently, it is not the English language itself which may cause "damage" to Czech; the main problem lies in the absence of a general language policy in the Czech Republic where care about the language has not been paid any political attention and has remained only within the walls of universities and scholarly institutes. Persons acting in the public area, such as politicians and many journalists, have disregarded and neglected this means of communication, thus contributing to the incomprehensibility and extreme vagueness of official texts including legislation and private legal documents. It is not only that little has been done since 1918 to legally purify our legislation and make it transparent (see 2.1. above), but also linguistic ignorance and want of attention, increasingly shown after 1990, have contributed to the chaotic situation in Czech law.

One authentic example of gross linguistic neglect shown in the Czech language can be provided here: the following extract is a paragraph from an official textbook of Czech business law for students studying law within the Socrates/Erasmus programme in the Law School of Charles University in Prague. The Czech text had been proofread and edited before printing. It was then translated and a parallel Czech – English text was formed. The extract is taken from the proofread and edited text:

Mezi tyto speciální důvody zrušení veřejné obchodní společnosti patří např. výpověď společníka, smrt společníka fyzické osoby, zánik společníka právnické osoby, [1]prohlášení‹m› konkursu na majetek některého ze společníků nebo zamítnutím návrhu na prohlášení konkursu pro nedostatek majetku, [2]zbavení‹m› nebo [2a]omezení‹m› způsobilosti k právním úkonům některého ze společníků. *(Numbers in brackets are inserted to visualize the problem.)*

Instrumentals in [1], [2] and [2a] are obvious mistakes which have apparently been left in the text as a result of an attempt to rephrase the original provision in the Commercial Code (sec. 88 (1): "Kromě případů uvedených v §68 se společnost zrušuje: [...] e) prohlášením konkursu

[...], f) zbavením nebo omezením způsobilosti [...]"). The translator had to identify the type of mistake by consulting the respective Code (to exclude the mistake in punctuation and a subsequently different interpretation of the thus formed complementary clauses: "zánik společníka právnické osoby prohlášením konkursu [...]"), and to translate the correctly construed paragraph:

> The special grounds for the dissolution of an unlimited company shall be, for example, a notice by a company member of termination of his/her membership, the death of a company member - natural person, the cessation of the existence of a member - juridical person, the adjudication of the bankruptcy order with respect to the property of any of the company members, the dismissal of the petition for the bankruptcy order due to an insufficient bankrupt's estate, the incapacitation or limitation of legal capacity of any of the company members.

The corpus of Czech legal texts in public law, or legal realia, consists not only of normative acts but also of other types of writings classified by Kořenský, Cvrček & Novák (1999: 16–17) as follows:

(a) legislation (all laws as well as secondary legislation published in an official journal entitled the "Collection of Laws of the Czech Republic");
(b) judicial decisions (published in various law reports);
(c) individual decisions and normative instructions of state administration bodies;
(d) explanatory memoranda published along with proposed legislation;
(e) proposed legislation and projects;
(f) parliamentary debate records;
(g) collected comments on draft bills resulting from their circulation within the comment procedure in the relevant government departments;
(h) commentary on enacted legislation;
(i) law textbooks and monographs;
(j) law journal articles;
(k) expert opinions (of outstanding lawyers, primarily with respect to the interpretation of legislation);
(l) itemized lists of legislation in force (in both chronological and subject arrangement).

All these texts are sources of legal language, which is of primary importance in understanding and interpreting the law in general. Each of the above types of texts represents a separate genre of Czech legal text and requires a different or modified approach in its translation. Comparative genre analysis of individual types of texts would go beyond the scope of this paper but remains our future task (cf. Chromá 2003a).

3.2.2. Levels of translation

The language of law is a rather formalized language at all levels: lexical, syntactic, textual and generic. Traditionally the vocabulary has been mentioned as the main discriminating factor, particularly with respect to the use of terminology. For example, Hohnhold (1982: 382) designates the terminological analysis of specialized texts in the source language and the target language as a "terminological approach to translation". Later, however, he (1982: 386) admits that translation must go beyond the level of nomenclature and cover phraseology and may even include whole passages for special text categories. Legal language is not just composed of technical terms, of a specific terminology. As Reed (1993: 81) emphasizes, it also contains idioms, syntagms that are peculiar to the legal field, if not to each of the sub-fields of the law. He complains that too little attention is given to the acquisition of the sentence structures of the law; what is meant here is that the legal discourse should be analyzed in more detail, before tackling the equally important issue of the terminological problems posed by translation in a bi-legal and bilingual context.

Since law belongs to a wider category of humanities, the vocabulary of which is based on abstract words and expressions however bearing quite a precise meaning, legal terminology consists primarily of abstract terms deeply and firmly rooted in the domestic culture and intellectual tradition. Bergenholtz & Tarp (1995: 60) use the attribute "culture-dependent" to denote subjects or knowledge such as law that have historically and culturally developed their own specific features within delimited geographical areas. Unlike natural or exact sciences, technology or medicine, law remains first and foremost a national phenomenon (Šarčević, 2000: 13). Therefore, Bachrach's view (1982: 375) that to properly fulfil their task translators ought to be able to use terminology as well as the language of the specialist in the field, Riley's (1995: 68) precision of this idea that understanding the legal vocabulary of the law is in itself a legal task, and Smith's definition (1995: 181) of three prerequisites existing for the successful translation of legal texts, (namely (a) a basic knowledge of the legal systems, (b) familiarity with the relevant terminology, and (c) competence in the target language's specific legal style of writing) constitute the practical rules which should be respected by each translator and correspond with our own experience: the translation of legal texts should not be undertaken without an extensive knowledge of the respective legal topic in both the source language and the target language, i.e. the knowledge of concepts, terms denoting these concepts, sentence patterns visualizing the information, genre classification of the text, the knowledge and legal culture and so on, in both languages and legal systems. Next, the translator should consider the skopos / purpose of the target legal text and, preferably, the expectations of the ultimate recipient.

Rogers and Ahmad (1998: 194) point out that specialist translators always operate in a highly specific context, beginning with a particular source text which has a purpose in a known communicative situation and producing a target text which is customised for a new situation. They add:

> [...] they do not just translate, say, a text in legal English into Spanish, but rather a letter in English from a British solicitor representing a UK company in a trade dispute with a company in Madrid into Spanish for the UK Managing Director, who wishes the letter to be assessed by his Spanish lawyer with a view to future action.

This is an example of a typical situation: the need for Czech legal texts to be translated into English in order to mediate the information contained in the source legal text so that further action may be considered and planned. The lexical information which translators require is therefore highly specific with regard to the language variety, subject-matter, text type and level of communication. Thus, Beyer and Conradsen's (1995: 175) assumption that legal translation requires both linguistic skills and some basic understanding of legal concepts seems to be rather underestimating. Smith (1995: 180) mentions that "intralingual translation", or translating the legal language into the standard language, can be extremely challenging whenever legal phrases or terms are imprecise or open to interpretation. Intralingual translation in such an understanding is a component part of the interpretation of legal clauses and provisions. Correct interpretation of the source legal text and its reasonable transposition into the target legal text may be practicable only if we know the respective legal topic in both systems. Tomášek (1990: 113) points out that legal translation is a procedure based on both linguistic and legal comparative approaches. He asserts that the content of legal information should be fully preserved and transposed into the target language so that the target legal text corresponds with the usage in the target legal environment. What is denoted as "intralingual" translation by Beyer and Conradsen above, Tomášek (1991: 147) calls "intrasemiotic" translation and describes as the transfer of information from the first to the second semantic level of the source language, i.e. the interpretation of law by means of transfer from the legal language to the legal metalanguage. "Intersemiotic" translation is then understood by Tomášek as the translation of a legal text from the source language to the target language.

As can be assumed from the above, the quality of legal translation is fully and primarily dependent on the ability of a translator to adequately interpret the original text and to transpose it into the language and legal culture of the recipient. Šarčević (2000: 72) extends such assumptions stating that the goal of legal translation is to produce a text that will preserve the unity of a single instrument by guaranteeing its uniform interpretation and application. Joseph (1995: 33–34) in his analysis of the practice of legal translation concludes that translators should interpret rather than merely translate (for example, by interrupting the translation with an informed commentary); they should intervene in the text, semantically, stylistically, intellectually, to the extent called for. He adds:

> It should be insisted that where law is concerned, the desire to provide easy reading should not lead one to sacrifice fully interpretative translation in favour of the simple legal convention of the target language anytime the systems differ or anytime the original includes resonances and connotations that the simple target-language equivalent cannot capture.

We claim that the primary objective of legal translation is that the target recipient should be provided with as explicit, extensive and precise legal information in the target language as is contained in the source text, complemented (by the translator) with facts rendering the original information fully comprehensible in the different legal environment and culture.

It is obvious that the problems of translation are not all situated at the same level, and that what is called "legal translation" comprises quite an array of sub-disciplines and genres, each with its own terminology and its own discourse (Reed, 1993: 82). Translation of judicial decisions and other documents issued by courts, translation of legislation, translation of private acts such as deeds, contracts, letters, or individual legal opinions, etc., all require different approaches, work with different concepts and serve different purposes in the target language. Trosborg (1997b: 154–155) maintains that there are two basic types of legal translation in relation to the skopos theory, namely a 'documentary' translation and 'instrumental' translation (referring to Nord, 1991: 72). The former serves as a document of a source culture communication between the author and the source text recipient. The latter is a communicative instrument in its own right, which can focus on some features of the source text, while pushing others into the background. Trosborg claims that translations of legal texts may generally fall into the group of documentary translation. She rightfully admits, however, that not all target legal texts would have the same function as the original and that the translation procedure adopted by the translator of a legal document depends on the purpose of the text. Referring to Rogers and Ahmad (1998: 194) mentioned above, as well as to our own translation experience (cf. a comment on the executive memorandum in 3.2. above), we would argue that instrumental translation of legal texts has become regularly used in certain environments and for certain purposes. Our teaching experience shows that if a translation is done by a Czech lawyer proficient in English he or she would use techniques which are closer to those of instrumental translation than documentary translation. Chart 1 may visualize the process of legal translation described above (cf. Chromá, in print b).

3.2.3. The issue of equivalence

Equivalence has been usually mentioned in relation to the vocabulary of different languages where words or phrases having equal or corresponding import, meaning or significance are matched, particularly in the process of translation. We will confine the term to this limited sense although equivalence may apply to larger syntactic structures, texts, genres or even discourse (communicative situations or speech acts).

Whatever approach to translation may be chosen the issue of equivalence remains one of the crucial aspects of a translator's as well as a lexicographer's work. Each of them would treat the problem in a rather different way: the lexicographer has to operate in much more general conditions than the translator does, and is prevented from availing him or herself of various levels of context determined by a concrete translation situation including the purpose of the target text and the expectations of the target recipient. Steiner (1989: 255) rightfully complains of some translation dictionaries being "a stock-pile of equivalencies that were once translations in a certain context. These translation equivalents, divorced from their original speech acts, provide only a repertoire of choice" from which a translator can select or adapt whatever seems useful for his or her translation, however, without any guarantee that what has been chosen will be appropriate for his or her specific context. Moreover, as Gémar (2001: 122) points out, the problem of achieving equivalent legal effects in the translated texts is not the same for the translator and jurist. Ideally, the translator is also a lawyer, which is rare; however, a non-lawyer-translator generally strives for linguistic equivalence, whilst a translating lawyer strives for legal equivalence. Gémar concludes that in both cases, it is the meeting and harmonious fusion of the two constitutive ingredients of the text – form and content – that produce the desired equivalence. It should be added that linguistic equivalence will be based on and primarily result from semantic interpretation of the source legal text whilst the search for legal equivalence will be induced by legal interpretation of the source information.

Zgusta calls as an equivalent such a lexical unit of the target language which has the same lexical meaning, i.e. designation, connotation, or range of applications, as the respective lexical unit of the source language (1971: 312). Where only one of its senses is covered by the target language counterpart it should be called a "partial equivalent". He also suggests (1971: 314) that the equivalent should be a real lexical unit of the target language which occurs in real sentences. Such a requirement may seem redundant, but when referring to the note by Steiner above and to the somehow regular practice of compiling bilingual specialist dictionaries in the Czech Republic, where authors sometimes provide equivalents which, they think, might work in the target language, the requirement should become a rule applied and supervised ultimately by publishers. The degree of equivalence should be carefully measured by the translator; he or she must decide how to compensate in the target language what is missing, whether it suffices to use an explanatory term or whether other means should be employed such as glosses or translator's comments. Referring to the research on the conceptual analysis of legal terms pursued by the "Internationales Institut für Rechts- und Verwaltungssprache" in Berlin, Germany, Šarčević (2000: 238) distinguishes among three basic degrees of equivalence: (a) "near equivalence", where concepts in the source language and target language expressed by the respective terms share all of their essential elements and most of their accidental characteristics; (b) "partial equivalence", where concepts in the source language and target

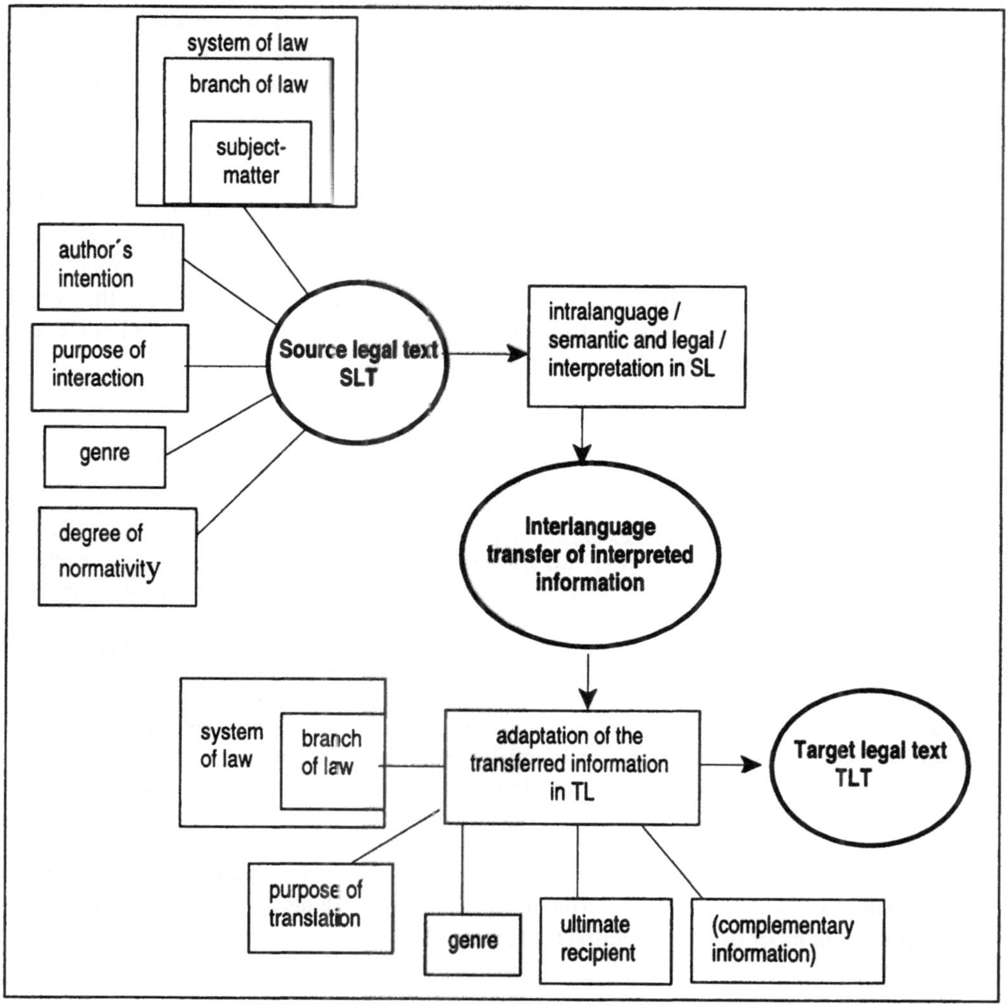

Chart 1

language share most of their essential elements and only some of their accidental characteristics; and (c) "non-equivalence", where concepts in the source language and target language share a few or none of their essential elements and no accidental characteristics.

Another issue has been raised in this context. Zgusta (1971: 319) and Al-Kasimi (1983: 159) distinguish between "translation(al)" and "explanatory" (or descriptive) equivalents. The former is a lexical unit which can immediately be inserted into a sentence in the target language whilst the latter cannot always be inserted into a sentence in the target language. In the legal area, a significant number of equivalents would be of a descriptive nature simply because the systems of law differ, and many terms would belong to a large category of expressions that may be called 'legal realia', i.e. culturally rooted in the national law and language but having no, or an incomplete, counterpart in the target language and target legal system. Therefore, we would argue that an explanatory equivalent should always be inserted in a sentence whichever form of insertion may be chosen (translator's note, gloss, etc.). For example, the Czech term *obchodní jmění* should be translated into legal English using its explanatory equivalent 'corporate assets and liabilities'; the Czech *způsobilost mít práva a povinnosti* should be explicatively translated as 'legal personality of an individual' ('an individual' may be replaced by 'a natural person', which is the proper legal term used in civil law). Whilst the former (*corporate assets and liabilities*) would always be inserted into the sentence without any problem, one might hesitate how to use the whole terminological phrase in the following Czech sentence: *Způsobilost mít práva a povinnosti je pro všechny rovná a nemůže být omezena*. The terminological phrase should be loosened; its core part 'legal personality' would serve as the terminological equivalent for *způsobilost mít práva a povinnosti*, and the postmodifying determining attribute 'of an individual' would change its position to complement the verbal phrase. The translation would be as follows: 'Legal personality shall be equal for every individual and may not be limited.'

Čermák (1995b: 238) provides an extensive definition of equivalence:

> Ekvivalence je vztah mezi lexémem v určitém významu výchozího jazyka a formou cílového jazyka založený na jejich (téměř) identickém, resp. vysoce podobném významu a funkci. Členy, koncovými termíny tohoto vztahu jsou ekvivalenty. Tento vztah přitom obvykle není symetrický a ekvivalentem nemusí být nutně lexém, ale jiná forma. Je to mj. důsledkem toho, že lexikálně-sémantické vztahy dvou jazyků jsou zásadně anizotropní. V tomto pojetí ekvivalent tudíž zprostředkuje informaci o sémanticko-pragmatickém systému druhého jazyka, popř. o jeho potenciálu.
> (Equivalence is the relationship between a lexeme of a certain meaning in the source language and the form in the target language based on their (almost) identical, or highly similar senses and functions. Members, or ultimate terms of the relationship are equivalents. The relationship, however, is not always symmetric, and the equivalent need not be a lexeme, it could be a different form. This is due, among other things, to essentially anisotropic relations between two languages. In such an understanding, the equivalent would mediate information on the semantic and pragmatic system of the other language, or on its potential.) *(Translated by author)*

Examples supporting Čermák's definition of equivalence may be found among Czech-English legal equivalents. There are (a) multiverbal translational equivalents of one-word Czech terms, or (b) a limited number of Czech multiverbal terms which have only a one-word equivalent in English law.

(a) There is a limited number of Czech monosemous terms which have no legal equivalent in English and an explanatory (or descriptive) equivalent should be found or coined:

Bezúhonnost may be translated as 'probity' or 'moral integrity' in general language. However, the Czech legal term should be translated as 'having no criminal records' since this is the only requirement prescribed for *bezúhonnost* under Czech law;

Delát has no one-word equivalent in English and should be translated by explanation as 'heir called to assert his succession rights'.

Dobírka is the Czech term for the English abbreviation C. O. D. (collect/cash-on-delivery) which is rarely used in its full form in legal documents.

Hejtman has no literal equivalent in the administrative nomenclature of any English-speaking country; we should use an explanatory equivalent such as 'the chief executive officer of the region' or 'regional chief executive officer' to denote his or her position in regional government. The 'chief executive officer' is a neutral term denoting the head of indiscriminate bodies or authorities of administration of public or private entities in the US or UK.[50]

Přestupek, as emphasized above, should be translated into English as 'administrative delict' to accurately denote the legal substance of the violation of law.

Skartace is a Czech legal term which has no counterpart in legal English; therefore explanation should be provided, such as the 'safe destruction of official documents'. The physical act of destruction would depend on the technology used, for example, shredding, burning, etc. under the supervision of a person in charge.

Vznik (společnosti) as well as *zánik (společnosti)* are terms precisely defined by Czech law and should be translated into English in such a manner that their legal substance may be preserved. Thus we should have 'the commencement of the legal existence (of the company)' and the 'cessation of the legal existence (of the company)' respectively according to the legal definitions as they are stated under the Commercial Code (Act N. 513/1991 Coll., as amended).

(b) One-word English equivalents may be found for the following Czech phrases:

Právní odpovědnost is 'liability ' in English, although 'legal responsibility ' may be used as well;

Subjektivní právo should be translated as 'right' without any attribute;

Dočasné přerušení (řízení) would be 'suspension (of proceedings)' since a suspension is always temporary in the legal understanding of the word;

Předmět doličný has its English counterpart 'exhibit'; under limited circumstances the Latin term 'corpus delicti' can also be used;[51]

Věcné břemeno means 'easement' in English law;

Povinný ze závazku and *oprávněný ze závazku* will be simply translated as 'obligor' and 'obligee' respectively;

Odnětí svobody as a type of punishment will be translated as the derivative 'imprisonment' in Anglo-American systems of law;

Nesprávný úřední postup will be translated as 'maladministration', representing the same legal definition as the Czech multiword term.

Since, as noted several times, law is a part of national culture, concepts, and words or phrases expressing them, are firmly culture-bound. Such words or phrases cannot generally be transferred into another language, usually because the concept as such has been absent or different in the target legal environment. The problem is not confined only to law but generally to what Newmark (1988: 82) calls "cultural words". He suggests that a SL cultural word can be translated by a TL cultural word thus becoming the so-called "cultural equivalent". The Czech term *maturita* would be a typical example: where the target recipient of the target text is British he or she can perfectly understand what is meant if the English term 'A-levels' is used. Should he or she be, for example, an American without previous knowledge or experience in this area, 'A-levels' could mean almost nothing to him or her and as such may not be considered an equivalent; the general phrase 'school-leaving examination' should be

---

50 However, the representatives of 13 regions in the Czech Republic have convened recently and decided to call themselves in English "the President of the Region".

51 The Latin term has a two-fold meaning: in a stricter sense it is "the body of a crime"; more generally, it means evidence by which the crime may be proven before court.

used instead and a gloss or brief explanation would have to be attached. Interestingly, English-speaking specialists in Central Europe (of Czech, German, Austrian, Polish, etc. origin), when dealing with this topic at seminars or meetings, often use a mixed Austrian-German English term 'matura-exam'. Such processes are sometimes denoted as "naturalization", i.e. transference and adaptation of a SL word or phrase into the target language (Newmark,1988: 82; Šarčević, 1989b: 215). Borrowings and naturalizations are usually used as equivalents for culture-bound terms; in fact, literal equivalents are not equivalents in the traditional sense of the term; they are newly coined words in the target language, created by transcription of the SL word into the target language, and serve merely as a means of identifying a source term. Typical examples of original SL borrowings having become well-established in general English, are, for example, *art nouveau*, *guerrilla*, *robot*, etc. American legal English has acquired a few Spanish borrowings relating to criminal justice, such as *incommunicado*, regularly used instead of *solitary confinement*. One example partially[52] illustrating the issue may be given in relation to Czech law: before 1990 the Czech legal language did not possess a term denoting one source of English law, namely *equity*. The Czech word 'ekvita' did exist as a sophisticated philosophical term in the meaning of fairness, however, it was considered rather formal, rare and archaic in usage, and in practice was not used. After the 1990s' influx of information, the Czech 'ekvita' has acquired a new meaning in legal contexts denoting the English law of equity; the derivative *equitable* has been translated as 'ekvitní' although, unlike 'ekvita', it was missing in the comprehensive dictionary of the Czech language "Slovník spisovného jazyka českého" (1989, Praha: Academia). As has been already emphasized the skopos and the target recipient of the translation are decisive factors in selecting a comprehensible word or phrase in the target text so that the information contained in the source text may be transferred or mediated. Therefore the English adjective *equitable* should be translated into Czech as an explicative postmodifying attribute 'podle práva ekvity' (E. 'according to the law of equity') rather than as a simple premodifying adjective 'ekvitní', which is less explicit.

3.2.3.1. Functional equivalence

The term "functional equivalence" is used in general translation theory and in comparative law (cf. Šarčević, 2000: 236). In translation theory (Newmark, 1988: 83; Knittlová, 1991: 213), a functional equivalent is understood to result from a cultural componential analysis and serves as the most accurate way of translating (deculturalising) a cultural word. The selection of a functional equivalent is based upon the comparative semantic and genre analysis of the source text and corresponding texts in the target language. Šarčević (1989a: 278; 2000: 236) explains that "functional equivalence" as a term in comparative law was coined by Canadian lawyers in their bilingual legal environment.[53] Therefore she regards a functional equivalent as a term

52 "partially" is used here because no coinage of a new word occurred, however, the existing, although unused, word was revived and acquired a new meaning.

53 Recently, the process of searching for functional equivalents between common law and civil law in Canada has been quite intensive. As can be seen at http://www.canada.justice.gc.ca/en/ps/bj/harm/, the main motivation is to harmonize bijural legislation serving both Quebec (civil law jurisdiction) and other Canadian provinces (common law jurisdictions). Canadian bijural terminology records may serve as an excellent source of translational equivalents for anyone translating from civil law source texts to common law target texts, or the other way round, where either SL or TL is English.

in the target legal system designating a concept or institution, the function of which is the same as that of the source term. Šarčević (2000: 238) also admits that most functional equivalents are only partially equivalent, and asserts (1989a: 279) that lexicographers should take the initiative and use conceptual analysis to measure the degree of actual equivalence achieved by each supposedly equivalent term.

Functional equivalence in the Czech-English legal context can be illustrated by a Czech term from corporate law, *společník*: there are basically two English expressions that may serve as equivalents in legal English, namely 'member (of company)' and 'partner'. The Czech *společník* is used in three types of Czech companies, [1] an unlimited company ('veřejná obchodní společnost'), [2] a limited partnership company ('komanditní společnost') and [3] a limited liability company ('společnost s ručením omezeným'). *Member (of the company)* would be the functional equivalent in [1] and [3] since it has the same function, application and can be identically construed in the same types of companies in the Anglo-American system of law, whilst *partner* would be functional in [2] as it serves as a term referring to any partnership(-like) business organization in the UK or US. Concepts of different legal systems can be regarded as functional equivalents only if they are capable of solving the same factual problem (Šarčević, 1989a: 283).

Another example would be the Czech *společenská smlouva* as a document proving that a company is to be formed. Basically, there are at least two equivalents in legal English: the term 'articles of incorporation' used primarily in US corporate law, and 'memorandum of association' employed primarily in British company law. If the translation is to reach an American target recipient, the US equivalent would be regarded functional; similarly, the British term would be functional where the target legal text is produced for a British recipient. A problem occurs, however, if the target recipient is unknown or unidentifiable; in such cases the selection of either option should be terminologically consistent with the rest of the translated text, and the alternative equivalent should be mentioned in a translator's note or gloss. This would help the target recipient avoid misunderstanding if his or her previous knowledge has been incidentally oriented towards the other legal system. As Gémar (2001: 122) points out, the principle of functional equivalence that applies to the translation of pragmatic (i.e. communicative) texts also applies to legal texts. Regardless of the nature of the text to be translated, the principle is the same: the message in one text is transferred to another text in order to make it understood by the recipient.

Some researchers (Riley, 1995: 72; Šarčević, 1989a: 282) have noted one discrepancy in law, namely the unusual importance of achieving precision on the one part, and, on the other hand, a large number of indefinite or vague concepts which are undefined or inaccurately defined. Vagueness and indeterminacy in legislative texts are usually intentional: there are instances in which the law consciously opts for broad terminology to allow flexibility of application in relation to varying circumstances. It would be a task for a court to determine whether, for example, the care taken is still reasonable under the concrete circumstances, or a bank has executed due diligence in screening the prospective investor. There are vague and indefinite terms in Czech law, too: [1] *nepřiměřené použití síly* (to be preferably translated as 'excessive force'), [2] *s péčí řádného hospodáře* (literally 'with the care of a proper husbandman'; but this adverbial phrase can simply be translated as 'duly') or [3] *řádný občan* (literal translation is 'good citizen' or 'orderly citizen' but the functional English equivalent is 'a law-abiding citizen'). The English equivalent in [1] is more concrete: the literal translation of the Czech original would be 'inadequate use of force' which may be either insufficient (i.e. less than required) or excessive: the circumstances in which such an allegation may be brought in court would always suggest that the force used in self-defence was excessive resulting in the death or serious injury of the offender by the victim of the committed crime. The equivalent in [2] is as vague as the Czech original, although reduced to one adverbial complement in lieu of the Czech metaphorical phrase. The English equivalent 'law-abiding citizen' in [3] is more concrete than the Czech term and confines the proper conduct of a person to his or her observance of laws. These English equivalents would be functional in most contexts, however, this does not mean that the implications of all equivalents of all other Czech terms are the same.

To facilitate a better understanding by the user of the degree of equivalence of equivalents provided in translation dictionaries, glosses should be used to specify partial equivalents (Zgusta, 1971: 329) and clarify borrowings, naturalizations and literal equivalents. Glosses should be provided in the form of generalizations, explanatory equivalents and cultural equivalents of third societies (Šarčević, 1989b: 217). The use of explanatory equivalents is the most common method of glossing. The initial part of one entry in our "Czech-English Law Dictionary with Explanations" may be provided as an example of glossing (glosses are typed in smaller letters; *LU* stands for Louisiana whose legal system is based on civil law thus essentially using civil law terminology in English, and the equivalent was taken from Louisiana Civil Code 1996):

> **příslušenství** appurtenance usually to real property, accessory usually of personal property, accessions usually of intangibles, civil fruits (LU); [...]

One problem should be mentioned here. As Toury (1990: 290) suggests, sometimes an equivalent is coined for one specific situation without previous research in the target language and without intention to use it in the future (for example, in the course of conference interpreting). In the course of time, some of these ad hoc translational solutions may well be picked up by a growing body of translators as a means of solving the same, or similar, problems, and gradually become part of the norm themselves. The English equivalent 'joint-stock company' of the Czech term *akciová společnost* would serve as an example. It was used in the beginning of the 1990s when the new Czech Commercial Code was passed in order to regulate, among other things in business, newly introduced registered companies. The term *joint-stock company* exists in British, Irish, Canadian or US law, but denotes rather a different concept compared to the Czech *akciová společnost*. In the US and Canada, it is an unincorporated (i.e. not registered) business entity partially resembling the so-called *partnership*. In the UK and Ireland, it is an archaic name for companies now registered as *public limited companies*.[54] Nonetheless, as can be seen on the Internet, *joint-stock company* as a term denoting more or less identical types of companies as in the Czech Republic, may be found in English translations in the whole of the post-soviet region, in Scandinavian countries, and Austria. Paradoxically, the term may be uniformly understood everywhere but in native English-speaking countries. If we wished to be more precise we would use the term *stock company* or *stock corporation* instead, which is more comprehensible and without any peculiarities in status.

---

[54] Laws regulating joint stock companies in the UK were passed in the 19th century, subsequently replaced by Companies Acts, providing for public limited companies instead.

3.2.3.2. Interference

Generally, the linguistic term "interference" denotes the use of features belonging to one language while speaking or writing another. In translation, and particularly in interpreting (i.e. oral translation), interference has played rather a mean role often leading to the destruction of communication that should have been mediated. Gabrovšek (1998: 165) lists "false friends, deceptive cognates, false pairs, false cognates, faux amis" as terms denoting inter-language homophones (at the level of vocabulary) and suggests that the compilation of a dictionary of false friends must be assessed primarily against the background of the users' needs and expectations.

Obviously, interference affects various linguistic levels (Tomaszczyk, 1983: 43). Newmark (1981: 123) calls them varieties of interference:

(a) Collocations or lexemes of the source language and the target language which are similar in form and different in meaning are the most frequent variety. Only a few examples are provided here:

Czech	English	English	Czech
protokol (policie)	report (on st. made by the police)	protocol	diplomatický protokol
evidence	files, records, archives	evidence	důkaz(y)
aktuální	current, recent; topical	actual	skutečný, vlastní
paragraf (§)	section	paragraph	odstavec
provize	commission	provision	ustanovení; poskytnutí
komise (zboží v komisi)	consignment	commission	provize
subjekt (práv)	(legal) person	subject	předmět

(b) Source language morphological features inappropriately superimposed on the target language features: the English uncountable term *damage* denotes the harm or injury caused or suffered. Its plural form *damages* means exclusively the compensation for such damage. In Czech, both *škoda* (singular) and *škody* (plural) are used in the meaning of harm, therefore, a Czech translator often tends to use the plural in English as well. The Czech clause *byly napáchány podstatné škody* should be translated as 'substantial damage has been caused'.

(c) SL word order, or word-phrase order, inappropriately reproduced in the target language: the Czech *trestní právo procesní* as the name of one branch of law should be translated as 'criminal procedure' although there is a separate English term 'procedural / adjective / adjectival law ' for a more general Czech term *procesní právo* not denoting the type of procedure (civil, criminal or administrative). The Czech *mezinárodní právo veřejné* (literally 'international law public') has its English equivalent 'international public law'; similarly, *občanské právo hmotné* (literally 'civil law substantive') has its counterpart 'substantive civil law', etc. The Czech *podnikatelský subjekt* is usually 'body corporate' but premodifying 'corporate body' is also possible in legal English.

(d) Primary meaning of words or phrases interfering with appropriate contextual meaning: the Czech *právnická osoba* has often been mistakenly translated into English as 'legal person'; however, the latter has its Czech equivalent *právní subjekt*. The former was widely used as *právnická osoba* in European Union English texts which partly is a result of the varying quality of translators.

(e) Interference from a third language known to the translator: this often happens, for example, when a Czech translator or interpreter translates from legal English into legal Russian. Czech may interfere particularly in the use of proper Russian terminology.

(f) Stylistic predilections of the translator; for example, the English statutory terms *bankruptcy* and *bankrupt* have often been translated into Czech as 'bankrot' and 'bankrotář' respectively although the Czech words belong to a lower register and do not serve as legal terms (the legal terms being 'konkurs' for the former, and 'úpadce' or 'konkursní dlužník' for the latter).

(g) Finally, the translator's idiolect, including his or her regional and social dialect, is mentioned as one possible source of interference in translation.

3.2.3.3. Lacunas

Traditionally, it has been admitted that certain onomasiological gaps exist, thus some words, expression or phrases have no translational equivalents (Zgusta, 1971: 325). Šarčević (2000: 239) speaks about non-equivalence in the target legal system. Fischer (2000: 4) asserts that any lexical gap is only a structural and not a functional one, which is close to Čermák's (1995b: 238) assertion:

> Pragmaticky a nevhodně se mluví o lakunách, mezerách ve slovníku, a naznačuje tak ovšem i neschopnost druhého jazyka vyjádřit určitý význam jazyka prvního, což je očividný nesmysl. Každý jazyk je vždy schopný vyjádřit vše, co potřebuje; jakým způsobem to však dělá, je jiná věc. Nemusí to být nutně, v případě uvažované výchozí roviny lexémů, koncový lexém, ale jejich kombinace.
> (Pragmatically, and inappropriately, lacunas, or gaps in vocabulary are mentioned, thus suggesting the incapability of the other language to express a certain meaning in the source language, which is an obvious nonsense. Each language is always capable of expressing everything it needs to; another matter is in which way it does so. It does not necessarily need to be an ultimate lexeme, considering the level of lexemes, but, for example, a combination of lexemes.)
> *(Translated by author)*

Our experience and research in legal languages suggest that a translator should be able to express everything that is in the source legal text; it is always possibile to use explicative (explanatory) and descriptive techniques to mediate the source information. Problems with English equivalents of the Czech term *přestupek* were mentioned in 2.2. above, and this Czech term may serve as an example of the non-existence of semantic or onomasiological gaps in English in this field. Legally, no identical concept exists in the Anglo-American system of law. The definition of the Czech *přestupek* can be found in s. 2(1) of Act N. 200/1990 Coll., as amended:

> Přestupkem je zaviněné jednání, které porušuje nebo ohrožuje zájem společnosti a je za přestupek výslovně označeno v tomto nebo jiném zákoně.

(An administrative delict shall be an action based on fault, which is in violation of the interests of society and is explicitly listed as an administrative delict by the Act herein or any other statute.)
(Translated by author)

To further complicate the situation, Czech Administrative Law distinguishes two types of administrative violation, namely *přestupek* and *jiný správní delikt*, the former being committed by individuals (natural persons), the latter usually by artificial legal persons and it is similar to administrative delicts as understood in the Anglo-American system of law. The analysis of any unlawful behaviour should be considered from two aspects: "the issue (matter, question, point) of fact" and "the issue (matter, question, point) of law". Factually, the Czech *přestupek* may be found among English torts (such as a private nuisance between neighbours), or within criminal offences (minor violation of traffic regulations, for example). Legally, they are qualified in the Anglo-American system of law as either civil wrongs, i.e. torts, entitling the injured person to compensation, or crimes, rendering the guilty person to punishment and to a criminal record kept of his or her conviction. In Czech law, the violator, when found guilty of *přestupek*, is liable to a fine (or to a caution under limited circumstances) and no criminal conviction is entered in his or her records.

The respective entry in the CELDE suggests the following solution (explanations are printed in smaller letters and the original entry is shortened):

přestup|ek protiprávní čin podle správního práva (CZ) administrative infraction a wrongful act committed by an individual and governed by administrative law; more generally administrative delict; transgression / violation of administrative law; **dopravní ~** breach of traffic regulations as an administrative infraction; [...], **~ky a jiné správní delikty** administrative infractions and other administrative delicts, [...]

Generally, it can be recommended that the Czech *přestupek* should be translated as 'administrative infraction' or 'administrative delict'; the premodifying attribute "administrative" is crucial in the English equivalent as it suggests that the wrongful act is to be judged according to administrative law and not civil law (no liability to damages) or criminal law (no criminal conviction). Czech society does not consider an administrative infraction to be serious enough to amount to a crime, nor is it legally understood as the primary cause of an action for damages. Subsequently, after administrative proceedings before a competent administrative body have been closed, the victim may sue the violator for compensation in court, however, the costs of the proceedings would be much higher that the actual damages to be sought.

4. Lexicographical framework

4.1. Theory of lexicography

Lexicography, as a branch of applied linguistics, can be subdivided into two parts: theory and practice, or theoretical and applied lexicography. The latter, in Landau's terms, represents both the art and craft (1993: title) of writing (or making) dictionaries.

Ladislav Zgusta[55] is considered one of the founders of modern bilingual lexicography. His comprehensive work entitled "The Manual of Lexicography", published in Prague and the Hague in 1971, became a bible for lexicographers. Zgusta (1993: 137) formulated the basic principles of theoretical lexicography. The theory of dictionary-writing concentrates on:

(a) the study of specifically lexicographic methods and their problems;
(b) the selection of those results of linguistic (and computational, psychological, cognitive, etc.) research which are potentially useful to lexicography and
(c) the transformation of those results into useful components of lexicographic practice.

The theory of lexicography, however, was subsequent to the practice of dictionary-making; it was developed through analysis of existing dictionaries and commentaries of lexicographers, through the process of generalization of common features, thus forming general concepts, metalanguage, methods, procedures and approaches which could be synthetically applied, and transformed to practical steps, by a dictionary compiler.

Dictionaries can be divided and classified according to many distinctive features. Generally, dictionaries are subdivided into monolingual (to provide basic information on linguistic units), and bi- or multilingual dictionaries (i.e. for the purposes of translation). Unlike monolingual dictionaries which may be arranged according to various criteria being written primarily for native speakers and containing definitions of entry-words, translation dictionaries written for speakers of at least two languages are almost always arranged alphabetically, and the source language words or phrases are provided with their target language equivalents. Al-Kasimi (1977: 20) provides the following classification of bilingual dictionaries:

(a) dictionaries for the speakers of the SL vs. dictionaries for the speakers of the TL;
(b) dictionaries of the literary language vs. dictionaries of the spoken language;
(c) dictionaries for production vs. dictionaries for comprehension;
(d) dictionaries for the human users vs. dictionaries for machine translation;
(e) historical dictionaries vs. descriptive dictionaries;
(f) lexical dictionaries vs. encyclopaedic dictionaries; and
(g) general dictionaries vs. special dictionaries.

Most bilingual dictionaries are intended primarily for the speakers of the source language, based on literary language and intended for comprehension; they are descriptive and synchronic and concentrate on vocabulary; dictionaries of general language are much more widely used than special-purpose bilingual dictionaries.

Considering the future users of a bilingual special-purpose dictionary, Bergenholtz & Tarp in their comprehensive "Manual of Specialised Lexicography"[56] claim, surprisingly, that (1995: 77): "Lexicographical work often proceeds without any prior knowledge of the potential user group, and the dictionary may therefore be said to be the result of the lexicographer's own conjectures concerning user needs for lemmata, collocations, sentence examples, encyclopaedic and linguistic information, etc." We will argue that to consider the potential users of the dictionary is of extreme importance at as early as the preparatory stage of writing any of the above categories of dictionaries, and the more so in the case of a bilingual special purpose

---

[55] L. Zgusta is a Czech scholar who was forced to leave Czechoslovakia during the communist regime. He assisted the process of founding and/or establishing several world-wide journals dealing with lexicographical topics, and retired as a professor of linguistics at the University of Illinois, Urbana, USA.

[56] The "Manual" is one of the major outcomes of a 3-year research project held within the Danish Research Council for Humanities, entitled "Translation of LSP Texts".

dictionary. Needless to say, the making of a bilingual law dictionary requires quite a profound knowledge of the respective legal systems and of the two languages, as well as extensive experience in translation between the two languages within the whole subject-area, otherwise the lexicographer may face considerable trouble in selecting relevant excerpts to create the initial lexicographical database.

Van der Meer (1998: 217) emphasizes (with respect to translating dictionaries) that dictionary writers should try to compile genuine users' dictionaries: "[...] dictionaries that try to reflect the user's knowledge and their ways of dealing with semantic complexity, rather than those of the lexicographers, who by their very nature tend to organize, schematize, streamline, and above all to economise on space". It should be noted, however, that the lexicographer is not always the only person to be blamed for the inadequate format of a dictionary or even for individual entries: a bilingual special-purpose dictionary where one of the languages is minor and relevant to a small territory thus addressing a limited number of potential users, sometimes induces publishers to reduce the costs of publication as much as possible; as a result, the dictionary becomes a two-column alphabetically arranged list of isolated source language terms and their (isolated) target language equivalents providing insufficient context to help the translator decide whether he or she can rely on them.

Čermák (1995b: 233), analysing the dichotomy of "encoding" and "decoding", recognizes four types of dictionaries from the user's perspective. For example, a Czech-English dictionary is an encoding dictionary for Czechs (or speakers of Czech), thus intended for production, and decoding for English speakers whether native or not, i.e. intended for comprehension; an English-Czech dictionary would be an encoding one for English speakers and decoding for the speakers of Czech. The processes of encoding and decoding in their clear form would apply, however, to the native (or native-like) users of either the source language or the target language. Should the speakers be non-native, e.g. speakers of Czech and English as a foreign (or second) languages, the processes of encoding would be preceded by decoding and encoding the source and target language information respectively.

Steiner (1989: 254) notes that a translation dictionary is much more efficient for decoding than it is for encoding. We would argue that such an assertion fully depends on the primary purpose of the dictionary, i.e. whether the dictionary is intended for production or only for comprehension, and whether the dictionary is made with a special group of users in mind. The "Czech English Law Dictionary with Explanations" was written primarily to help produce legal texts in English, and our recent experience suggests that it has done so. Surprisingly, it has even helped English speakers, who are non-lawyers, to produce English legal texts.

Opitz (1983a: 56) uses the term "segmental dictionaries" to denote dictionaries (both mono- and bilingual) concentrating on languages for specific purposes. In his understanding, segmental dictionaries play a normative and distributive role in reducing the confusing effects of polysemy on the unrestricted core of the language (1983a: 64). In this context, we prefer to speak about terminography (i.e. a lexicon of terms), since polysemy applies to individual terms whether reduced to one word or not (cf. 3.1.2.6. above). Pearson (1998: 2) understands terminography as specialised lexicography; Thomas (1993: 43) explains that terminography "is to the language for specific purposes what lexicography is to the language for general purposes". We would argue, however, that dictionaries of languages for special purposes should not deal only with terms. They should also cover phrases, clauses or even larger syntactical units that can be regularly found in the source language for specific purposes, and provide their possible counterparts or equivalents in the target language for specific purposes (cf. 3.1.2.1.). Opitz (1983b: 171) concludes that the success of a technical dictionary is largely determined by the correct degree and method of subject specialization, which lies in a sound balance of the principle of inclusiveness and exclusiveness. We would further claim that finding such a sound balance is the task for the lexicographer who should be knowledgeable of the subject area in both the source and target languages for specific purposes.

Obviously, special-purpose dictionaries serve as a means of codification of both the source and target languages for specific purposes. Hartmann (1983a: 5) points out that the writers of dictionaries sometimes find themselves – together with grammarians and language teachers – in the role of "arbiter or authority on question of usage, they willy-nilly contribute to the continuous development of linguistic standardization". Standardization, or codification, is a highly responsible task requiring rather a sensitive approach to finding corresponding equivalents as well as an extensive knowledge of the subject area. For example, it should be found out that the two Czech terms *péče* (E. 'care') and *výchova* (E. 'upbringing'), as they are used in the Family Act (N. 94/1965 Coll, as amended), are not two different terms, but only two synonyms used indiscriminately (and neglectfully) in the Act; to prevent misunderstanding in translation they should be translated either by one English equivalent, i.e. 'care' (encompassing both notions as the English term in English family law), or by an explicit phrase combining the two Czech expressions, i.e. 'care and upbringing'. It should be noted in this context that translators should always resist the temptation to show off all their knowledge and skills, for example what chains of synonyms they can compile and how sophisticated are the terms with which they are familiar. Translators' creativity has a very restricted place in the translation of legal texts.

Snell-Hornby (1990: 224), extending the idea of standardization, maintains that the dictionary can be placed between the language system and an idiosyncratic text, and its function would be to "indicate the norm or prototype along with those variants lexicalized in normal language usage". She points out that the task for the translator is not to hunt for the insertable item, but to use the given information as an aid in his or her all-important decision-process in recreating the text. The issue of equivalence and the existence of readily insertable expressions or phrases were discussed in 3.2.3. above, however, one more point made by Snell-Hornby (1990: 210) should be mentioned: the basic guiding factor for bilingual lexicography should be "the more sceptical principle of varying interlingual relationship, the simplest relationship existing at the level of terminology and nomenclature, and the most complex being conditioned by the 'dynamic' factors of sociocultural norm, perception and evaluation, with varying stages of gradation in between". Such an assumption applies even more to law as a branch firmly rooted in national culture, and to legal language since, as noted above in 3.2.1., legal translation should be based primarily on comparative legal, linguistic and genre analyses in order to make the transfer of legal information as precise, accurate and comprehensible as possible. Thus, Riley (1995: 83) recommends that bilingual law dictionaries "for the foreign reader need to be encyclopaedic in scope and provide the necessary contextual explanation of legal concepts which will allow the reader to put the terminology meaningfully into its context in the English (or other) legal system".

In conclusion it should be admitted, however, that any bilingual dictionary for specific purposes can serve only as a first aid to those who consult it. No bilingual dictionary can be fully exhaustive to cover all situations that a translator may possibly face. Translators should also work with monolingual specialized dictionaries, lexicons and encyclopaedias in all languages they work with. On the other hand, dictionaries are also consulted by interpreters not only when they prepare for their performance but particularly in the course of their interpreting (depending on the type of interpreting activity). In such situations, they have to fully rely on information provided by the respective dictionary, which instantly becomes a "life-saving" first aid; subsequently, having completed their job, they should seek more information in the above-mentioned resources in order to avoid similar situations in the future. Not only that any bilingual dictionary as such is an exercise in contrastive lexicology (Tomaszczyk, 1983: 45), but a good translator or interpreter should engage himself or herself in a SL – TL comparative study of the subject-area he or she is supposed to deal with. No dictionary can replace one's own experience acquired during the search for relevant information.

4.2. Conceptual dictionary

Every dictionary essentially has three stages: planning, writing and producing which includes proof-reading (Landau, 2001: 343). Planning and writing are the most important stages with respect to the content of the dictionary; the producing stage is crucial for formatting, final appearance, and user-friendliness. As emphasized above, a translation dictionary in law should be preceded by an extensive comparative study of the two (or more) legal systems and their reflection in the languages: how identical legal concepts can be expressed in different languages, how concepts not entirely agreeing in their qualities, properties or functions should be treated for the purposes of translation, and so on. As Lind (1998: 209) complains, "the transposition or translation of legal terminology is a virtual minefield, since there will rarely be complete or direct equivalence between concepts in two languages." In order to find the differences and agreements between the source language and the target language and the legal systems they express, a conceptual analysis should be pursued.

Traditionally, methods of semantic analysis are followed at various levels. Sekaninová (1993: 36) emphasizes that semantic confrontation of the lexical systems of the respective languages should be made by comparing their macrosystems and microsystems through their immediate constituents (in Chomsky's understanding), i.e. the deep structure analysis should be pursued in order to achieve tertium comparationis (comparative base). Applying the processes of semantic analysis to translation, Nida (1975: 84) argues that there are also certain theoretical considerations with respect to the deep structure analysis which should be carefully weighed. He assumes that in the first place, an analysis of the deep structures of different languages will show rather startling similarities:

> In fact, the deeper the analysis, the more alike, or even identical, the structures appear to be. It would seem that ultimately, the deepest structural level involves simply a pool of semantic universals – what any language can say. Rather than go through the complex procedures involved in back-transforming in the source language to this lowest level of universals, and then forward-transforming the results again to the level of kernels in the receptor language, the translator instinctively concludes that it is best to transfer directly from the kernel level in one language to the corresponding kernel level in the receptor language.

We maintain Nida's conclusion above: deep structural analysis cannot be applied if the practical activity of translation is to be considered. The language of law is primarily to communicate legal concepts (or, as lawyers say, institutions) that must be precisely defined and comprehended so that the legal environment, wherein appropriate subsequent action may be taken or omitted, can be reasonably determined. Concepts are usually expressed through special words or phrases, i.e. terms; not only the differences in the linguistic structure of the source and target languages must be taken into account, but also those differences which result from the legal systems themselves. Thus, whenever an identical term in the target language does not exist, the lexicographer must not only 'translate' a legal term from one language into another, but at the same time he should – which is more important – make a term from one legal system accessible and comprehensible to a person familiar with the other legal systems (Arntz, 1993: 16). As emphasized earlier, legal concepts are bound to a particular national legal system and culture (culture-dependent system). As a result, the legal terminology of different legal systems is inherently incongruent; it can be shown that the boundaries between the meanings of concepts of different legal systems are also incongruent (Šarčević, 1989a: 278). Conceptual analysis should reveal the incongruities and help identify ways in which the term in question can be transposed into the target legal language in a manner comprehensible to ultimate recipients of the target legal text.

For example, the English term *tort* has no legal counterpart in Czech law. *Tort* is defined as "a civil wrong for which a remedy may be obtained, usually in the form of damages"; it is further specified as "a breach of a duty that the law imposes on everyone in the same relation to one another as those involved in a given transaction." (Black's Law Dictionary, 1999: 1496). The Czech Civil Code (Act N. 40/1964 Coll., as amended) does not provide for any definition of a concept of a similar nature. It is mentioned, however, that an act giving rise to liability for damage in the Czech civil law may be called *civilní delikt* (Madar, 1995: 220). As mentioned earlier, however, each act or conduct should be considered as a question of law and as a question of facts. Legal qualification of an English *tort* and Czech *civilní delikt* (or *občanský / občanskoprávní delikt*) is quite close: both of them are understood as a breach of civil law, therefore a civil law remedy should follow (i.e. no punishment). Regarding the point of facts, the category of *torts* is much wider than the Czech *civilní delikt*. Certain facts that belong to the category of *torts* in the Anglo-American system of law are classified as *přestupek* in Czech law (for example, *private* or *public nuisance* – 'soukromoprávní' and 'veřejnoprávní rušení'). The following chart may illustrate the relationship between the English *tort* and *crime* on the one hand, and the Czech *civilní delikt* and *přestupek* on the other, but strictly considered from the perspective of the facts (C. 'skutkově').

Explanations of Chart 2:
Considering facts committed (not the questions of law), the Czech *civilní delikty* (E. 'civil delicts') makes up only a part of the Anglo-American *tort*. However, there are some overlaps:

I. This is an overlap based on the example described above in relation to the Czech *přestupek* (sg.) or *přestupky* (pl.) (see 2.2.). The primary grounds for the different approach of the two systems lie in the general philosophy of law: whilst the Anglo-American system of law is construed upon the ultimate principle that damage incurred by an individual should be compensated by the wrongdoer (and, if need be, consequently, or simultaneously, a criminal prosecution should be pursued by the State), the tradition of Czech (and Central European) law is based on the strong position of the State which should primarily punish any misdeeds, and, consequently, the damage might be sought by the innocent party, and compensated as a result of a separate judicial action.

II. As explained in 2.2., some acts called *přestupek* in Czech law, and thus constituting only an administrative wrong, would be treated as crimes in the Anglo-American system of law; the most obvious example is the area of minor traffic violations (such as wrong parking, speeding, etc.), which would be considered *přestupek* in Czech law and a crime[57] in the English-speaking countries.

[57] This would be a crime of low gravity called *infraction* for which the only punishment may be a fine.

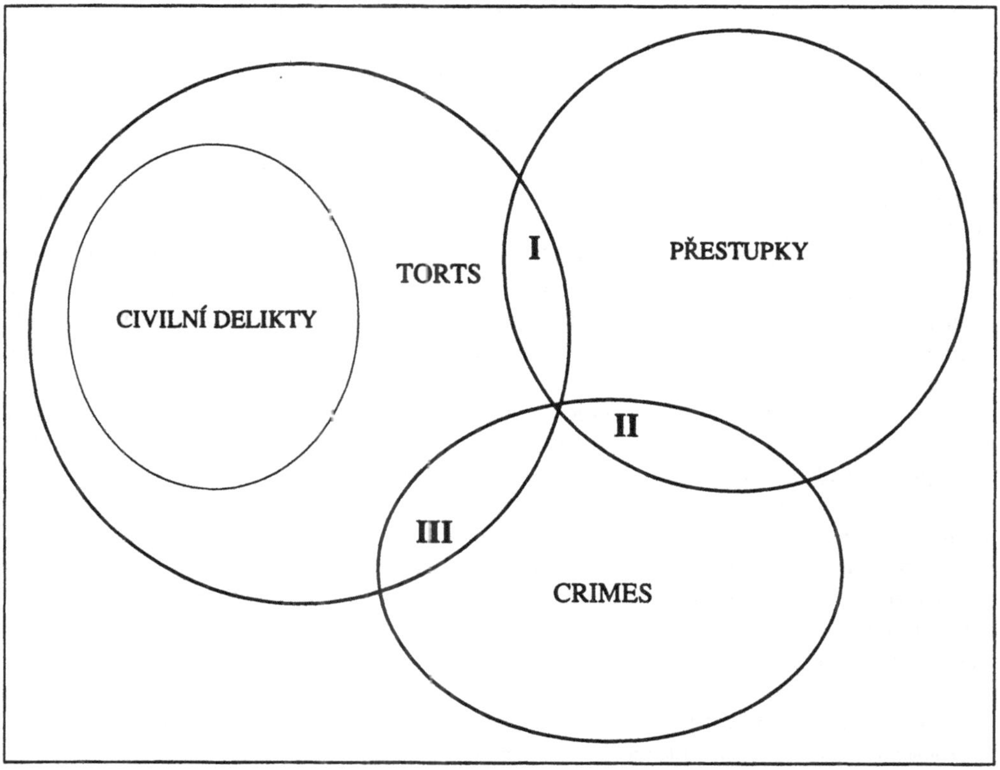

Chart 2

III. Some torts may also constitute a crime. For example, an *assault* (C. 'napadení') may be both a tort, as a result of which the injured party should be compensated, and a crime for which the court imposes a punishment.[58] Whether the respective act is to be assessed as both a tort and crime would usually depend on the gravity of the damage inflicted as a result of the assault, and the danger for the society of such an act. Other examples of torts usually constituting a crime are those forming the category called *trespass to the person* (C. 'delikt proti osobě'), such as *battery* (C. 'ublížení na zdraví') or *false imprisonment* (C. 'omezení osobní svobody'). Another tort which may also amount to a crime is *libel* (C. 'pomluva'). Libel is a type of defamation that is in a permanent form, i.e. recorded, printed, etc. In Czech law such a wrongful act is legally qualified as a crime. The other type of defamation is termed *slander* (C. 'urážka na cti'). This can only be a tort in the Anglo-American system of law and would be considered a civil delict in Czech law also. However, such acts would belong to a wide category of the Czech *ochrana osobnosti* (E. 'protection of personal rights', i.e. rights other than property rights) and the phrase *to bring an action for slander* would be translated as 'podat žalobu na ochranu osobnosti'.

In conclusion it should be emphasized that no term denoting an unlawful act in the Anglo-American system of law may be translated as *přestupek* into legal Czech. Should the term

[58] The standard of proof is also different: to prove a tort only needs the preponderance of evidence whereas a crime must be proved beyond all reasonable doubt.

civilní delikt occur in an original Czech law text it might be translated into English as 'a tort' if the general nature of the unlawful act is to be expressed. It is suggested, however, that the English term *civil wrong* or *civil delict* should be used instead.

As assumed above, conceptual analysis must be pursued whenever no identical term in the target language exists. The more general the legal term in question, the higher degree of probability there is that a terminological counterpart in the target language and legal system exists. For example, the English constitutional term *a state* can freely be translated as 'stát' into legal Czech; *a crime* in English is the Czech 'trestný čin', etc. When dealing with terms denoting more particular concepts, one must always undertake conceptual analysis in order to determine the boundaries of the SL and TL concepts and to decide the manner in which the source language term should be transposed into the TL term, preserving the maximum characteristics of the former.

A concept is to be understood as a set of common characteristics which can be observed by human beings in a certain number of objects (Felber, 1982: 123). The structure of a system of concepts depends upon the selected type of characteristics. Felber rightfully assumes that a change in the type of characteristics even in a subsystem of concepts may lead to the alteration of the whole system of concepts; this is usually the reason why systems of concepts in the same subject field are different in various languages. This can be shown through the example of the Czech term *výrok* and English *verdict* that the description of a concept by explanation consists in the enumeration of those characteristics which are significant for the concept. The following example is a shortened entry of *výrok*:

> **výrok** statement, holding in Czech law, where no jury exists, it combines the issues of fact and law, and is pronounced by the court; verdict delivered by the jury where such exists, considering only the facts of the case; judicial dictum pronounced by a judge; **jednomyslný ~** **poroty** unanimous verdict of a jury, **oddělitelný ~ rozsudku** *(CZ)* separable statement / holding of judgment; **odsuzující ~** statement of the court determining the guilt as a part of judgment; verdict of guilty delivered by jury; **rozhodčí ~** arbitral award, arbitration sentence; *(obsolete)* arbitrament; **soudní ~** judicial statement / holding, statement / holding of the court; **zprošťující ~** statement in the judgment determining the acquittal, [...]; **~ o náhradě škody** statement of the court / in the judgment specifying / determining damages; **~ o nevině** statement of the court determining the innocence of defendant; verdict of not guilty delivered by jury; [...]; **~ o trestu** statement of the court / in the judgment specifying punishment, **~ o vině** statement of the court determining the guilt; verdict of guilty, guilty verdict rendered by jury; [...]

The equivalents of the headword are contextualized with brief explanations given in smaller letters. Examples of usage are also interlaced with glosses that can be used as a part of an equivalent in certain contexts thus explaining the specificity of the term. Whether to make glosses a part of the target language equivalent or not would depend on the context of the target legal text as well as the experience of the translator and his or her ability to determine if the target text requires more information to be communicated or not.

As mentioned earlier, the unequivocal meaning of a term and its relation – without ambiguity – to a concept is undoubtedly generally accepted; it should be noted, however, that one term can be used for more than one concept (Leclercq, 1982: 141). Thus, conceptual analysis within the source language should be made in order to determine the polysemy of a term and its different meanings in different contexts (cf. 3.1.2.6. above regarding the Czech terms *věc* and *právo*).

Conceptual analysis as a basis for dictionary-making should be based on the so-called "parallel topical excerption" (Tomaszczyk, 1983: 45), i.e. reading extensively on narrowly defined topics in both the source language and the target language, and looking for the ways in which the native speakers of the two languages characteristically write about them. For example, the Czech phrase *předběžná vykonatelnost nastává ze zákona* is an elliptical shortening of the clause *vykonatelnost rozsudku nastane před jeho vyhlášením a tato možnost je stanovena zákonem*. To make this clear in English the following solution was chosen for the dictionary:

> **vykonatelnost** rozhodnutí enforcement of a decision; enforceability *(EU)*; **předběžná ~ rozsudku** enforcement of judgment before it is declared legally effective final and conclusive, [...] **předběžná vykonatelnost nastává ze zákona** v případě plnění výživného nebo pracovní odměny za tři měsíce před vyhlášením rozsudku pre-judgment enforcement i.e. before the judgment is legally effective is established by virtue of law / under statute in the case of a maintenance order or reimbursement of wages due for three months preceding the award of judgment; pre-judgment writ of attachment *(US)*

The Czech phrase is contextualized with the determination of the possible occurrence of the situation "v případě plnění výživného nebo pracovní odměny za tři měsíce před vyhlášením rozsudku" and the English equivalent phrase is interlaced with glosses. Finally, the similar order issued by US courts is given: "pre-judgment writ of attachment".

As a result of the inherent incongruity of the terminology of different legal systems, legal lexicographers cannot be expected to provide translation equivalents which are identical to their source terms at the conceptual level, argues Šarčević (1989a: 278). Nonetheless, it is perfectly legitimate to require, she adds, that they cite equivalents of the target legal system which most accurately convey the legal sense of the source term. The following examples may be shown here:

> A.
> **prokurista** *(CZ)* proctor, procurator one who is duly authorized to act in behalf of another in any business; chief / confidential clerk; proxy; **jednatel je statutární orgán jednající jménem společnosti, zatímco ~ je zástupcem společnosti jednajícím za společnost** a corporate agent shall be an authorised representative acting on behalf of the corporation while a proctor shall be a representative of the corporation acting for the corporation within the scope of corporate business

The Czech *prokurista* is a Czech company law term having no counterpart in the Anglo-American system of law. His responsibilities were quite obscure and unclear, confused with those of a corporate agent or a director (known as concepts in the Anglo-American law), until the Supreme Court of the Czech Republic determined the difference between a corporate agent and a proctor in the functioning of a company. This differentiating definition declared by the Supreme Court was used in the entry to clarify the meaning.

> B.
> **rozsudek** judgment; judgement *(gen)* final disposition of the case; in the US the narrow disposition of the case, generally found at the end of opinion; judicial opinion reasoning and decision of the court *(US)*; judicial decision; decree *(obs)*; holding that portion of the opinion that answers the legal question raised by the facts of the controversy before it *(US)*; [...]

The Czech term *rozsudek* may be translated into legal English in more than one way. To avoid confusion in English and to clarify the variations in meaning, brief explanations follow the English equivalents. Even an inexperienced translator should be able to distinguish between *a judgment* and *opinion* if the target legal text is to reach an American lawyer without previous experience in continental law.

As Šarčević (1989a: 290) further maintains, the results of conceptual analysis should be used to measure the degree of equivalence of the functional equivalent and its source term. It is obvious that only essential information should be provided in a specialist bilingual dictionary, based on a comparative conceptual analysis of the source and target legal systems, which is needed by translators to enable them to make the final decision as to whether an equivalent is adequate for their particular purpose. To facilitate this decision, entries should include brief descriptions of both the functional equivalent and its source terms, noting their essential differences and similarities in scope of application, structure, and legal effect. The term *rehabilitace* may serve as an example here:

> **rehabilitace** **prominutí nebo zmírnění následků odsouzení** rehabilitation the remission or moderating of consequences of conviction; exoneration, disburdening / relieving from blame or reproach; reinstatement of s.o. in any previous position / privilege; the action of re-establishing a person in a former standing with respect to rank and legal rights; **mimosoudní** ~ out-of-court / extra-judicial rehabilitation; ~ **odsouzených** rehabilitation of convicts, **soudní** ~ **zahlazení odsouzení** judicial rehabilitation i.e. expungement of conviction from s.o.'s criminal records

The headword is followed by a definition as provided by Czech law. English equivalents are followed by explanations as provided by various books on Anglo-American law. Exemplification of the use of the term contextualizes the meaning, providing more specific nuances of the concept.

4.3. Types of explanations

The title of the dictionary "Czech-English Law Dictionary with Explanations" is to suggest that the dictionary contains more than simple equivalents of Czech legal terms. Fillmore (1978: 167) claims that the law has its own sort of semantic principles; the semantics of the technical stratum of legal language is founded on stipulative definitions. Such assumptions, however, would not apply to dictionary-making since the purpose of definitions contained in bilingual dictionaries is rather different.

Producing definitions can have different discoursal functions (Swales, 1981: 111), and our intention in writing the CELDE was to provide as much conceptual information as permitted by the scope and size of the dictionary (and by the publisher) and needed by translators in order to decide what equivalent to select for their particular purpose. The term "explanation" was chosen to avoid an authoritative connotation of the word "definition". However, we maintain Swales' conclusion that the function of definitions "is more to furnish explanations of terms than to establish axioms which form part of a logical system of postulates and theorems" (1981: 107). Pearson (1998: 117) supports this conclusion claiming that dictionaries are rephrasing, i.e. clarifying usage, rather than defining in the sense of prescribing, i.e. that dictionary definitions are merely reporting rather than defining for the first time. Such characteristics can be seen in the following entries from the dictionary:

A.

srocení tumult public disturbance; disorderly or riotous proceeding; mobbing violent or threatening action taken in an effort to obtain a definite end and this distinguishes it from rioting and breach of the peace which are disorderly conduct at large; riot a violent disturbance of the peace by an assembly or body of persons; an outbreak of active lawlessness or disorder among the populace; commotion public disturbance; disturbance breaking up of peace

This is an example of an entry without exemplification. The translator should choose the appropriate equivalent according to the explanation following each of them and the (legal and linguistic) context of the source text.

B.

spis file a collection of papers placed on / in a file; document evidence or information upon any subject; pleadings formal allegations, written documents setting forth the cause of action or the defence; docket an endorsement on a document, briefly indicating its contents or subject; records an authentic or official report of the proceedings; **obžalovací ~** accusatory instrument, indictment; **osobní ~ zaměstnance** personal files on a worker; cards; personnel records; **přípravný ~** pro soudní řízení trial brief; **soudní ~** pleadings in civil proceedings; judicial file of a certain case in criminal proceedings; docket *(UK)* register of legal judgements; *(US)* list of causes for trial; **~ k navrhované osobě** *(CZ)* files on a candidate [...]

Explanations are provided here for the equivalents of the headword; glosses are inserted to clarify the context in exemplification.

Although the concept of a hybrid dictionary format containing definitions together with equivalents (Mackintosh, 1998: 138) is mentioned in relation to L2-L1 (decoding) dictionary users research (i.e. translation from a foreign language into a native one) there is no doubt that the same principle should apply the other way round for L1-L2 (encoding) dictionaries. As true equivalence of terms does not exist between languages, definitions can be very helpful, but should not be taken at their face value (Bachrach, 1982: 375). As emphasized many times before, translating legal texts requires a certain degree of substantive knowledge of law in both the source and target languages. Explanations may help to choose the most adequate equivalent but the dictionary would still be a first aid and, in the case of a more complex problem, the choice should be supported by further research. The following entry may serve as an example of quite explicit explanations:

smluvit ***(v)*** **co** contract *(v)* to do st., for st.; stipulate to specify st. as an essential part of the contract; covenant agree formally or solemnly; concert to arrange by mutual agreement primarily in international law; agree upon

Pearson (1998: 189) describes various approaches to defining, or explaining, expressions in dictionaries:

1. synonyms are used where equivalence in meaning and usage can be traced, such as in the example of use in the following entry:
   subvence subsidy a grant or contribution of money

2. substitution involves the use of a general language word or phrase to explain a term, such as:
   střelivo ammunition articles used for loading guns

3. paraphrase is an expression in other words, usually fuller and clearer, of the sense of any term or terminological phrase, for example:
   stížnost complaint a statement of injury or grievance laid before a court or judicial authority for the purpose of prosecution or of redress

Sager (1990: 42–43) provides an extended list of methods used for defining terms which may be used for the purposes of bilingual dictionary making (the examples are taken from individual entries in the CELDE):

1. definition by analysis; the following examples may illustrate this method:
   (i) **[...] agraciace je prominutí** trest není vykonán **nebo zmírnění** trest se sníží nebo se změní na mírnější druh **pravomocně uložených trestů** pardon / pardoning means the remission imposed punishment is not served or mitigation term is reduced or changed for a less severe one of punishment granted upon a final legally effective judgment

   (ii) **[...] příslušenství pohledávky** úroky nebo poplatek z prodlení a claim and related civil fruits (in civil law), accessions of a claim / debt interest on or charges for default (in common law)

2. definition by synonyms; for example:
   demise vzdání se úřadu / funkce, odstoupení resignation resigning one's office, withdrawal from office

3. by paraphrase, such as in:
   soukromě jako soukromá osoba in a private capacity, as a private person

4. by synthesis (i.e. identifying relations, by description), for example:
   [...] ilace je vnesení věci illation is the bringing of a thing onto premises

5. by implication (i.e. using the word in an explicative context); such as in:
   cedulový pertaining to bill, note; [...] **~á banka řídí peněžní oběh včetně vydávání bankovek a mincí, platební styk a zúčtování** the issuing / circulation / central bank shall govern the circulation of money, the issuance of notes and coins, money transfers and bank clearing [...]

6. by denotation (i.e. listing examples, by extension), for example:
   spolupachatelství complicity criminal assistance, partnership in a criminal action; *(rare)* accomplicity; accessoryship; criminal assistance; **~ zahrnuje podněcování, schvalování, nadržování, nepřekážení nebo neoznámení trestného činu** complicity includes inciting, encouraging, abetting, failure to prevent and failure to report a crime

7. by demonstration: naturally, this is a method of definition missing in dictionaries.

Since the language of law uses complex terms and phrases which are sometimes obscure for a layperson, we tried to provide simple explanations not only of equivalents of headwords and examples of their uses, but also of the headwords themselves; explanations were therefore used in both the source language (Czech) and the target language (English). Such an approach has proven to be efficient, particularly because most translators lack legal background, and not all of them have access to monolingual law dictionaries where they may look up the meaning of terms unknown to them in both the source and target legal systems.

4.4. Collection of material and entry-processing

The selection and collection of material for making excerpts should be tied to the purpose of the dictionary. Pearson (1998: 48) calls such collection a special purpose corpus, i.e. a corpus whose composition is determined by the precise purpose for which it is to be used. A corpus is any body of text collected with the aim of analyzing its features (Landau, 2001: 273). Since the main objective of the dictionary, as emphasized in the beginning, is to help all those trying to translate Czech legal texts into English so that such translations can be both linguistically and legally correct, precise and accurate and may serve their expected purposes, both Czech and English corpora of legal texts had to be created or compiled in our making of the CELDE, particularly because a translated text should be comprehensible not only to an English-speaking recipient in general, but also to lawyers who are native speakers of English and whose legal system and legal education is based on common law.

Naturally, the Czech corpus was compiled first. Since legal language is used in various discourses (Pearson, 1998: 36), it was crucial to decide what types of legal texts were to be chosen to create the basis for the database. Unlike the language of common law, continental legal language is represented primarily by the language of statutes. Legislation is the main source not only of new concepts expressed by prescriptive terms or terminological phrases, but also of syntactic structures and patterns subsequently applicable and applied in non-legislative legal discourses; even Czech legal jargon has its roots in legislation, usually subsisting in a syntactical ellipsis, and only partly in special vocabulary different to that of statutes.

Therefore, to create the Czech corpus, we relied on the annotated core laws representing the whole body of Czech law: the Civil Code, the Civil Procedure Code, and the Commercial Code in the area of private law, the Criminal Code, the Criminal Procedure Code, and the Administrative Procedure Code in public law. Other laws were also consulted primarily to clarify terms or structures used in the core legislation. In addition, about 3,000 pages of authentic legal documents were collected, such as law textbooks, university lectures, court documents and police reports, contracts, etc. Thirdly, monolingual dictionaries and lexicons of Czech law were also included.

Sinclair et al. (1996: 174) argue that, for comparative purposes, parallel corpora should be created, i.e. that texts in the source language be translated into the target language thus forming parallel corpora. Teubert (1996: 241), however, warns that translations, no matter how good and near-perfect they may be (but rarely are), cannot but give a distorted picture of the language they represent. We would strongly support Teubert's recommendation that linguists should never rely on translations when they are describing the language. The translated corpus is only a translation. with all its weaknesses and inaccuracies depending on the competence of its translator(s); such corpora would have minimum significance in determining the relationship between the source text and language on the one hand and the target language and text on the other. What should be used, however, are so-called comparable corpora, i.e. similar authentic texts are collected in the source language and the target language. These may be a valuable source of both legal and linguistic equivalencies to be utilized in a bilingual law dictionary. Therefore, our corpus of English legal texts encompasses legislation (Louisiana Civil Code, Canadian Penal Code, the US Rules of Civil and Criminal Procedure, etc.), monolingual law dictionaries, law textbooks and authentic documents and forms covering both private and public law. The most important part of the dictionary-making was to find relevant in topic English texts that would serve as a source of terminology and the language in general. As Teubert (1996: 247) complains, "syntax, and lexical syntax in particular, is the field where, basically, all dictionaries are deficient." To fill the gap we tried to include clauses and even whole sentences as exemplification in many entries so that the translator consulting the dictionary may get a certain degree of orientation in the target language sentence patterns. For example:

> **zletilý** being of legal / full age; major; adult; **Osoba mladší 18 let nesplňuje podmínku provozování živnosti ani tehdy, když je ~á.** A person under 18 shall not qualify for practising a trade even if s/he is an adjudicated adult.

There are two reasons for the inclusion of this sentence in the exemplification of use of the head-word "zletilý" (E. adult): (1) an apparent contradiction in general Czech between *osoba mladší 18 let* (E. 'a person under 18') and *je zletilá* (E. 'is of legal age') is explained in the English translation (although generally a person 18 or older is considered adult, under certain circumstances, usually for marriage purposes, a person younger than 18 years of age may be declared /*adjudicated*/ adult by court); and (2) although the obvious semantic and syntactic ellipsis of the Czech sentence has been taken from a law textbook it should be translated in such a way that the English translation may be generally comprehensible and two steps are to be taken: (i) interpreting the Czech legal statement (i.e. a person under 18 can become an adult only upon the decision of court), and (ii) translating such an explanatory construction into English.

4.4.1. Headword

There are four basic terms used to designate the main item of an entry, namely the head(-)word, main entry, entry word and lemma. Traditionally, the "head-word" is the name for the lexeme introducing the whole entry. Landau (1993: 76) uses "main entry" in the same meaning, Zgusta (1971: 249) uses "entry word" or "head word" interchangeably. "Lemma" is usually used instead of "headword" in computational lexicography (Čermák & Blatná, 1995: 97; cf. Bergenholtz & Tarp, 1995: 99); or, as Zgusta explains (1971: 250), it is a larger segment consisting of the entry word and its morphological, syntactical or other linguistic information determining the nature of the lexeme. Van der Meer (1998: 225) extends the meaning of "lemma" for bilingual dictionaries: it consists of context-free translational equivalents followed by contextualisation. We will use the term "headword" to designate the respective lexeme of the source language and the term "entry" to encompass the headword, TL equivalents and contextualized examples.

There are two types of decisions to be undertaken by a lexicographer: those relating to the macrostructure and those relating to the microstructure of the dictionary (Atkins, 1993: 16, Čermák & Blatná, 1995: 21–22). Macrostructure decisions apply to the word list, whether it is to be selective or comprehensive, how the arrangement of entries is to be made (alphabetical or otherwise), whether the headwords will be reduced to single lexemes or if phrases are to be allowed as well, what metalanguage is to be employed to describe an entry characteristics, and so on. As Zgusta (1980: 15) points out, in all European languages other than English the different parts of speech are treated in separate entries. The CELDE is arranged alphabetically; the list of headwords is not comprehensive, but adequate with respect to the excerpted material. Almost all headwords in the dictionary are simple lexemes except for Latin phrases which have become a regular part of the Czech legal language. In such cases, the whole Latin phrase was chosen to be the headword, for example, *de lege ferenda* or *de lege lata* arranged under "D" letter section. Since it is a bilingual special-purpose dictionary, grammatical features are added only exceptionally, for example, in the case of substantivized adjectives (*obviněný (adj)* /'accussed'; *obviněný (n)* /'the accussed'/). Abbreviations are used to denote different branches of law, lexicological information or to designate a word or phrase to a specific topic, and to denote grammatical information.

Microstructure decisions relate to the structure of an entry; the lexicographer should decide what constitutes the limits of a term in LSP and choose the headword which will represent a multi-word term or phrase (Thomas, 1993: 45). We can assume that a linguistically aware person may not see much difficulty in deciding which of the components of a compound should be the headword under which the entire expression is listed (Opitz, 1983b: 173); unsophisticated users, on the other hand, may have problems in identifying under which headword they will find the word or phrase they are looking for unless they can be sure of a certain principle that is applied throughout the dictionary and is at the same time simple enough to be acted upon by all users. For example, the adjective+noun phrase *koluzní vazba* (E. 'collusive custody') can be found both under adjective *koluzní* and noun *vazba*. Idiomatic phrases such as *vytěžený svědek* (E. 'debriefed witness') can also be found under both components. In verb+preposition phrases the verb acts as an entry and the prepositional collocations is shown in the examples of its usage. Nominalized verb+noun phrases, such as *podat žalobu* (E. 'bring an action') or *podat stížnost* (E. 'file a complaint'), can be found under the verb *podat* as well as the nouns *žaloba* and *stížnost* respectively. Terminological phrases, such as *ve znění pozdějších předpisů* (E. 'as amended'), can be found under the key word in the phrase *znění*, etc.

Since Czech is primarily a flexive language one more decision had to be taken with regard to the entry-formatting, namely when and where the morphematic juncture should be visualized in the headword. Čermák (1995b: 241) suggests that the juncture should be earmarked in the place of the headword where the inflexion starts. Having considered the type and objective of the dictionary, and its potential users, we concluded that the morphematic juncture should be visualized with a perpendicular (|) only where Czech examples contain paradigms of the headword in exemplification. For example:

> **účelný** meaningful; efficient; **~é rozdělení věci** meaningful partition of a thing, **~é uplatňování nebo bránění práva** meaningful application or protection of law, **~é vynakládání finančních prostředků** efficient spending of funds

Most headwords in the CELDE are autosemantic[59] words, primarily nouns, adjectives, verbs and adverbs. Several synsemantic[60] words are to be found in the dictionary, namely the prepositions *bez* (E. 'without'), *na* (E. 'on, upon'), *podle* (E. 'under, according to'), *proti* (E. 'against'), as these seem to be rather frequent in legal texts, as suggested by our corpora, and not always straightforward and simple in translation. Auxiliary verbs create separate headwords in two cases; in fact, there is only one Czech modal verb *moci* (E. 'be able to') as a separate entry. Another Czech verb only acts as an auxiliary in a particular context, namely *mít* (E. 'have') (cf. 3.1.2.4. above). For example, the Czech phrases *mít za to, že* (E. catenative verb 'appear that') or *mít za prokázané* (E. 'satisfy /a court/') have the core verbal component *mít* in its auxiliary function. Other elements in the phrases are either a preposition and participle

---

59 i.e. semasiological units of speech, those which give complete expression of psychic phenomena which are communicable in themselves.

60 "grammatical" words which are meaningful only when they occur in the company of other words, i.e. relational units.

(*za prokázané*) or an adverbialized preposition + pronoun unit (*za to*). Both phrases are not terms in the strict sense (i.e. terms of art); they are a part of the legal language causing problems in the accurate translation of legal texts since they have their functional counterparts in legal English. As such, they should be inserted in the dictionary, although they never appear as infinitives in any Czech legal text. Therefore, examples showing the usage and their translation into English have been included under the headword *mít*. Specification of the grammatical function of the verb in those phrases has been omitted as irrelevant for potential users and the type of dictionary.

Typological differences between the Czech (primarily flexive and synthetic) and English (primarily isolative and analytical) languages are not of an extreme importance to dictionary-making. Basic difference can be seen in headwords and examples of their use. Czech headwords are always in their basic grammatical (canonical) form, i.e. the nominative singular for nouns, the nominative singular masculine for adjectives, pronouns and numerals, and the infinitive form for verbs. However, examples of their usage may be represented by a phrase, or even a larger unit, where declension or conjugation would be used. In such a case, the headword is subdivided by a perpendicular to show the root (or the morphematic juncture) of the word and the position where the ending is attached.

One comment should be made in this context. Principles of so-called "political correctness" in language communication have been disregarded in the process of writing the CELDE. The level of enforcement of "politically correct" expressions, phrases or clauses substantially differs between Czech and English, i.e. legal Czech lacks any features suggesting that politically correct language might be an issue. Grammatical gender rigidly used in Czech may be the most significant example (although most conservative British law professors would also use the grammatical "he" to denote a party to a contract). Fillmore (1978: 157) comments on the conflicts sensed by anyone who takes seriously the effort to desex English:

> Since the system of pronouns in English is a closed class of words in which singularity for humans cannot be separated from sex, there is no way of choosing an anaphoric pronoun for an indefinite human antecedent without offending somebody. 'They' offend the grammarians, 'he' offends the feminists, 'he or she' offends the stylists, 'she' is downright hostile, and 'it' just cannot be taken seriously. We could get out of this by speaking Chinese, but that's bound to offend some people, too.

As can be assumed (and our experience also suggests so) the problems occur in translation from English into Czech rather than the other way round.

4.4.2. Exemplification

Exemplification can serve one of two purposes; it may be used to exemplify the meaning of the entry, or it may be used to exemplify its usage (Pearson, 1998: 81). When the meaning of the word is exemplified, exemplification involves citing examples of the word and may replace a definition. The following example may illustrate the approach:

> **aberace** aberration deviation / divergence from an intended course or mode of action; **~ je skutkový omyl, kdy čin namířený proti jednomu subjektu zasáhne jiný subjekt** aberration is a factual error an error as a matter of fact whereby an act aimed against one person causes injury to another

When usage is exemplified, a definition is also usually provided, and the exemplification allows the display not only of the meanings of words, but also of their syntax, selectional restrictions, collocations and stylistic level. For example:

> **požit|ek** profit attached to an office / position in addition to salary / wages; benefit pecuniary advantage; casual emolument, perquisite any casual emolument, fee, or profit, attached to an office or position in addition to salary or wages; **služební ~ky** emoluments of public servants; **~ky ústavních činitelů** perquisites and emoluments of government officials; **právo na ~ky z věci** right of beneficial use; **příjem ze závislé činnosti a funkčních ~ků** income from employment and perquisites/ emoluments thereof

We would maintain Landau's assumption (2001: 309) that collocations are of great importance in ESL (English as a second language) and bilingual lexicography, where readers are unfamiliar with the common associative patterns of the language they are trying to learn. Thus we have chosen a user-friendly approach in repeating examples under different entries. The repeatability rate is about 25%. For example, the Czech attributive terminological clause *ten, kdo se mohl při náležité péči o doručení usnesení dovědět* and its English counterpart 'one who, if diligent and careful, should have known of an attempted service of the resolution' can be found under the headwords *péče* (E. 'care'), *náležitý* (E. 'due') and *doručení* (E. 'service').

In setting a syntactic range of collocations we selected a communicative approach, i.e. larger units rather than individual words or binominal expressions with an emphasis on more difficult translational structures were chosen. The entry *usnesení* contains almost all phrases and clauses (44 examples) denoting various types of such a court decision that exist in Czech procedural law.

The entry *pokus* (E. 'attempt') consists of examples facilitating the analogous creation of terms denoting various attempted crimes. The entry *škoda* contains examples of two Czech statutory attributes *nikoliv malá* (E. 'not small') and *nikoliv nepatrná* (E. 'not insignificant') that may be crucial in determining the amount of subsequent damages to be awarded by the court.

4.4.3. Formatting an entry

Formatting an entry is a part of the microstructure of the dictionary. As mentioned earlier, limited grammatical characteristics were attached to the headwords. Unfortunately, no Czech-English dictionary published recently contains pronunciation of English equivalents although, logically, one would assume that the pronunciation of English words that are looked up and unknown to the user should have been included. Moulin (1983: 149) claims that, among other features, the UK and US spelling variants are to be inserted. Where appropriate, such differentiating notes were made, such as in the entry *obhajoba* ('defence' (UK), 'defense' (US)).

Atkins (1993: 18) points out that the presentation of lexical units should show the way in which the headword is divided into senses (either flat or hierarchical sense differentiation) and the order in which these senses are set out in the dictionary entry. She adds that the explanation of meaning should utilize, among other things, lexically relevant data external to the headword (e.g. cross-reference), paradigmatic information (e.g. parts of speech), usage information (e.g. 'obsolete'), status (e.g. 'dialect', 'slang'), and field (i.e. a branch of law, such as the Czech *OP* for "občanské právo" /civil law/ in the headword or Czech example).

Thus, Czech headwords in the CELDE are printed in bold type and listed alphabetically. They usually consist of one word, or of two words in the case of reflexive verbs (e.g. *podrobit se* /E. 'be subject to') or two verbal aspects of one verb (e.g. *zakázat, zakazovat* /E. 'prohibit'). Where necessary, a complement collocation immediately follows the headword (e.g. obligatory preposition in *nutit ‹k› čemu*).

An explanation, definition or interpretation of a headword is given exceptionally, only where the term is not frequently used in legal Czech, such as *agnoskace* (E. 'recognition'), *bonita* (E. 'solvency'), or if a Czech term does not have a legal equivalent in the Anglo-American system of law, such as *magistrát* (E. 'metropolitan authority') or *živnost* (E. 'trade' in the meaning of an ancient 'guild').

The following rules were observed in formatting the CELDE:

(1) The headword is represented by a swung dash (~) in examples of its use, for example:
adhézní accessory; adhesive; collateral; ~ **řízení** [...] .

(2) Polysemic (polysemantic, polysemous) terms (within one word category) and some functional synonyms are listed as separate headwords and distinguished by subscript numbers, for example the entries **právo**$_1$ (objektivní), **právo**$_2$ (subjektivní); **řízení**$_1$, **řízení**$_2$, **řízení**$_3$.

práv|o $_1$ **objektivní** law *(uncount)* as a system; **církevní katolické** ~ canon law; **daňové** ~ tax law, revenue law; **dědické** ~ law of succession, law of inheritance; **diplomatické** ~ ambassadorial law, law of diplomacy; **evropské** ~ European law; [...]

prá|vo $_2$ **subjektivní** right of / to do st.; interest in st.; title to st.; entitlement to st / to do st.; privilege to do st.; **dědická ~va** rights of inheritance, succession rights; rights to inherit, rights to take / acquire by descent / inheritance; **hlasovací** ~ voting right / power / privilege, right to vote; **hrobové** ~ right to bury in a grave; **majetkové** ~ proprietary / property right, right / interest in property, property interest; [...]

řízení $_1$ proceeding(s) a course of a particular case; procedure system and method of proceeding; process *(inform)*; **adhézní** ~ collateral / adhesion proceedings where the victim of crime may recover damages in the course of criminal proceedings; **arbitrážní** ~ proceedings in arbitration, arbitration proceedings; **blokové** ~ *(CZ)* hearing of an administrative delict / infraction; [...]

řízení $_2$ management; administration; governance; ~ **letového provozu** air navigation services, ~ **ministerstva** administration / management of a ministry, ~ **společnosti** corporate governance, management of a company; [...]

řízení $_3$ driving; **nepozorné** ~ **motorového vozidla** careless driving, ~ **vozidla pod vlivem alkoholu** driving while intoxicated; drink-driving, drinking-driving *(UK)*, drunk(-)driving *(US)*, ~ **vozidla pod vlivem omamných látek** driving while intoxicated with narcotics; [...]

(3) Verbal nouns are listed as separate headwords only when they are of a specific terminological value, such as the entry **braní**:

braní taking; receiving; seizing, seizure as crime prevention; ~ **rukojmích** taking hostages, ~ **úplatků** bribery, the taking / acceptance of a bribe, bribe-taking; corruption, ~ **užitků z nájmu** receiving / taking of proceeds of lease.

(4) Verbal aspect may serve as a distinctive feature of individual entries if exemplification of their use required the separation of entries in order to make the meaning of a word clearer and to prevent terminological confusion. Compare the headword **zakázat, zakazovat** where the swung dash (~) denotes either aspect indiscriminately, with two separate entries **vyžádat (si)** and **vyžadovat**.

zakáz|at, zakaz|ovat prohibit, forbid usually by law; ban usually by virtue of office; interdict usually by a command; impose a ban on st.; ~ **nezákonné shromáždění** prohibit unlawful assembly, ~ **parkování na ulicích** prohibit parking in the streets, ~ **prodej alkoholu nezletilým** prohibit the sale of alcohol to minors; [...]

vyžádat (si) request, require; ask for; command; ~ **(si) přítomnost** koho **na jednání** request the presence of s.o. at the trial / hearing, ~ **(si) spis** request the file to be submitted; [...]

vyžadovat call for; require; command; ~ **jiný volební systém** call for a different electoral system, ~ **většinu** command / require a majority; [...]

(5) Grammatical information is given only exceptionally to avoid the confusion of meanings, e.g. the headword **moci** *(v)* (E. 'be able to') where *(v)* suggests the verb since the same word *moci* may suggest the plural form of the frequent noun *moc* (E. 'power').

(6) If there are more English equivalents for one headword that are different in their meaning and function, they are listed according to their occurrence in legal usage and context, where it was possible to identify such information, i.e. a lower Arabic number signifies a more frequent equivalent. For example:

arbitrážní 1 pertaining to arbitration; ~ **doložka** arbitration clause; ~ **jednání** hearing in arbitration; arbitration hearing; ~ **řízení** arbitration procedure / proceedings; ~ **soud** arbitration court, court of arbitration; 2 pertaining to arbitrage; ~ **makléř** arbitrager, ~ **poplatek** arbitrage fee

mandát 1 **oprávnění k výkonu funkce; 2 příkaz, zmocnění** mandate 1 instruction or commission as to policy supposed to be given by the electors; 2 command, commission; ~ **člena obecního zastupitelstva** the mandate of a member of a community council / community councillor, ~ **poslance a ~ senátora vzniká zvolením ve volbách** the mandate of a Deputy or Senator shall arise upon their election in general elections

(7) An English equivalent follows the headword and is printed in regular type. Where it is possible to use more than one English equivalent for a Czech headword, synonyms are listed in an ascending order according to the frequency of their use starting with the equivalent used most frequently. Where it is important that individual synonyms should be distinguished within the chain of synonyms, a semicolon is used.

Considering the differences between Anglo-American and Continental systems of law, many equivalents are subject-matter (legal) rather than linguistic equivalents, for example the entry **vázaný**.

vázan|ý tied confined to st.; blocked restricted; bound by a duty, statute, etc.; bounded limited; **~á hypotéka** closed mortgage, **~é obchody** tied transactions, **~ý účet na splnění určitých smluvních podmínek nebo budoucí události** tied account the payment of which is made upon the fulfilment of certain conditions; blocked account; **~ý výrobek** tied product, **ohlašovací živnost ~á** *(CZ)* professional notifiable trade learned and skilled professions; **uložit na ~ý účet** put in a tied account; hold in escrow a deposit held in trust or as security

(8) Explanations, definitions and/or the interpretation of English equivalents, if necessary, are printed in smaller type, as can be seen in the entry **adhézní** below.

(9) An explanation, definition or interpretation attached to an English equivalent of a Czech example need not necessarily be the literal translation of the explanation, definition or interpretation attached to the Czech term. Where the legal content of an English equivalent suggests so, explanations, definitions or interpretation were taken from British and/or American law dictionaries as can be seen in **adhézní**:

adhézní accessory contributing in an additional and subordinate degree; adhesionary relating to adhesion contract; collateral subordinate, indirect; **~ řízení** collateral / adhesion proceedings the type of civil proceedings held within the criminal proceedings where the victim of a crime may recover damages; **~ smlouva** accessory contract assuring the performance of a prior contract; adhesion contract no possibility to bargain, the "take it or leave it" principle); collateral contract made prior to, or contemporaneous with, another contract on the same or similar subject

(10) Czech legal institutes not existing in the Anglo-American system of law are explained in a smaller type, and the closest in meaning and most legally adequate ways of translation are suggested, e.g. the entry **přestupek** below; exemplification encompasses the classification of administrative infractions as provided by the relevant Czech legislation.

(11) Czech examples of the use of a headword follow after a semicolon, and are printed in bold type (i.e. everything in Czech is in bold). Their English equivalents are printed in a regular type and size, whereas definitions, explanations or interpretations are printed in regular type but a smaller size; for example **přestupek**:

přestup|ek protiprávní čin podle správního práva (CZ) administrative infraction a wrongful act committed by an individual and governed by administrative law; more generally administrative delict; transgression / violation of administrative law; **dopravní ~** breach of traffic regulations as an administrative infraction; **hromadný ~** multiple administrative infraction; **kázeňský ~** breach of discipline; disciplinary transgression; **sbíhající ~ky** concurrent administrative infractions / delicts; **trvající ~** perpetual administrative infraction; **~ na úseku dopravy a na úseku silničního hospodářství** administrative infraction in the field of transport and highway management; **~ na úseku financí a měny** administrative infraction in the field of finances and currency; **~ na úseku kultury** administrative infraction in the field of culture; **~ na úseku ochrany před alkoholismem a jinými toxikomaniemi** administrative infraction in the field of protection against alcoholism and other types of drug addiction; ~ **na úseku podnikání** administrative infraction in the field of business; ~ **na úseku práce a sociálních věcí** administrative infraction in the field of labour and social matters; ~ **na úseku školství a výchovy mládeže** administrative infraction in the field of education and the upbringing of children; ~ **na úseku vodního hospodářství** water management administrative infraction; ~ **na úseku zdravotnictví** administrative infraction in the field of medical services; ~ **proti pořádku ve státní správě** administrative infraction against the state administration order; ~ **proti pořádku ve věcech územní samosprávy** administrative infraction against the order in territorial self-government; ~ **přecházení silnice mimo přechod** jaywalking crossing the street off the zebra crossing; **~ky a jiné správní delikty** administrative infractions and other administrative delicts; **objekt ~ku** a physical object of administrative infraction; **obviněný z ~ku** person accused of having committed an administrative infraction; **pokračování v ~ku** continued administrative infraction; **rozhodnutí o ~ku nelze doručit veřejnou vyhláškou** the decision with respect to an administrative infraction may not be served on the offender by a public notice; **řízení o ~cích** administrative hearing of administrative infractions; **subjekt a objekt ~ku** person committing an administrative infraction and a target thereof; **podkladem pro zahájení řízení o ~ku je oznámení státního orgánu o ~ku** the grounds for the commencement of administrative procedure shall be information that an administrative infraction has been committed

(12) A slash (/) separates expressions or phrases that can be linked to the preceding or following word, e.g. it suggests that a preposition or another synsemantic word may be linked to all the preceding synonyms, or if a definite or indefinite article or a preposition precedes a synonymical chain they may be connected to any of the synonyms if such a link is permitted by regular grammatical collocation.

(13) Grammatical information concerning English equivalents is given only where such information is relevant, such as the plural as well as singular of English *data* and *datum*.

(14) Irregular verbal forms of past tense and participle of Czech verbs are given with the respective irregular verbs and they are listed as possible equivalents of a headword, not in the examples of its use.

odebralt se withdraw /-drew, drawn/; retire; **soud se ~l k poradě o rozsudku** the Court withdrew / retired to consider judgment, the Court withdrew / retired to deliberate

(15) Words which are spelled differently in British and American English are given in both spelling varieties (e.g. offence-offense, labour-labor, centre-center, etc.) denoted *UK* or *US* for British English and American English respectively.

The structure of an entry depends on the part of speech in question:

(16) *Nouns.* The order of examples is as follows: phrases with an attribute in pre-modification; phrases with an attribute in post-modification; a noun serving as an attribute or any other part of speech in non-verbal collocations; prepositional phrases; verbal phrases; incomplete sentences, and full sentences.

(17) *Adjectives.* Phrases with an adjective serving as an attribute in pre-modification are listed first; other collocations follow.

(18) *Verbs.* The order is as follows: verbs with complements arranged alphabetically; incomplete sentences; sentences.

(19) *Other parts of speech.* Examples in an entry are arranged in alphabetical order.

(20) *The lozenge.* A few headwords are exemplified using phrases that can be assigned to none of the preceding equivalents. They follow after the lozenge (◆) and are of an idiomatic nature.

4.5. Software and Statistics

Dictionary-writing in the era of electronic media cannot dispense with reliable hardware and efficient software. Most publishing houses concentrating on lexicography possess prodigious corpora and databases worked on by efficient teams of lexicographers. Since our task was much more modest and the "team" consisted only of one member we had to choose reliable software that would help us fulfil our objective.

Paradox 5 for Windows is the database software used for storing and processing excerpts; the database consists of more than 50,000 records. The database consisted of six fields: (1) the key word in the source language according to which the database was alphabetically arranged, and later becoming a headword; (2) the whole excerpted phrase in the source language where the key word occurred in the excerpted text; (3) the source where the Czech phrase was found (for example, abbreviated references to statutes, textbooks, monographs, Internet, etc.); (4) the target language semantic equivalent or equivalents of the source language key word; (5) the target language phrase equivalent to the source language under (2); (6) the source of the target language equivalent phrase (again referring to a printed or electronic resource in an abbreviated form). It is suggested that information referring to the resources should be kept as precise and detailed as possible, i.e. not only the title of the excerpted book but also the page and paragraph or any other text format detail so that any subsequent searching for the original occurrence of a term can be as quick and straightforward as possible.

The OUP software "Wordsmith Tools" was selected not only to show the collocations of some problematic terms and equivalents but also to set basic statistical data about the corpus:

(1) the database of Czech excerpts consists of about 167,000 words, of which approximately 145,000 were selected to either serve as headwords or for exemplification of use on the Czech side of the dictionary;
(2) the database of English equivalents of headwords and examples of use consists of about 253,000 words, of which 215,000 were selected to be included in the dictionary.

Corel WordPerfect 8 was used as a word-processor for the ultimate processing of individual entries; the final version of the dictionary consists of approximately 9,200 Czech headwords, 29,000 Czech terms, terminological phrases and semi-sentences, and of about 46,000 of their English equivalents.

III. Conclusion

The main purpose of this comparative legal and linguistic study has been to analyse three main aspects forming the basis for the writing of the CELDE: (a) the language of law in the Czech Republic (legal Czech) and major English-speaking countries (legal English), (b) approaches to the translation of legal texts, and (c) approaches to dictionary-making in the area of bilingual special-purpose lexicography. We have tried not only to find well-grounded and justified solutions to be used in the dictionary but also to indicate directions for envisaged future research and pedagogical applications.

1. Summary of findings

Language for law purposes (LLP) is used to facilitate communication within legal discourse. It is a variety of language strongly determined by the respective discourse event. The research into this subsystem of the general language system consists of describing and analysing the selection, combination and use of existing morphological, lexical and syntactic units, structures and patterns that would best serve the specific stylistic, genre and discourse functions of a text in a concrete subject area and specific social context. Specificity of the discourse seems to be primarily a pragmatic category reflecting the communicative purpose and needs of the users – professionals in the respective subject field and, possibly, lay (or paralegal) persons charged with legal assignments.

Traditionally, terminology has been considered the most significant representative of language for specific purposes (sometimes, mistakenly, suggested as the only discriminating factor). Law terminology encompasses a wide range of special-purpose expressions, phrases and higher syntactic units that can be subdivided into five groups:

(a) Terms of art, or "pure" law terms, including legal Latin; it is a relatively limited in number group of words or phrases that are not used outside the branch of law unless stylistically marked. Examples are the Czech term *žaloba*, or English *demurrer*.

(b) Terms "generalized" in everyday non-legal communication; these are words with a related legal meaning (such as Czech *pozemek*, *nedbalost* and their English counterparts *land* and *negligence* respectively).

(c) Expressions of general import acquiring specific legal meaning if so defined by legislation; one example was mentioned – that of a British law called the Welfare of Pigs Act 1998 which provides a definition of "pig" for the purposes of that law. In Czech law, the Family Act introduced the Czech word *zodpovědnost* as a legal term in an unprecedented context of *rodičovská zodpovědnost*.

(d) Phraseological and semi-syntactical units; (i) so-called phrasemes are multi-word terms usually formed by elliptical nominalization (e.g. C. *zákonná domněnka svědčící manželu matky* or E. *maliciously damaging the property of another*); (ii) repeatedly used stipulating clauses hardened into terminological units, such as C. *pokud zákon nestanoví jinak* (E. 'unless the Act provides otherwise'), and (iii) clauses such as *má-li soudce za to, že,* (E. 'where it appears to the judge that'), or *žalovaný měl způsobit škodu*, (E. 'the defendant is alleged to have caused damage') where the legal usage has shifted their function from a simple assumption without significant implications to the determination of circumstances that would create legal consequences.

(e) Jargon makes up in both legal Czech and English a significant portion of terminology. Jargon may not be confined only to the lexicon of a subject-field; as a subvariety of language, it also covers morphology and syntax. It was shown that the elliptical language in everyday legal and judicial practice tends to condense and economize the legal speech (and unofficial writings), thus shifting to jargon.

Conceptual analysis is to be pursued whenever an identical term in the target language does not exist or its full equivalent is in doubt. The more general the legal term in question the higher the degree of probability that can be presumed with respect to the existence of a terminological counterpart in the target language. Dealing with terms denoting more particular concepts means that conceptual analysis is always to be undertaken in order to determine the boundaries of the source language and target language concepts and to decide the manner in which the source language term should be transposed into the target language, preserving the maximum characteristics of the former.

There are phrases in English law which are similar or identical in function although not necessarily accurate in the sense of literal translation. These are usually called functional equivalents and should be used whenever such an equivalent exists in the target language and the functional analysis proves it to be a counterpart of the source language unit (a word, phrase, syntactic unit). The language of law is a highly formalized language using settled vocabulary, phrase and sentence patterns; the more vocabulary, phrase and sentence patterns firmly established in the target language and used in the process of translation of the source text, or production of the target legal text, the more natural and comprehensible may be the final product. Comparative functional analysis should be made in order to set the scope of equivalence between source language and target language units.

Legal translation should be based primarily on the comparative genre analysis in order to make the transfer of legal information as precise, accurate and comprehensible as possible, and to shape the target text in a manner adequate to its purpose. The primary objective of legal translation is that the target recipient should be provided with as explicit, extensive and precise legal information in the target language as is contained in the source text, complemented (by the translator) with facts rendering the original information fully comprehensible in the different legal environment and culture. Three prerequisites existing for the successful translation of legal texts (a basic knowledge of the legal systems, familiarity with the relevant terminology, and competence in the specific legal writing style of the target language) constitute the practical rule which should be respected by each translator and is based on our own experience: the translation of legal texts should not be done without an extensive knowledge of the respective legal topic in both the source language and target language, i.e. a knowledge of concepts, terms denoting these concepts, sentence patterns visualizing the information, genre classification of the text, legal culture, etc., in both languages.

A dictionary which would help its users produce legal texts in the target language as well as adequately translate source legal texts into the target language must be founded upon a profound comparative legal and linguistic study that would (a) determine equivalents at the levels of vocabulary, syntax and, possibly, genres and (b) select the appropriate lexicographic material to be included in the dictionary. A bilingual law dictionary should contain not only the source language terminology but also syntactic units that are relevant for the language of law. Since Czech law is derived from continental law based on written codes and statutes, the source language and target language corpora, facilitating conceptual and functional analysis, should encompass essential legislation relating to private and public law, materials based on legislation, such as annotations and textbooks or authentic documents, and law dictionaries. Case law will play an important role in searching for relevant conceptual counterparts in legal

English. A user-friendly approach should be chosen for formatting the dictionary (for example, the repeatability of examples should be higher) as a linguistic background cannot be expected of all users.

2. Implications for future research

2.1. Applied linguistics

An English – Czech legal genre analysis will be pursued in order to find relevant ways of translating authentic legal documents between the two languages. The analysis will apply to individual text types in private law (e.g. contracts, corporate documents), public law (e.g. legislation, prosecution materials), and procedural law (decisions of court and other judicial documents and forms, as well as rules of procedure). The main purpose will be to create comparable corpora of English and Czech legal texts so that a translator or lawyer may find relevant information.

2.2. Lexicography

Extensive research will be pursued in order to prepare a comprehensive English-Czech law dictionary that would cover the legal systems of all major English-speaking countries. An English law corpus will be compiled encompassing case law, core legislation, authentic legal documents and law dictionaries. An analysis will be made at the levels of terminology, genres and discourse (primarily written). The main purpose of the dictionary will be to provide and explain concepts of the Anglo-American system of law and to find their conceptual and/or functional equivalents and counterparts in Czech law and legal language.

IV. Zusammenfassung

Die vorliegende Arbeit ist eine rechtslinguistische Studie, deren Ziel darin besteht, die Ausgangsbasis für die Schaffung eines tschechisch-englischen Rechtswörterbuchs unter dem Titel "Česko-anglický právnický slovník s vysvětlivkami" (Tschechisch-englisches Wörterbuch mit Erklärungen) zu analysieren und die praktischen Methoden und Vorgänge seiner Bearbeitung zu begründen. Den Ausgangspunkt dieser Studie bildet eine komparative rechtslinguistische Untersuchung zweier Rechtssysteme, und zwar des in der Tradition des europäischen Kontinentalrechts verankerten tschechischen Rechtssystems und des angloamerikanischen Systems, das auf Gewohnheits- und Richterrecht beruht; wir befassen uns mit den Sprachmitteln, Vorgängen und Stilen, die in dem jeweiligen System zur Vermittlung von Rechtsinformationen verwendet werden.

1. Ziele des Wörterbuchs

Die Studie besteht aus vier Kapiteln. Im ersten Kapitel werden die entscheidenden Gründe für die Schaffung des Wörterbuches und die bei seiner Bearbeitung verfolgten Ziele erklärt. Das Hauptmotiv unserer Bemühung war es, den Benutzern des Wörterbuchs (vor allem den Übersetzern und Dolmetschern), die bestrebt sind, tschechische Rechtstexte ins Englische zu übertragen, Hilfe zu leisten, damit ihre Übersetzung außer der sprachlichen Korrektheit auch sachgemäß ist, sowie jenen Benutzern (vor allem den tschechischen Juristen), welche die Realität der tschechischen Rechtsordnung auf Englisch wiedergeben müssen. Der übersetzte oder neu erschaffene Text sollte auch jenen Juristen verständlich sein, deren Muttersprache Englisch ist, wenn das Ausgangsrechtssystem, mit dem sie sich befassen und in dem sie tätig sind, das allgemeine angelsächsische Recht (Common Law) ist. In diesem Sinne bemühten wir uns um eine "Begriffsanalyse", die Susan Šarčević für die Schaffung eines Rechtswörterbuches empfiehlt (1989: 290). Die Basis dieser Analyse bildet der Vergleich der Rechtsbegriffe in den beiden Rechtssystemen (Ausgangssystem und Zielssystem), um das Äquivalenzmaß zwischen potentiell äquivalenten Termini zu erstellen.

Ein weiteres Ziel des vorliegenden tschechisch-englischen Rechtswörterbuchs ist es, zur Vereinheitlichung verschiedener Herangehensweisen an die Übersetzung tschechischer Rechtstexte ins Englische beizutragen. Die Standardisierung der (sachlichen und sprachlichen) englischen Äquivalente der tschechischen Rechtsterminologie ist dringend notwendig, besonders im Kontext der Verhandlungen der Tschechischen Republik um Mitgliedschaft in der Europäischen Union. Bereits die zwölf Amtsprachen der Union verursachen beträchtliche Probleme bei der Übersetzung der Rechtsvorschriften; es ist anzunehmen, dass falls zumindest die elementare Standardisierung der englischen Übersetzungsäquivalente der tschechischen Termini nicht schon vor dem Beitritt der Tschechischen Republik zur Europäischen Union am 1. Mai 2004 durchgeführt wird, die Lage sehr unübersichtlich werden und zu vielen unnötigen Auslegungsunklarheiten führen kann.

Es ist zwar offenkundig, dass kein Übersetzungswörterbuch in allen seinen Aspekten absolut verbindlich und normativ sein kann. Der Benutzer muss sich selbst entscheiden, inwieweit und in welcher Hinsicht er es für normativ halten wird (Barnhart, 1980; 39). Trotzdem ist es notwendig, solche Wörterbücher zu erarbeiten. Dabei wird eine umfangreiche

Datei geschaffen, die bei der Vorbereitung eines großen elektronischen zwei- oder mehrsprachigen Wörterbuchs verwendbar sein könnte, das neben der Gemeinsprache auch das Vokabular verschiedenster humanistischer oder technischer Fächer einschließt.

Nicht zuletzt haben wir versucht, die Grundcharakteristika der tschechischen Rechtssprache einschließlich deren Abweichungen vom Standard zu erfassen. Zum Beispiel der Fachausdruck *odvolání [Berufung]* (E. *appeal*) ist meistens mit der Präposition *proti [gegen]* (E. *against*) verbunden. Diese Präpositionalverbindung wird sowohl in der tschechischen Gemeinsprache[1] als auch in der Rechtssprache standardmäßig gebraucht und ermöglicht die nominale sowie verbale Valenz (*odvolání proti rozsudku [Berufung gegen das Urteil]* – E. *an appeal against the judgement*; Tsch. *odvolat se proti zamítnutí stížnosti* – E. *appeal /against/ the dismissal of complaint*, etc.). In der tschechischen Rechtssprache werden jedoch noch zwei weitere Präpositionen verwendet: Tsch. *z* – E. *from* und Tsch. *do* – E. *to*. Die tschechischen Präpositionalverbindungen *odvolání ‹z› rozsudku* a *odvolání ‹do› rozsudku* haben dieselbe Bedeutung und Rechtswirkung wie die Verbindung *odvolání ‹proti› rozsudku*. Die ersten zwei präpositionalen Kollokationen gehören dem Rechtsjargon an und kommen sehr oft in Äußerungen der Parteien im Gerichtssaal vor. In schriftlicher Form sind sie dagegen viel seltener. Im Rechtsenglisch findet man ein entsprechendes Präpositionalgefüge für die tschechische Verbindung *odvolání z rozsudku*, nämlich *an appeal ‹from› judgement*. Unser Korpus verschiedener englischsprachiger Rechtstexte, das zirka sechs Millionen Belege umfasst, zeigt jedoch, dass die englische Verbindung *an appeal ‹from› /a judgement, a decision/* viel häufiger ist, als die tschechische Kollokation *odvolání ‹z› /rozsudku/*. Im Gegensatz zum Rechtstschechisch kommt das englische Präpositionalgefüge *an appeal ‹from›* auch in Gesetzestexten vor (z.B. im amerikanischen Gesetz "Criminal Alien Deportation Amendments 1990", §4 Abs. 5 lit. a), Satz 3 oder im britischen "Criminal Appeal Act 1995", § 7 Abs. 2 lit. b); zusammen mit der Verbindung *appeal against* dienen sie deshalb als akzeptable Synonymverbindungen des tschechischen Gefüges *odvolání proti rozsudku*. Die tschechische Präpositionalkollokation *odvolání do rozsudku* besitzt zwar kein Äquivalent im Rechtsenglisch, kann jedoch ohne sprachliche oder rechtliche Sinnesstörung als *an appeal against the judgement* übersetzt werden.

Wir haben fernerhin versucht, in der anglo-amerikanischen Rechtssprache authentische (d.h. funktionelle) englischsprachige Äquivalente für tschechische Ausdrücke bzw. terminologische Einheiten zu finden, die schon früher unrichtig ins Englische übersetzt wurden, wobei diese falschen Übersetzungsäquivalente immer wieder, häufiger oder weniger häufig, überliefert werden. In erster Linie handelt es sich um die Termini *právní subjekt* [*Rechtssubjekt*] und *právnická osoba* [*juristische Person*]. *Právní subjekt* wird wiederholt unpassend als *legal subject* übersetzt, besonders deshalb, weil sowohl das tschechische Substantiv *subjekt* als auch der englische Ausdruck *subject* Polyseme sind, wobei ein unerfahrener Benutzer der englischen Rechtssprache (sei es Übersetzer oder Jurist) annehmen mag, dass in diesem Fall die tschechische und englische Bedeutung zusammentrifft; zweifellos wirkt hier auch die zwischensprachliche Interferenz mit. Der tschechische Terminus *právní subjekt* wird oft als natürliche Person (fyzická osoba) (E. *natural person*), bzw. als juristische Person (E. *legal entity*) definiert, die imstande ist, Rechtsbeziehungen einzugehen und somit Rechte zu erlangen und Pflichten einzugehen. Diese Charakteristik entspricht dem englischen Ausdruck *legal person*, der das einzig richtige und zugleich funktionelle Äquivalent des

---

[1] Wir halten die Gemeinsprache für eine Variante der Schriftsprache, d.h. als Gegensatz der Fachsprache, nicht als Synonym für Gemeintschechisch. Sowohl die Gemeinsprache, als auch die Fachsprache sind Bestandteile der Schriftsprache.

besagten tschechischen Terminus im anglo-amerikanischen Recht darstellt. Der englische Terminus *legal subject* kann nur im Sinne eines gesetzmäßigen Objekts (eines Vertrags, einer Vereinbarung) gebraucht werden. Der tschechische Rechtsausdruck *právnická osoba* wird oft unrichtig als *legal person*[2] übersetzt; wie wir bereits gezeigt haben, hat dieser englischsprachige Terminus eine andere Bedeutung. *Právnická osoba* ist ein künstlich geschaffenes Rechtssubjekt, das imstande ist, Rechte zu erlangen und Pflichten einzugehen. Somit kann es auch Rechtsbeziehungen eingehen. Dieser Begriff der tschechischen Rechtssprache kann also mit Hilfe der überaus geläufigen Termini des anglo-amerikanischen Rechts *artificial legal person* oder *artificial person* übersetzt werden. Daneben gibt es dafür noch weitere anglo-amerikanische Entsprechungen, zum Beispiel *legal entity*; *juridical person*; *body corporate (corporate body)*.

Das Definieren der Zielgruppe der Benutzer ist einer der wichtigsten Faktoren der Vorbereitungsarbeiten am Wörterbuch (Atkins 1993: 12, Malkiel 1890: 55), der seine Konzeption und Bearbeitungsweise grundsätzlich beeinflusst. Man darf annehmen, dass die Benutzer des Wörterbuchs eine motivbedingt und erfahrungsbedingt verhältnismäßig diversifizierte Gruppe bilden werden. Im Grunde kann man jedoch sagen, dass die potentiellen Benutzer in zwei Grundkategorien eingeteilt werden können, und zwar in eine Gruppe, deren Mitglieder primär sprachorientiert sind (ausgebildete Linguisten) und eine andere Gruppe, deren Mitglieder zwar Juristen sind, aber nicht unbedingt eine eigentliche formale Sprachbildung genossen haben. Zweifellos wird es noch eine zahlenmäßig geringere Gruppe derer geben, die zwar weder juristisch noch linguistisch ausgebildet sind, aber in ihrem Beruf manchmal die tschechische Rechtsrealität auf Englisch ausdrücken müssen (z.B. Journalisten). Man kann jedoch mit hohem Sicherheitsgrad behaupten, dass für das Verwenden des tschechisch-englischen Rechtswörterbuchs durch tschechische Muttersprachler Kenntnisse der englischen Gemeinsprache und zumindest ausreichende Kommunikationsfertigkeiten in englischer Sprache notwendig sind; dasselbe betrifft entsprechende Kenntnisse und Fertigkeiten im Tschechischen, falls ein Englischsprechender das Wörterbuch benutzen will.

2. Rechtsrahmen

Bei der Übertragung der Rechtstexte aus dem Tschechischen ins Englische kann man vielen potentiellen Problemen begegnen, die insbesondere durch die folgenden Faktoren beeinflusst werden:

Weder die tschechische Rechtsterminologie noch die gesamte tschechische Rechtssprache auf allen ihren Ebenen (in morphologischer, lexikalischer, syntaktischer und stilistischer Hinsicht) können als stabilisiert betrachtet werden. Sie sind in stetiger Entwicklung, Erweiterung und Verschiebung begriffen, befinden sich unter starkem Druck und Einfluss des Europarechts und in den letzten zwölf Jahren werden sie keiner strengen Rechts- bzw. Legislativkontrolle oder Prüfung ihrer sprachlichen Korrektheit unterworfen.

---

[2] Ihren negativen Einfluss üben hier zweifellos die in der englischen Sprache verfassten Rechtsdokumente der Europäischen Union aus, wo (besonders früher) auch der Terminus *legal person* im Sinne der tschechischen Rechtsperson vorkam. Über die Gründe, warum dies der Fall ist (oder war), kann man nur Spekulationen anstellen. Das Grundproblem ist anscheinend die Tatsache, dass die Übersetzer der Union meistens keine Juristen sind, und umso weniger Juristen, die im Rechtssystem der Sprache, in die sie übersetzen, versiert wären.

Die System- und Begriffsunterschiede zwischen dem europäischen Kontinentalrecht, dessen Zweig das tschechische Recht ist, und dem anglo-amerikanischen Rechtssystem, das auf Common Law beruht, stellen besonders für Übersetzer ein Problem dar, das nur dann gelöst werden kann, wenn sie imstande sind, die intrasemiotische Analyse (Tomášek 1991: 153) anzuwenden, d.h. die Rechtsauslegung des rechtlichen Ausgangstexts vornehmen können.

Das anglo-amerikanische Recht besteht aus Rechtssystemen, die in den bedeutendsten englischsprachigen Ländern, nämlich in den USA, in Großbritannien, Kanada, Australien und Irland vorherrschen. Weitere Staaten, wo Englisch immer noch Amtssprache ist, tragen zur Bereicherung und Erweiterung der englischen Rechtssprache bei, sowohl in rein linguistischer Hinsicht, als auch auf dem Gebiete der Rechtsterminologie (Begriffsbildung). Dabei kommt es auch zur Vermehrung der terminologischen Synonymie bzw. zur Verzweigung von Lexemen in polysemische Bedeutungen.

Einer der Faktoren, die die Erforschung der Rechtssprache im tschechischen Kontext grundsätzlich beeinflussen, ist die Validität der tschechischen Rechtsvorschriften. Nach Kořenský, Cvrček und Novák (1999: 32–33) wurde seit 1918 fast nichts für die Purifikation der Rechtsvorschriften und Sicherstellung ihrer Transparenz getan. Ein Sechstel der seit 1918 in der Gesetzessammlung veröffentlichten fast 30 000 Dokumente sind überhaupt keine Legislativakte, 10 000 Vorschriften wurden explizit aufgehoben und die restlichen 15 000 befinden sich in verschiedenen Phasen der Gültigkeit bzw. Ungültigkeit. Ein Drittel dieser Dokumente geht auf "legislative Unordnung" zurück, denn einige ihrer Teile wurden aufgehoben, andere traten außer Kraft, aber grundsätzlich wird kein Verzeichnis über den Stand dieser Vorschriften geführt. Das zweite Drittel sind Gesetze, die zwar ihre Gültigkeit behalten haben (d.h. sie sind nicht explizit aufgehoben worden), aber inzwischen außer Kraft traten (z.B. Gesetze über den Staatshaushalt, die alljährlich verabschiedet werden, wobei die alten Haushaltsgesetze nicht aufgehoben werden). Das letzte Drittel, ungefähr 5000 Legislativakte, bildet den Grundstock unserer gültigen rechtlichen Regelung.

Das sich beschleunigende Tempo der Vorbereitungen der Tschechischen Republik für den Beitritt zur Europäischen Union beeinflusst in einer grundsätzlichen Weise den Legislativprozess. Das ganze Korpus der Rechtsnormen, das nie hinlänglich "gereinigt" worden ist, wird alljährlich um Dutzende Gesetze erweitert, die in einem gewissermaßen hektischen Legislativprozess verabschiedet werden, welcher als "Legislativwirbelsturm" bezeichnet wird[3]. Das Grundproblem besteht in der Tatsache, dass die Gesetzentwürfe nicht nur von Fachleuten auf dem Gebiet der Gesetzgebung, sondern auch von verschiedenen Privatpersonen vorbereitet werden, die öfters keine entsprechende Bildung besitzen und als Assistenten oder Berater der Abgeordneten tätig sind; die auf diese Weise entstandenen Entwürfe werden der Abgeordnetenkammer des Parlaments als Gesetzesvorschläge der Abgeordneten zur Billigung vorgelegt. Wenn der politische Wille dazu vorhanden ist, wird ein solcher Vorschlag angenommen, ohne dass im Laufe des Legislativprozesses oder im nachhinein die Zeit und die Möglichkeit vorhanden sind, alle Auswirkungen zu identifizieren, die das betreffende Gesetz auf die restlichen gültigen Rechtsvorschriften haben könnte. Das vorrangige Problem solcher Gesetze aus linguistischer Sicht ist ihre begriffliche und terminologische Uneinheitlichkeit (wenn man die oft ziemlich linkischen syntaktischen Konstruktionen außer Acht lässt), die eine eindeutige Auslegung des Gesetzestextes oder eines seiner Teile erschweren. Im Gegensatz zu den in den englischsprachigen Ländern angenommenen Gesetzen beinhalten unsere Gesetze keine als "Definition der Begriffe"

---

[3] Während im Jahre 1998 45 Gesetze angenommen wurden, waren es im Jahre 2001 insgesamt 96.

betitelte Passage. Deshalb geschieht es, dass ein Terminus in zwei verschiedenen Gesetzen in unterschiedlichen Bedeutungen verwendet wird.

Ein weiteres Problem der tschechischen Gesetzgebung ist die wachsende Zahl der novellierten Gesetze und der novellierten Novellen. Wie Kořenský, Cvrček und Novák zeigen (1999: 38), wurden im Jahre 1990 159 neue Gesetze, davon 70 novellierte Vorschriften angenommen; im Jahre 1994 waren es 69 Gesetze einschließlich 52 Novellen; und 46 der im Jahre 1997 angenommenen 57 Gesetze waren Novellen. Unsere Untersuchung zeigte, dass 60 der im Jahre 2001 insgesamt angenommenen 96 Gesetze novellierte Gesetze waren. Wiederholte Novellierungen betreffen vornehmlich jene Gesetze, die für den Gang der Gesellschaft während der Übergangsperiode vom totalitären System zur Demokratie von grundsätzlicher Bedeutung sind. Zum Beispiel die im Jahre 1963 angenommene tschechische Zivilprozessordnung hatte man bis 1990 nur fünfmal novelliert; seit 1990 wurden bereits 36 Novellen der tschechischen ZPO angenommen. Das tschechische Handelsgesetzbuch, das im Jahre 1991 angenommen wurde, wurde bis Ende 2001 einundzwanzigmal novelliert; weitere Vorschläge wurden bereits dem Abgeordnetenhaus unterbreitet. Das im Jahre 1991 angenommene Gewerbegesetz wurde bis Ende 2001 fünfzigmal novelliert. Überstürzte Novellierungen stellen grundsätzliche Eingriffe in den Gesetzestext dar, sowie Veränderungen und Verschiebungen hinsichtlich der Begriffe und Termini, die in den betreffenden Gesetzen verwendet werden, und nicht zuletzt kommt es dadurch zur Novellierung von weiteren Rechtsvorschriften, deren Übersicht nicht hinlänglich erfasst ist.

Die Unterschiede in der Rechtsterminologie in den einzelnen englischsprachigen Ländern verursachen zahlreiche Probleme oder Unklarheiten bei der Übertragung tschechischer Rechtstexte ins Englische. Zum Beispiel der britische Begriff *company* nach der Definition im Companies Act 1985 ist in seiner rechtlichen Bedeutung und hinsichtlich seiner Rechtswirkung mit dem Terminus *corporation* identisch, der im Gesetz Revised Model Business Corporation Act 1984 als eingetragene Handelsgesellschaft definiert ist. Wenn man lediglich die linguistische und bedeutungsmäßige Charakteristik dieser beiden Termini in Betracht nimmt, könnte man zum Schluss kommen, dass sie Vollsynonyme sind. Der Kontext jedoch, in dem sie korrekt gebraucht werden können, ist unterschiedlich, oder, anders gesagt, es sind keine Funktionssynonyme. Diese zwei Termini darf man nicht einmal im Kontext des britischen bzw. des US-amerikanischen Rechts verwechseln. Der Terminus *company* im Recht der Vereinigten Staaten bezeichnet üblicherweise eine nichtregistrierte Person[4], während der Begriff *corporation* ein Subjekt bezeichnet, das im Register der Gesellschaften eingetragen ist; der Terminus *corporation* in ursprünglichen britischen Texten bezeichnet eine Gesellschaft, die nicht primär zu Handelszwecken gegründet wurde und dessen tschechisches Äquivalent *korporace* [*Korporation*] ist, wobei der Terminus *company* eine Handelsgesellschaft bezeichnet, die im Register der Gesellschaften (im sog. Companies House) eingetragen ist.

Ein anderes Beispiel ist der britische Terminus *frustration* (Vereitelung der Vertragserfüllung), dessen US-amerikanisches Gegenstück *impossibility* ist; der britische Begriff *theft* (im Theft Act 1967 als Rechtsterminus für den Diebstahl definiert) wird in den US-Gesetzen als *larceny* bezeichnet.

Ähnlich gilt in Großbritannien das Wort *jail* als volkstümliche Bezeichnung für Gefängnis; in der US-amerikanischen Rechtssprache bezeichnet *jail* eine von der örtlichen Behörde verwaltete Haftanstalt oder "Zelle der vorläufigen Festnahme" (Arrestzelle im Wortlaut der

---

4 Die letzte Ausgabe des Rechtswörterbuchs Black's Law Dictionary lässt zu, dass der Terminus *company* ein Synonym des Begriffs *corporation* ist, wobei jedoch nur der Begriff *corporation* ein Terminus des Gesetzes ist, das eingetragene Handelsgesellschaften in den USA regelt.

tschechischen Gesetzes), deren Synonyme *police cell* oder *holding cell* sind. Man begegnet auch verschiedenen Bezeichnungen für den tschechischen Begriff *podzákonný právní předpis*: dem britischen oder kanadischen Terminus *statutory instrument* steht die in den Vereinigten Staaten gebräuchliche Bezeichnung */executive/ regulation* oder der australische Terminus *legislative instrument* gegenüber.

Die Frage ist nun, welche der zwei oder mehr möglichen Varianten als das beste Äquivalent im zweisprachigen Rechtswörterbuch anzuführen ist und mit welchem Anmerkungsapparat die einzelnen Äquivalente zu versehen sind. Die Antworten werden völlig vom Sprach-, Sach- und Sozialkontext abhängen, in dem das jeweilige Äquivalent verwendet werden soll. Nicht zuletzt hängt es auch von der Verlegerpolitik ab, inwieweit man Instruktionen für die Übersetzung von juristischen Texten im Wörterbuch eingliedern kann. Nach unserer Ansicht und nach unseren Erfahrungen kann kein tschechisch-fremdsprachliches Fachwörterbuch den Benutzer hinreichend unterweisen, wie und wann das jeweilige Äquivalent zu verwenden ist. Die Wahl wird immer von dem Motiv abhängen, warum der Benutzer im Wörterbuch nachschlägt (z.B. Suche nach einem unmittelbar verwendbaren Äquivalent bei der Übersetzung oder beim Dolmetschen, oder nur zur Inspiration, die dann durch das Studium der erklärenden einsprachigen Lexika oder anderer Quellen weiterentwickelt wird); weiterhin wird es von den Sprach- und Rechtskenntnissen des Benutzers abhängen und nicht zuletzt wird der Adressat des Zieltexts bestimmend sein. Instruktionen, wie man mit der rechtlichen Zielsprache umgeht, die mit dem Wörterbuch vereinbar wären, wären sehr schwierig zu bearbeiten. Die Genretypologie der Rechtstexte und deren Funktionen sind so umfangreich und in der tschechisch-englischen Vergleichsebene noch unbearbeitet, dass es in dieser Phase unmöglich war, konkrete Anweisungen im Wörterbuch einzugliedern; eine vergleichende typologische und Genrestudie der tschechischen und englischsprachigen Rechtstexte wird Gegenstand einer künftigen selbstständigen Untersuchung.

3. Linguistischer Rahmen

3.1. Fachsprache und Terminologie

Im Gegensatz zum Tschechischen, das nur einen Begriff zur Benennung der Sprachvarietät besitzt, den es in verschiedensten Disziplinen der Grundforschung oder der applizierten Forschung und in diversen Wissenschaftsfächern verwendet, nämlich *odborný jazyk* [*Fachsprache*] kann man im Englischen mehrere Benennungen finden: *language for special / specific purposes, sub-language, scientific language, specialized language* (Pearson 1998: 28).

Die Fachsprache ist ein gewissermaßen schwer definierbarer Begriff, der von verschiedenen Blickwinkeln betrachtet werden kann. Aus pragmatischer Sicht ist sie ein Subsystem des allgemeinen Sprachsystems, das auf konkreter Wahl, Kombinatorik und Verwendung der bestehenden morphologischen, lexikalischen und syntaktischen Einheiten (bzw. Paradigmen) beruht, die am besten den Stil-, Genre- und Kommunikationszielen des jeweiligen Textes in einem konkreten Fachbereich und einem konkreten Sozialkontext dienen. Die "Fachmäßigkeit" dieses Subsystems ist eine primär-pragmatische Kategorie, welche die Kommunikationsziele und Bedürfnisse seiner Benutzer, nämlich der Fachleute auf einem konkreten Gebiet, widerspiegelt. Aus linguistischer Sicht handelt es sich um eine Analyse der vorhandenen Fachtexte und um die nachfolgende Definierung der Prozesse, die zu deren Bildung geführt haben, d. h. um die Festsetzung der Regeln auf dem Niveau des Wortschatzes, der Syntax und des Textes, bei deren Einhaltung ein allgemeinannehmbarer Fachtext geschaffen wird. Die Laien halten jede Äußerung, in welcher Fachterminologie und kompliziertere syntaktische Konstruktionen vorkommen und die ein Thema hat, welches kein Bestandteil der üblichen tagtäglichen Praxis bildet, für Fachsprache. Obwohl Picht und Draskau (1985: 3) die Fachsprache (LSP) als eine "formalisierte und kodifizierte Sprachvariante, die zum besonderen Zweck und im jeweiligen entsprechenden Kontext verwendet wird", ansehen, nehmen wir an, dass eine solche Definition vielmehr dem entspricht, was die Vorgenannten als eine Varietät der Fachsprache bezeichnen, d.h. die "Sprache" eines konkreten Faches, zum Beispiel die tschechische oder englische Rechtssprache, Handelssprache, Maschinenbausprache u. ä. Man kann annehmen, dass eine Durchdringung aller dieser Varietäten existiert, die als "vergegenständlichte" Fachsprache an sich betrachtet werden könnten, aber soviel wir wissen, gibt es vorläufig keine die tschechische oder englische Sprache betreffende Studie, welche die "Sprachen" verschiedener Fächer vergleichen und das selektieren würde, das allen diese "Sprachen" gemeinsam wäre.

Pearson (1998: 31) führt sechs Faktoren an, die bei der Abgrenzung einer Variante der Fachsprache von Nutzen sein können:

(1) ein bestimmtes Fach (z.B. das Recht);
(2) lexikalische, semantische und syntaktische Begrenzungen (z.B. Benutzung der Terminologie);
(3) grammatische "Abweichungen" (z.B. Zählbarkeit des sonst unzählbaren Substantivs *an information* in der Bedeutung *trestní oznámení* [*Strafanzeige*];
(4) die hohe Frequenz bestimmter Verbindungen und syntaktischer Strukturen (z.B. feststehende Satzverbindungen in Gesetzestexten);
(5) bestimmte Texttypen (z.B. Gesetze oder Verträge);
(6) Benutzung von Sonderzeichen oder Symbolen;

Die ersten drei Faktoren werden in dieser Studie in unterschiedlichem Maße analysiert, der vierte und fünfte Faktor geht über den Rahmen dieser Arbeit hinaus und erfordert eine selbstständige vergleichende Untersuchung. An diesem Ort erwähnen wir den letzten Punkt, nämlich die Benutzung des Symbols "§", das in tschechischen Gesetzen den Paragraphen bezeichnet, denn aus der Sicht der Übersetzung handelt es sich um ein mehr oder weniger grundsätzliches Problem. Während die tschechischen Gesetze in Paragraphen, Absätze, Literä und Sätze unterteilt werden, haben die im Englischen verfassten Gesetze zwar dieselbe Struktur, aber eine andere Benennung der Strukturunterteilung, die für den Benutzer anfänglich verwirrend wirken kann: *section, subsection, paragraph, subparagraph.* In tschechischen Zitationen wird der Paragraph als "§" bezeichnet, wonach eine arabische Ziffer folgt; der Absatz (*odstavec*) wird als "odst." abgekürzt, wonach wieder eine arabische Ziffer folgt; die Litera (*písmeno*) wird durch die Abkürzung "písm." oder "lit." ausgedrückt, wonach ein Kleinbuchstabe folgt (oder mehrere Buchstaben in alphabetischer Ordnung), der letzte Strukturteil – der Satz ("věta") – wird nicht abgekürzt und die jeweilige Ordinalzahl wird in Kleinbuchstaben ausgeschrieben. In anglo-amerikanischen Gesetzen werden einzelne Paragraphen nur in Gesetzessammlungen durch das §-Symbol bezeichnet, und zwar hauptsächlich in US-amerikanischen Gesetzeswerken; in einzelnen Gesetzen wird nur eine fett gedruckte arabische Ziffer verwendet; der Absatz (*subsection*) wird durch eine arabische Ziffer in beiderseitigen runden Klammern bezeichnet; die Litera (*paragraph*) wird durch Kleinbuchstaben in beiderseitigen runden Klammern ausgedrückt und der Satz (*subparagraph*) durch kleingeschriebene römische Ziffern in beiderseitigen runden Klammern.

Dementsprechend wird der Hinweis auf eine Bestimmung im tschechischen Gesetz – § 12, odst. 3, písm. a), věta třetí – auf folgende Weise ins Englische übertragen: s. 12 (3) (a) (iii). Für einen mit diesem System nicht vertrauten Übersetzer, der bemüht ist, sich bei der Übertragung an den Ausgangstext zu halten, wird die Übertragung aus dem Englischen ins Tschechische viel komplizierter vorkommen, weil er nicht imstande sein wird, den numerischen Verweis in verständlicher tschechischer Form wiederzugeben. Sollte er versuchen, die englische Zitation unter Verwendung von Abkürzungen der einzelnen Strukturteile eines Paragraphen Wort für Wort ins Englische zu übertragen, wird die Übersetzung schwerfällig, wenn auch die mitzuteilende Information verständlich bleibt.

Eines der wichtigsten Merkmale der Fachsprache ist die Benutzung der Terminologie, obwohl der Wortschatz in jedem gegebenen Fach nicht ausschließlich aus Fachtermini besteht. Verschiedenste Ermittlungen sowohl im Tschechischen (Poštolková 1984: 16–17) als auch im Englischen (Riley 1995: 73–79) oder Russischen (Zimová, Koníčková 1989) haben gezeigt, dass die juristische Fachsprache eine viel breitere Skala von Ausdrucksmitteln umfasst; üblicherweise werden hier drei Gruppen definiert:

a) "Reine" Rechtsterminologie, z.B. *aberace [Aberration]* (E. *aberration*), *cedent [Zedent]* (E. *assignor*), *estoppel [Hemmung der Klage]* (Tsch. *překážka uplatnění žalobního nároku*) oder *demurrer [Rechtseinwand]* (Tsch. *procesní námitka*). Es handelt sich um eine verhältnismäßig begrenzte Gruppe von Termini, die außerhalb des Rechtsgebiets nicht verwendet werden, in die Gemeinsprache nicht übergingen und auch außerhalb eines bestimmten Kontexts als Rechtstermini zu identifizieren sind. Hierher gehört auch das begrenzte Repertoire der lateinischen Rechtstermini.[5]
b) Rechtsausdrücke, die in der Gemeinsprache verwendet werden (allerdings nicht wie genau definierte Termini), die jedoch im jeweiligen Rechtskontext rechtlich genau abgegrenzt sind, z.B. *pozemek* [*Grundstück*] oder *nedbalost* [*Fahrlässigkeit*] und deren englische Äquivalente *land* und *negligence*; ihre Benutzung, Distribution und Funktion in der tschechischen und englischen Sprache ist identisch. Zu dieser Gruppe gehören auch Ausdrücke, deren allgemeine und rechtliche Bedeutung sich in einem bestimmten Maß unterscheidet. Zum Beispiel das tschechische Wort *titul* [*Titel*] besitzt in der tschechischen Alltagssprache eine andere Bedeutung als die terminologisch benutzten Ausdrücke *titul* und *title* in der jeweiligen Rechtssprache.
c) Einige Ausdrücke der Gemeinsprache können eine konkrete rechtliche Bedeutung annehmen, falls sie das Gesetz für einen bestimmten Zweck definiert. Zum Beispiel das Wort Schwein (Tsch. *vepř*) im Sinne des britischen Gesetzes "Welfare of Pigs Act 1998" bezeichnet nur ein Zucht- oder Masttier. Falls also ein Exemplar dieser Tierart für andere als die im Gesetz vorgesehenen Zwecke gehalten wird (zum Beispiel als ein Lieblingstier), handelt es sich um keinen *vepř* im Sinne des genannten Gesetzes, dessen Bestimmungen in diesem konkreten Falle keine Anwendung finden.

Obwohl Newmark (1988: 160) anführt, dass die Terminologie annähernd 5–10% des Fachtextes ausmacht, halten sie die meisten Personen ohne linguistische Bildung

---

[5] Die im tschechischen Recht benutzte lateinische Rechtsterminologie entspricht nicht vollkommen den im anglo-amerikanischen Recht verwendeten lateinischen Ausdrücken. Zum Beispiel die Verbindungen *de lege lata* (gemäß dem geltenden Recht) und *de lege ferenda* (entsprechend der vorgeschlagenen oder beabsichtigten rechtlichen Regelung), die in den tschechischen Rechtstexten öfters vorkommen, sind im anglo-amerikanischen Recht unbekannt geblieben. Umgekehrt kommen die umschreibenden Termini *obiter dicta* und *ratio decidendi* als zwei grundlegende Begriffe des anglo-amerikanischen Präzedenzrechts in tschechischen Rechtstexten nicht vor.

(einschließlich Juristen) für den einzigen und fundamentalen Faktor und betrachten die Termini "Fachsprache" und "Terminologie" als Synonyme, wobei sie den Ausdruck "Terminologie" vorziehen, wenn sie über die Fachsprache reden.

Felbers Definition des Begriffs Terminus (1984: 181–2) kann man auch auf Rechtstermini anwenden, allerdings nicht ohne Vorbehalt. Ein Rechtsterminus sollte genau, treffend und sprachlich korrekt sein, und sollte darüber hinaus die Ableitung anderer Wortarten gestatten. Zugleich sollte er möglichst einwortig (aus einem einzigen Wort bestehend) und monosemisch (nur eine Bedeutung tragend, eindeutig) sein. Während die Genauigkeit, Prägnanz und sprachliche Korrektheit jene Forderungen darstellen, die jeder Terminus erfüllen muss, weil er sonst im gegebenen Sprachsystem kaum verwendbar wäre, sind die Bedingungen der Ableitungsfreiheit, Einwortigkeit und Eindeutigkeit schwerer zu erfüllen, besonders deshalb, weil die meisten Rechtstermini Benennungen sind, die aus mehreren Wörtern bestehen oder syntaktische Einheiten darstellen. Die aufgrund des amerikanischen Rechtswörterbuchs Black's Law Dictionary durchgeführte Grobschätzung des Verhältnisses der einwortigen und mehrwortigen Termini deutet an, das ungefähr 33% der Termini einwortige und 67% mehrwortige Ausdrücke sind. Eine ähnliche Schätzung aufgrund des tschechischen Rechtswörterbuchs[6] ergab, dass das Verhältnis bei 26% der einwortigen zu 74% der mehrwortigen Termini liegt[7].

Die Termini kann man nach verschiedensten Kriterien in Gruppen einteilen; unsere Gruppierung konzentriert sich auf zwei Aspekte, d.h. dass die Termini nach ihrer Bezeichnungsqualität oder Funktion und ihrer grammatischen (morphologischen, lexikalischen, bzw. syntaktischen) Charakteristik gegliedert werden. Wir neigen zu Bečkas qualitativ-funktioneller Einteilung (1992: 73) in Fachtermini (die klar definiert, genau und meistens eindeutig sind) und beschreibende Termini (die ihrerseits die Taxonomie der jeweiligen Fächer oder ihrer Subdisziplinen bilden), sowie in technische (technologische) Termini, welche die Erscheinungen der praktischen Anwendung wissenschaftlicher Erkenntnisse bezeichnen. Sowohl die englischsprachige als auch die tschechische Rechtsterminologie beinhaltet insbesondere die ersten zwei Terminustypen. Wie Fillmore bemerkt (1978: 168), enthält die Rechtsprache eine hohe Zahl verschiedenster taxonomischer Aufzählungen – das von ihm angeführte Beispiel ist der Terminus *murder* (Tsch. *vražda*), der sich nach dem Typ und Gewicht der absichtlichen Tötung weiter gliedert. Natürlich kann man nicht annehmen, dass solche Aufzählungen im tschechischen Rechtssystem einerseits und im anglo-amerikanischen Rechtssystem andererseits kompatibel und vergleichbar sein werden – in dem Sinne, dass sie korrekte Äquivalente für die Übersetzung aus der einen Sprache in die andere zur Verfügung stellen würden. Es ist stets notwendig, zuerst eine Begriffsanalyse in beiden Sprachen vorzunehmen (Šarčević 1989: 290), welche die Übereinstimmung und Unterschiede zwischen dem Inhalt der Termini in den beiden Sprachen erkennen lässt; erst dann kann man entscheiden, ob der jeweilige Ausdruck in einer Sprache als Äquivalent in der Zielsprache dienen kann, beziehungsweise welches Maß an Explizierung gewählt werden sollte.

Ein weiterer Faktor, den wir in unserer Studie erwähnen, ist die Normativität der Terminologie. Galinski (1982: 189) gibt die folgende Einteilung der Terminologie:

---

[6] Madar, Zdeněk: Slovník českého práva (Prag, Linde 1995).

[7] Die prozentuelle Berechnung wurde aufgrund einer Zählung der einwortigen und mehrwortigen Termini mit den zahlreichsten Anfangsbuchstaben, die in den besagten Wörterbüchern vorkommen, durchgeführt: die Einträge unter Buchstabe C im Blacks Rechtswörterbuch (S. 202–388, d.h. 186 Seiten) ergaben 1239 einwortige und 2531 mehrwortige Termini; der Buchstabe P im tschechischen Wörterbuch (S. 924–1157, d. h. 233 Seiten) ergab 565 einwortige und 1596 mehrwortige Termini.

Deskriptivterminologie, die ihre Anwendung in der täglichen Fachpraxis widerspiegelt und Normativterminologie, welche ihrerseits die durch eine zuständige Institution empfohlenen Normen darstellt. Diese Einteilung wird zutreffend durch den Prozess charakterisiert, zu dem es in der juristischen Terminologie kommt: die zuständige Institution, d.h. das gesetzgebende Organ, verabschiedet eine Norm, nämlich ein Gesetz, in dem es bestimmte Termine definiert und ihre Anwendung in der Rechtspraxis voraussetzt. Darüber hinaus, wie Tiersma (1999: 109) richtig bemerkt, schließt die Deskriptivterminologie neben den im Gesetz definierten Begriffen auch den Rechtsjargon ein, mit dessen Hilfe ein bestimmtes Maß an Kondensierung in der geläufigen Rechtskommunikation erreicht wird. Aus der Sicht eines Übersetzers kann hier ein bestimmtes Problem entstehen, und zwar welcher Ausdruck als Äquivalent verwendet werden soll. Zum Beispiel führt die tschechische Strafprozessordnung für den geläufigen Ausdruck *kauce* [*Kaution*] den mehrwortigen Terminus *peněžitá záruka* [wörtlich "*pekuniäre Sicherheit*"] (E. *pecuniary security*) ein. *Peněžitá záruka* ist daher der normative Terminus, aber in der geläufigen Rechtspraxis wird das Wort *kauce* [*Kaution*] (E. *bail*) gebraucht. Im anglo-amerikanischen Recht wird sowohl in Gesetzestexten als auch in der Rechtspraxis der Terminus *bail* verwendet; nur in juristischen Bedeutungswörterbüchern wird zwecks Erklärung *pecuniary (monetary, cash) security* angeführt. Wenn man den tschechischen Terminus *peněžitá záruka* ins Englische übersetzen will, muss man wissen, dass es sich um eine Kaution handelt; ferner muss man in Erwägung ziehen, welcher Usus im anglo-amerikanischen Milieu überwiegt. Man kann feststellen, dass es in allen vorstellbaren Kontexten und für jeden Adressaten der Übersetzung verständlicher sein wird, wenn man die sklavische Übersetzung des tschechischen Gesetzesterminus *peněžitá záruka* vermeidet und statt dessen den englischsprachigen Gesetzesterminus *bail* verwendet.

Die grammatische Charakteristik der Termini und der terminologischen Verbindungen gliedert sich nach deren distinktiven Zügen in morphologische, kategorielle (d.h. grammatische Kategorien widerspiegelnde), lexikalische und syntaktische Ebenen (Hoffmann 1982: 399). Zu den interessantesten Erscheinungen kommt es zweifellos auf dem Niveau der Morphologie und Syntax. Das englische Agenssuffix *-er* wird in vielen Fällen durch das Suffix *-or* ersetzt, wobei in der Gemeinsprache die Substantive mit dem *-er*-Suffix ihre ursprüngliche Bedeutung bewahren, während das *-or*-Suffix in den meisten Fällen einen Rechtsterminus signalisiert. Der Gegenpol dieser Nachsilbe ist das Suffix *-ee*, das die Person bezeichnet, auf die sich die Handlung bezieht (Dativ)[8]. Auf diese Weise werden Wortpaare wie *lessor – lessee, assignor – assignee, obligor – obligee, promisor – promisee, grantor – grantee, mortgagor – mortgagee* usw. gebildet, wo das erste Glied den aktiven Teilnehmer einer Beziehung bezeichnet, d.h. jene Person, die irgend etwas zugunsten oder hinsichtlich ihrer Gegenseite in diesem Paarverhältnis bewirkt.

Terminologische Phraseme sind syntaktische Einheiten, die in einem bestimmten Rechtskontext stehende Bedeutung haben. Filmore (1978: 170) lässt zu, dass es in der Rechtssprache notwendig sei, mehrgliedrige terminologische Verbindungen als lexikalische Einheiten zu betrachten. Zum Beispiel die syntaktische Konstruktion vom Typ *maliciously damaging the property of another* stellt einen mehrwortigen Terminus dar, der in den USA eine minder schwere Straftat bezeichnet, die in der Beschädigung fremden Eigentums besteht. Die

---

[8] In der (saloppen) englischen Umgangssprache bleibt das Suffix *-ee* (trotz verschiedenen Empfehlungen der Linguisten und Juristen) produktiv, denn es hilft, unterschiedlich motivierte Wörter mit verschiedenartigen Konnotationen zu bilden (ohne die Person zu bezeichnen, mit der oder für die etwas geschieht, wie es in der rechtlichen Grundbedeutung dieser Nachsilbe vorkommt); z.B. escapee (Flüchtige/r), standee (Stehende/r), arrivee (Ankömmling), asylee (Asylbewerber).

Bezeichnung der Straftat *vražda novorozeného dítěte matkou* (ungefähr *Tötung eines Kindes bei der Geburt,* wörtlich: *von der Mutter verübter Mord am neugeborenen Kind*) im tschechischen Recht ist auch ein Terminus, wenn es auch nicht der strikten Charakteristik eines Terminus nach ISO entspricht.

Aus der Sicht der Übersetzung ist die terminologische Polysemie ein verhältnismäßig wichtiger Faktor. Das relativ hohe Vorkommen der Polysemie erfordert eindeutig, dass der Übersetzer die betreffende Rechtsproblematik wirklich versteht, statt sich lediglich an die Oberflächenbedeutung zu halten. Er oder sie sollte Kenntnisse der gegebenen Materie sowohl im Rechtssystem der Ausgangssprache als auch in der Zielsprache besitzen und imstande sein, funktionelle Äquivalente aufeinander abzustimmen, sowie auch deren Maß an Begriffs- bzw. Funktionsäquivalenz richtig zu erkennen. An dieser Stelle könnte man das verhältnismäßig einfache Beispiel von zwei tschechischen Rechtstermini *právo* [*Recht*] und *věc* [*Sache*] anführen. Das Wort *právo* hat zwei Grundbedeutungen: es bezeichnet sowohl das *Objektiv*recht (als System der Rechtsnormen), als auch das *Subjektiv*recht (als individuellen Anspruch). In den meisten Fällen kommen in den tschechischen Rechtstexten die Attribute *objektiv* oder *subjektiv* nicht vor, und der Übersetzer muss selber erkennen, um welche Bedeutung des Polysems *právo* es sich handelt: im erstgenannten Fall kann man den tschechischen Terminus mit dem unzählbaren englischen Substantiv *law* übersetzen, im letztgenannten Fall mit dem zählbaren Hauptwort *right*: anders gesagt handelt es sich im Englischen keinesfalls um ein Polysem. Ein anderes Beispiel der terminologischen Polysemie im Tschechischen ist der Terminus *věc*. Im Kontext des Prozessrechts bezeichnet es eine Rechtssache, womit es das funktionelle Äquivalent des englischen Begriffs *case* darstellt; auf dem Gebiete der Sachenrechts kann man diesen tschechischen Terminus mit dem unzählbaren Substantiv *property* bzw. dem zählbaren Hauptwort *thing* übersetzen.

Der Problemkreis des Jargons in der (tschechischen und englischen) Rechtssprache ist sehr weit und seine Behandlung würde wegen seiner Kompliziertheit den Rahmen der vorliegenden Arbeit sprengen. Gleichwohl muss betont werden, dass man über den Jargon nicht nur im Zusammenhang mit dem Wortschatz sprechen muss, sondern auch im Zusammenhang mit dem Gesamtcharakter des elliptischen und metaphorischen Ausdrucks (d.h. auf morphologischer, lexikalischer und syntaktischer Ebene). Die Entscheidung eines tschechischen Rechtsanwalts, dass er "*bude žalovat vyklizení*" [*/auf/ Räumung klagt*] und die Feststellung im Laufe eines Gerichtsverfahrens, dass "*the prosecutor rests*", sind typische Beispiele des Juristenjargons im weiten Sinne des Wortes.

3.2. Übersetzungslinguistik

Der dritte Teil der Studie befasst sich mit der Übersetzungslinguistik: wir beschreiben den Prozess des Übersetzens der Rechtstexte und die einzelnen Schritte, aus denen dieser Prozess in seiner Gesamtheit besteht. Das Ziel besteht nicht nicht darin, Regeln zu schaffen, wie man einen Rechtstext richtig übersetzen sollte, sondern auf jene Probleme aufmerksam zu machen, die bei der Übersetzung auftreten können, um eine Lösung solcher Probleme vorschlagen zu können.

Im Grunde existieren zwei Übersetzungsschulen. Trosborg (1997: 153) unterscheidet zwischen dem auf dem linguistischen Prinzip beruhenden Übersetzen, dessen Grundlage Äquivalenz ist, und dem sich auf das pragmatische (funktionelle) Prinzip stützende Übersetzen, dessen entscheidender Aspekt die Funktion des Zieltexts ist. Das erstgenannte Herantreten spiegelt sich in den klassischen Werken der Übersetzungstheorie wider (Catford 1965, Nida

1964, Newmark 1988); die funktionelle Auffassung der Übersetzung findet in den neueren Werken (Nord 1977, Šarčević 2000, Trosborg 1997) ihre Verfechter. Das pragmatische Modell berücksichtigt den Situationskontext eines Kommunikationsaktes und nimmt darüber hinaus die Erwartungen und Bedürfnisse des Empfängers des Zieltextes in Betracht. Die Qualitätsübersetzung eines Rechtstexts muss jedoch beide Gesichtspunkte in sich vereinen: der Problemkreis der Äquivalenz schließt außer dem Wortschatzniveau (Terminologie) auch höhere syntaktische Einheiten, ganze Texte und Kommunikativsituationen ein; die Äquivalenz ist also keine rein linguistische Angelegenheit, sondern auch eine Begriffs-, Sach- und Funktionskategorie. Die Äquivalenz wird somit als eine Kategorie der vergleichenden rechtslinguistischen Beschreibung von Rechtstexten betrachtet (Gémar 2001; 122).

Jede Übersetzung der Rechtstexte sollte gleichfalls auf einer vergleichenden Genreanalyse der Rechtstexte beruhen (Bhatia 1997: 206–7), die es ermöglichen soll, die jeweilige Rechtsinformation möglichst genau in die Zielsprache zu übertragen, wobei diese Information für den Adressaten verständlich bleiben muss. Wenn man zum Beispiel ein tschechisches Gesetz ins Englische übersetzten will, muss man die Legislativregeln der anglo-amerikanischen Gesetze, sowie deren Formstruktur und inhaltliche Organisation studieren. Neben den Kenntnissen der gesetzlich geregelten Materie muss man eine verhältnismäßig geschlossene Vorstellung von der Sprache haben, in der die anglo-amerikanischen Gesetze verfasst werden, man muss wissen, wie die Normativität eines solchen Texts ausgedrückt wird u. ä.

Die Theoretiker der Übersetzung von Rechtstexten (Šarčević, 2000: 72, Joseph, 1995: 33–34) stimmen darin überein, dass das Ziel darin besteht, einen so organisierten Text in der Zielsprache zu schaffen, der die gleiche Interpretation und Anwendung gewährleistet, die der in der Ausgangssprache verfasste Text voraussetzt. Ein Übersetzer von Rechtstexten interpretiert in erster Linie den Ausgangstext und erst danach überträgt er das Ergebnis einer solchen Interpretation in die Zielsprache. Der Adressat des Zieltexts sollte darin jene klare, genaue und möglichst vollkommene Information finden, die im Ausgangstext enthalten war – die jedoch nunmehr um solche Tatsachen und Informationen ergänzt ist, die ihm das Verständnis des Ausgangstexts in einer sprachlich, rechtlich und kulturell verschiedenen Umwelt ermöglichen.

Wie wir bereits oben unterstrichen haben, bleibt die Äquivalenz im breiten Sinne das Grundprinzip der Übersetzung von Rechtstexten. Begreiflicherweise spielt auch hier das Übersetzungswörterbuch eine wichtige Rolle, wenn es auch auf dem Gebiete der Rechtswissenschaft nur das erste Hilfsmittel darstellt, nach dessen Benutzung die eigene Komparativanalyse folgen sollte, die der Übersetzer in jedem Einzelfall vornimmt.

4. Lexikographischer Rahmen

In diesem Teil der Studie befassen wir uns mit den Grundregeln und -prinzipien, die bei der Schaffung eines Fachwörterbuchs zur Geltung kommen, und die wir bei der Verarbeitung des "Tschechisch-englischen Rechtswörterbuchs mit Erklärungen" (Leda Prag, 2001, 2003) angewandt haben. Im Gegensatz zu einsprachigen Wörterbüchern, die formell im Einklang mit dem Zweck, für den sie geschaffen wurden, geordnet sind (alphabetische, rückläufige oder nach dem Nestprinzip geordnete Wörterbücher usw.) sind zweisprachige Fachwörterbücher immer alphabetisch geordnet. Dazu muss jedoch bemerkt werden, dass kein Übersetzungswörterbuch so erschöpfend sein kann, um alle Situationen zu erfassen, denen der Benutzer bei der Übersetzung oder Schaffung eines fremdsprachigen Texts begegnen kann.

Jedem Übersetzungswörterbuch liegen vergleichende und lexikologische Studien zugrunde (Tomaszczyk, 1983: 45); bei den Rechtswörterbüchern kommt zusätzlich noch das Studium der Rechtssysteme der betreffenden Sprachgebiete hinzu. Wie bereits bemerkt wurde, sollte die Rechtskomparatistik bei der Bearbeitung eines zweisprachigen Rechtswörterbuchs, dessen Zielsprache Englisch ist, die grundlegenden Rechtssysteme jener Länder berücksichtigen, in denen Englisch die Amtssprache (und ursprüngliche Sprache) ist, denn gerade die Abweichungen der einzelnen Teilsysteme und die Unterschiede zwischen ihren Rechtsinstituten tragen unter anderem zur Entstehung synonymer Reihen möglicher Übersetzungsäquivalente bei. Jede Einheit einer solchen synonymen Reihe spielt jedoch in der konkreten Übersetzungssituation, die von den durch die Rechtsübersetzung bestimmten Grundfaktoren determiniert ist, ihre unvertretbare Rolle, und in der überwiegenden Mehrheit der Fälle kann man in einer konkreten Lage (und dann folgerichtig in dem gesamten zu übersetzenden Text) nur *ein* Glied der synonymen Reihe verwenden.

Den quantitativ umfangreichsten Teil bildet dabei begreiflicherweise die Terminologie. Um dem Benutzer des Wörterbuchs ein möglichst exaktes funktionelles (d.h. rechtliches) Äquivalent der Ausgangs- und Zielsprache zur Verfügung zu stellen, muss man die Begriffsanalyse der potentiellen Äquivalente der Ausgangs- und Zielsprache mit dem Ziel vornehmen, das Maß ihrer Äquivalenz bzw. Unstimmigkeit genau festzustellen (Šarčević 1989a: 278), wobei man den Begriffsüberhang oder umgekehrt das Begriffsdefizit im Wörterbuch beispielsweise mittels Erklärungen oder Glossen präzisieren kann.

Zudem ist es notwendig, die Begriffsanalyse überall dort durchzuführen, wo es auf den ersten Blick kein Äquivalent gibt, um die Weise zu finden, wie man einen solchen Begriff der Ausgangssprache verständlich in die Zielsprache übertragen kann. An dieser Stelle führen wir als Beispiel den tschechischen Terminus *přestupek* [*Übertretung*] an, der im anglo-amerikanischen Rechtssystem kein Rechtsäquivalent besitzt. Nachdem wir allerdings die tatsächliche und rechtliche Seite dieser rechtswidrigen Handlung analysiert haben werden, können wir eine Weise finden, den tschechischen Terminus rechtlich relevant und sprachlich adäquat ins Englische zu übertragen.

Die Begriffsanalyse sollte aufgrund eines extensiven parallelen Exzerpierens (Tomaszczyk, 1983: 45) oder anhand der Vergleichskorpora (Teubert 1996: 244) durchgeführt werden. Man muss sich mit authentischen in der Zielsprache verfassten Rechtstexten vertraut machen und diese analysieren, um erstens die Rechtsäquivalente der tschechischen Termini und zweitens die Weise zu finden, wie ein Begriff der Ausgangssprache, den es in der Zielsprache nicht gibt, in dieser auszudrücken sei. Ein Wörterbuch kann natürlich nur ein Bruchstück der durch die Begriffsanalyse gewonnenen Informationen enthalten, aber die grundlegende Information muss auf eine adäquate Weise zur Verfügung gestellt werden (vgl. zum Beispiel das Stichwort *rehabilitace* [*Rehabilitierung*]). Der Titel des Wörterbuchs "Tschechisch-englisches Wörterbuch mit Erläuterungen" deutet an, dass dieses Werk nicht nur englische Entsprechungen der tschechischen Rechtstermini enthält, sondern auch weitere Informationen in Form von Erläuterungen bietet, die zuweilen in einem bestimmten Fall ein tschechisches Stichwort, in den meisten Fällen jedoch seine englischen Äquivalente und in Exemplifizierung die betreffenden Anwendungsbeispiele erklären. Der Ausdruck "Erklärungen" wurde deshalb gewählt, weil es sich um keine autoritativen Definitionen der Termini handelt, sondern um die Deutung oder Spezifizierung des jeweiligen Begriffes, der durch den betreffenden Terminus repräsentiert wird.

Die Mehrheit der exzerpierten Materialien bildeten kommentierte tschechische Gesetze (und ein einsprachiges Sachwörterbuch), die im bibliographischen Teil der vorliegenden Arbeit angeführt sind. Eine weitere wichtige Quelle stellten ungefähr 3000 Seiten authentischer Texte tschechischer Rechtslehrbücher, authentischer privatrechtlicher Instrumente, sowie auch veröffentlichter Musterdokumente, authentischer Gerichtsentscheidungen und Polizeiprotokolle dar. Im Wörterbuch sind außer Fachtermini oder terminologischen Verbindungen und Satzeinheiten auch allgemeinwissenschaftliche und allgemeinrechtliche Ausdrücke vertreten, deren Unkenntnis, wie es sich in der Praxis zeigt, oft Probleme beim genauen Verständnis verursacht.

Das zur Äquivalenz der tschechischen Termini dienende Korpus besteht aus amerikanischen, britischen, irischen, australischen und kanadischen Gesetzen, juristischen Deutungswörterbüchern, Rechtslehrbüchern und aus authentischen Rechtsdokumenten. Das Manuskript des Wörterbuchs enthält 9 200 tschechische Stichwörter und 29 000 tschechische Termini, terminologische Verbindungen und größere syntaktische Einheiten mit Exemplifizierung, sowie etwa 46 000 englischsprachige Äquivalente.

5. Schlusswort

Seit Jahrzehnten steht die Rechtssprache im Mittelpunkt der Aufmerksamkeit der Juristen und Linguisten. Während sich die Juristen auf die Aufgabe konzentrieren, die Rechtsinformation im Text zu identifizieren, um das Recht anwenden zu können (juristische Textauslegung), stellen die Linguisten fest, durch welche Sprachmittel die Rechtsinformation ausgedrückt wird und wie sie aus linguistischer Sicht zu erfassen wäre (linguistische Textinterpretation, die oft auf semantische Interpretation reduziert wird). Zur dritten Gruppe der Fachleute, die sich mit der Rechtssprache befassen, gehören Übersetzer, die den juristischen und linguistischen Gesichtspunkt kombinieren. In überwiegender Mehrheit handelt es sich um ausgebildete Linguisten, die sich jedoch als Übersetzer von Rechtstexten mit der Rechtsproblematik befassen: sie gehen von einer komplizierten linguistisch-rechtlichen Analyse des Ausgangstexts aus und sind bemüht, die darin enthaltenen Informationen und das betreffende Rechtssystem in die Zielsprache so zu übertragen, damit der zu übersetzende Text in rechtlicher Hinsicht verständlich bleibt, um seine Funktion erfüllen zu können. Die rechtlich-linguistische Komparatistik erscheint umso komplizierter, je entfernter das Sprach- und Rechtssystem des Ausgangstexts vom dem des Zieltexts ist.

Das "Tschechisch-englische Rechtswörterbuch mit Erläuterungen" ist eines der Instrumente, die dem Übersetzer helfen sollen, sich in der sprachlichen Umwelt des tschechischen Rechts im Bezug auf die anglo-amerikanische rechtssprachliche Kultur zu orientieren. Es ermöglicht dem tschechischen Juristen, die tschechische Rechtsrealien auf verständliche Weise auf Englisch auszudrücken, in Abhängigkeit davon, wer der Endadressat der vorgelegten Information ist.

Die an diesem Wörterbuch geleistete Arbeit wird selbstverständlich zu einer weiteren Untersuchung führen, die sich in der ersten Phase auf den Vergleich zwischen der rechtlichen und der semantischen Textinterpretation und deren Auswirkungen auf die korrekte Übertragung der Rechtsinformation zwischen verschiedenen Sprach- und Rechtssystemen konzentrieren wird. In der nächsten Phase werden wir uns auf die vergleichende tschechisch-englische und englisch-tschechische Analyse der frequenten rechtssprachlichen Stiltypen (Genres) konzentrieren, deren Resultat die Bearbeitung der Regeln und Vorgänge für die Übersetzung einzelner Typen von Rechtstexten sein soll. Wir werden jedoch durchgehend weiteres Material für die Bearbeitung eines großen englisch-tschechischen Rechtswörterbuchs sammeln, das den Benutzern helfen soll, sich einerseits im anglo-amerikanischen Rechtssystem (im Vergleich mit dem tschechischen Rechtssystem) besser zu orientieren, und andererseits der Unterschiede zwischen der Sprache des anglo-amerikanischen Rechts und dem Englischen des Rechts der Europäischen Union gewahr zu werden.

V. Résumé

L'ouvrage présenté est une étude juridico-linguistique dont le but est d'analyser les points de départs de la création du dictionnaire juridique tchèque-anglais et de justifier les méthodes et les procédés pratiques de son élaboration. Le caractère fondamental de l'étude consiste dans un examen comparatif juridico-linguistique de deux systèmes juridiques, c'est-à-dire du droit tchèque en tant que partie du droit continental et du système anglo-américain fondé sur le droit coutumier et sur le droit des précédents, et des moyens linguistiques, des procédés et des styles que ces systèmes utilisent pour exprimer une information juridique.

1. Buts du dictionnaire

La partie principale de l'étude est composée de quatre chapitres. Le premier chapitre explique les motifs qui étaient à l'origine du travail sur le dictionnaire, et les buts que nous nous sommes proposés pour l'élaboration de ce dictionnaire. Le motif fondamental consiste dans un effort d'aider tous ceux qui s'efforcent de transposer les textes juridiques tchèques en anglais (surtout les traducteurs et les interprètes) à ce que la transposition soit correcte non seulement du point de vue linguistique, mais aussi du point de vue de la fidélité à la réalité extra-linguistique, et ceux (surtout les juristes tchèques) qui sont obligés à expliquer la réalité juridique tchèque en anglais. Le texte, qu'il soit traduit ou nouvellement créé, devrait être compréhensible aussi pour les juristes, pour qui l'anglais est la langue maternelle et le Common Law, droit commun anglo-saxon, le système juridique de base dans lequel et avec lequel ils travaillent. C'est dans ce sens que nous avons essayé d'effectuer une "analyse conceptuelle" telle qu'elle est recommandée par Susan Šarčević (1989: 290) pour la création d'un dictionnaire juridique bilingue. Cette analyse est basée sur la confrontation des concepts juridiques dans le système juridique de départ et dans celui d'arrivée pour pouvoir établir le degré de l'équivalence entre les termes équivalents potentiels.

L'autre but du dictionnaire juridique tchèque-anglais est de contribuer à l'unification des différentes approches à la traduction des textes juridiques tchèques en anglais. La standardisation des équivalents anglais (conceptuels et linguistiques) de la terminologie juridique tchèque est d'autant plus urgente dans le contexte des négociations en vue de l'adhésion de la République tchèque, le 1er mai 2004, à l'Union européenne. Déjà, à l'heure actuelle, les 12 langues officielles de l'Union causent des problèmes non insignifiants lors de la traduction des règles de droit; et l'on peut supposer qu'en défaut d'une standardisation au moins élémentaire des équivalents de traduction des termes tchèques effectuée déjà avant l'adhésion de la République Tchèque à l'Union européenne, la situation sera embrouillée et créera beaucoup de confusions inutiles.

Malgré l'évidence du fait qu'aucun dictionnaire bilingue ne peut avoir une force obligatoire absolue et normative dans tous ses aspects et que ce sont ses utilisateurs qui décideront dans quelle mesure et dans quels indices ils lui reconnaîtront une valeur normative (Barnhart, 1980: 39), il est nécessaire d'élaborer les dictionnaires bilingues. Il se crée ainsi une vaste base de données qui peut servir à la création d'un grand dictionnaire bilingue électronique comprenant outre la langue générale aussi les expressions de la langue des différentes branches scientifiques humaines ou techniques.

Non en dernier lieu, nous avons essayé de dégager des traits caractéristiques du tchèque juridique, y compris ses écarts par rapport à la langue standard. Par exemple, le terme *odvolání* (A. *appeal*) est utilisé, dans la majorité des cas, avec la préposition *proti* (A. *against*). Cette collocation prépositionnelle est standard dans la langue commune[1] ainsi que dans le tchèque juridique et concerne la possibilité de s'associer soit avec un substantif, soit avec un verbe (*odvolání proti rozsudku* - A. *an appeal against the judgment*; Tch. *odvolat se proti zamítnutí stížnosti* - A. *appeal /against/ the dismissal of complait*, etc.). Mais en langue tchèque juridique on peut trouver, dans ce contexte, encore deux prépositions : Tch. *z* - A. *from*, et Tch. *do* - A. *to*. Les constructions prépositionnelles tchèques *odvolání ‹z› rozsudku* et *odvolání ‹do› rozsudku* ont la même signification et le même effet juridique comme l'expression *odvolání ‹proti› rozsudku*. Les deux premières collocations prépositionnelles font partie du jargon juridique et on les trouve assez souvent dans les discours des parties présentes dans les salles d'audience, moins souvent dans les textes écrits. En anglais juridique on trouve une construction prépositionnelle équivalente à l'expression tchèque *odvolání ‹z› rozsudku*, A. *an appeal ‹from› judgment*. Mais notre corpus de différents textes juridiques, qui compte environ 6 millions de mots, montre que la construction anglaise *an appeal ‹from› /a judgment, decision/* est beaucoup plus fréquente que l'expression tchèque *odvolání ‹z› /rozsudku/*. A la différence du tchèque juridique, la construction prépositionnelle anglaise *an appeal ‹from›* se trouve dans la langue des lois (par exemple, la loi américaine "Criminal Alien Deportation Amendments 1990", § 4, alinéa 5, lettre a, phrase trois, ou le britannique "Criminal Appeal Act 1995", § 7, alinéa 2, lettre b); de même que la construction *appeal against*, elle sert donc comme une construction prépositionnelle synonyme à la construction tchèque *odvolání ‹proti› rozsudku*. La collocation prépositionnelle tchèque *odvolání ‹do› rozsudku* n'a pas d'équivalent en anglais juridique, mais elle peut être traduite comme *an appeal against* sans que le sens linguistique ou juridique soit violé ou détourné.

Nous avons aussi essayé de trouver dans la langue juridique anglo-américaine des équivalents authentiques (c'est-à-dire fonctionnels) des expressions ou des unités terminologiques, qui, une fois traduites en anglais d'une manière incorrecte, ont trouvé une grande persistance, dans leur acception erronée, dans la pratique de nos traducteurs et interprètes. Nous avons en vue surtout les termes *právní subjekt* et *právnická osoba*. Le premier d'entre eux est souvent traduit, d'une façon erronée, comme *legal subject* surtout pour le motif que tant le substantif tchèque *subjekt*, tant le substantif anglais *subject* sont des polysèmes et l'utilisateur pas très expérimenté (traducteur ou juriste) de l'anglais juridique peut croire que la signification tchèque est identique avec la signification anglaise, et, sans doute, on peut y voir les effets de l'interférence interlinguale. Le terme tchèque *právní subjekt* est défini comme la personne physique (A. *natural person*) ou personne morale (A. *legal entity*) apte à entrer dans les rapports juridiques, et être ainsi titulaire de droits et assujetti à des obligations. Cette caractéristique correspond à l'expression anglaise *legal person*, ce qui est l'unique équivalent fonctionnel correct dans le droit anglo-américain. Le terme anglais *legal subject* peut être compris seulement comme objet (d'un contrat, d'une convention) qui est conforme à la loi. Le

---

1 Nous considérons la langue commune comme une variante de la langue littéraire, c'est-à-dire comme une opposition de la langue de spécialité, et non comme un synonyme de ce qu'on apppelle "le tchèque commun". La langue commune, ainsi que la langue de spécialité, font partie de la langue littéraire.

terme tchèque *právnická osoba* est incorrectement traduit en anglais comme *legal person*[2]; mais ce terme anglais a une autre signification, comme nous l'avons montré ci-dessus. *Právnická osoba* est un sujet de droit artificiellement créé apte à être titulaire de droits et assujetti à des obligations et entrer dans les relations juridiques; on peut donc traduire aussi ce terme comme *artificial legal person* ou *artificial person*, ce qui sont des termes courants du droit anglo-américain. En outre, il existe encore d'autres équivalents anglo-américains, par exemple *legal entity, juridical person, body corporate (corporate body).*

La définition du groupe de base des utilisateurs est l'un des facteurs les plus importants dans la phase préparatoire des travaux sur le dictionnaire (Atkins 1993: 12, Malkiel 1980: 55) qui, d'ailleurs, exerce une influence décisive sur sa conception et sur le mode de son élaboration. On peut supposer que les utilisateurs du dictionnaire formeront un groupe hétérogène assez varié et différencié du point de vue de leur motivation et de leurs expériences. En général, on peut dire que les utilisateurs potentiels peuvent être divisés en deux catégories fondamentales: les personnes dont l'orientation linguistique est primaire, c'est-à-dire les personnes ayant une formation linguistique, et les personnes ayant une formation juridique, mais ne disposant pas souvent d'une formation linguistique formelle. Il existe aussi un groupe pas nombreux de ceux qui ne disposent ni d'une formation linguistique, ni d'une formation juridique, mais qui, de temps en temps, sont amenés à exprimer en anglais la réalité juridique tchèque (par ex., les journalistes). Mais on peut, avec une grande certitude, constater que pour que n'importe qui soit capable d'utiliser d'une manière acceptable et intelligente le dictionnaire juridique anglais-tchèque, il doit posséder des connaissances de la langue générale et des capacités de communiquer en anglais au moins au niveau du degré intermédiaire, si l'on parle des Tchèques d'origine, et il en est de même en ce qui concerne les connaissances de la langue tchèque et les capacités respectives, si c'est un locuteur anglais qui voudrait utiliser ce dictionnaire.

2. Cadre juridique

Lors de la transposition des textes juridiques du tchèque en anglais on trouve une grande quantité de problèmes potentiels qui sont influencés surtout par les facteurs suivants :

La terminologie juridique tchèque et la langue juridique entière dans tous ses niveaux (morphologique, lexical, syntaxique et stylistique) ne sont pas stabilisées; elles se développent sans cesse, elles s'élargissent et subissent des glissements de sens sous l'influence fondamentale du droit européen, et, au cours des douze dernières années, sans contrôle rigoureux de l'exactitude juridique (législative) et linguistique.

Les différences systématiques et conceptuelles entre le droit continental, le droit tchèque étant son rejeton, et le système anglo-américain fondé sur le Common Law, présentent surtout pour les traducteurs un problème que l'on peut résoudre seulement si l'on est capable de

---

2 Sans doute, on y rencontre les effets négatifs des documents de l'Union européenne écrits en anglais, où l'on utilisait aussi (surtout dans les temps plus éloignés) le terme *legal person* dans le sens de la personne morale du droit tchèque. On ne peut que spéculer sur les motifs de cette situation actuelle (ou passée), mais le problème fondamental est le fait que les traducteurs des textes de l'Union européenne ne sont pas, pour la plupart, les juristes, d'autant moins les juristes ayant une bonne connaissance du système juridique de la langue d'arrivée.

réaliser, avec succès, une analyse intrasémantique (Tomášek 1991: 153), c'est-à-dire une interprétation juridique du texte de départ.

Le droit anglo-américain se compose des systèmes juridiques appliqués dans les plus importants pays où l'on parle anglais, c'est-à-dire aux Etat-Unis, en Grande-Bretagne, au Canada, en Australie et en Irlande. Les autres pays, dans lesquels l'anglais est toujours la langue officielle, contribuent à l'enrichissement et à l'élargissement de l'anglais juridique non seulement dans le domaine purement linguistique, mais aussi dans le domaine conceptuel (juridique). De ce fait, il se produit aussi un accroissement de la synonymie terminologique ou une ramification des lexèmes en significations polysémiques.

L'un des facteurs, qui exercent une influence fondamentale sur l'examen de la langue juridique dans le contexte tchèque, est la validité des règles de droit tchèques. D'après Kořenský, Cvrček et Novák (1999: 32–33), dès l'année 1918 rien n'a été fait pour purifier les règles de droit et pour assurer leur transparence. Du nombre total de presque 30 000 documents publiés dès 1918 dans le recueil des lois ("*Sbírka zákonů*"), une sixième du nombre de ces documents n'a pas de caractère d'un acte législatif, 10 000 règles ont été explicitement abrogés et les 15 000 documents restant se trouvent dans de différentes phases de validité ou invalidité. Un tiers d'eux peut être mis sur le compte du "désordre législatif", car certaines de leurs parties ont été abrogées, d'autres sont devenues caduques, mais, en général, on ne tient pas de tableaux récapitulatifs concernant l'état actuel de ces règles. Le deuxième tiers est représenté par les lois qui sont valides (c'est-à-dire, les lois qui n'ont pas été explicitement abrogées), mais qui sont devenues caduques (par ex., les lois de finances qui sont adoptées pour chaque année budgétaire, sans que les lois précédentes aient été abrogées). Le dernier tiers, c'est-à-dire 5 000 actes législatifs environ, c'est la base de notre réglementation juridique en vigueur.

Le rythme accéléré des préparatifs de la République Tchèque en vue de l'adhésion à l'Union européenne influence d'une manière fondamentale la procédure législative. Non seulement que tout l'ensemble des normes juridiques n'est pas suffisamment "appuré", mais chaque année il est complété par des dizaines de lois adoptées dans une procédure législative hectique, appelée "ouragan" législatif.[3] Le problème fondamental est le fait que les projets ou propositions de lois sont préparés aussi, outre les spécialistes de législation, par différentes personnes privées qui, souvent, sans qu'ils disposent d'une formation juridique convenable, travaillent comme assistants ou conseillers des députés, et les propositions de lois ainsi créées sont présentées à la Chambre des députés pour leur approbation. Et, s'il y a la volonté politique respective, une telle proposition est adoptée sans qu'il soit possible, au cours de la procédure législative, identifier tous les impacts que ces lois peuvent produire sur les autres règles de droit en vigueur. Du point de vue linguistique, le problème principal est la diversité conceptuelle et terminologique, et l'on passe sous silence les constructions syntaxiques souvent un peu maladroites qui rendent difficile une interprétation univoque du texte ou de ses parties. A la différence des lois adoptées dans les pays de la langue anglaise, nos lois n'ont pas de passage appelé "définition des concepts". Il arrive donc qu'un terme est utilisé dans deux lois différentes dans des acceptions tout à fait différentes.

Un autre problème de la législation tchèque, c'est le nombre croissant des lois modifiées et des modifications modifiées. Kořenský, Cvrček et Novák (1999: 38) montrent qu'en 1990 on a adopté 159 lois nouvelles, dont 70 règles modifiées; en 1994 on a adopté 69 lois, dont 52 modifications; en 1997 on a adopté 57 lois, dont 46 modifications. Notre recherche a montré qu'en 2001 on avait adopté 60 lois modifiées des 96 lois adoptées au total. Les modifications réitérées concernent dans la plus grande mesure les lois dont l'importance est primordiale pour

---

3 Tandis qu'en 1998 on a adopté 45 lois, en 2001 on en a adopté 96.

le fonctionnement de la société dans la période de la transitions du système totalitaire au système démocratique. Par exemple, le code de procédure civile, adopté en 1963, n'a été, avant l'année 1990, modifié que cinq fois; dès l'année 1990 on a adopté 36 modifications. Le code de commerce, adopté en 1991, a connu, avant la fin de l'année 2001, vingt-et-une modifications, d'autres propositions ou projets ont déjà été présentés pour examen à la Chambre des députés. La loi relative à l'activité artisanale, adoptée en 1991, a connu, avant la fin de l'année 2001, cinquante modifications. Les modifications précipitées et irréfléchies entraînent des interventions essentielles dans le texte de la loi, des changements et des glissements de sens des notions et des termes utilisés par la loi respective, et, non en dernier lieu, ces modifications donnent lieu à la modification des autres règles de droit dont l'état et l'énumération ne sont pas suffisamment établis.

Les différences entre la terminologie juridique des différents pays de la langue anglaise se trouvent à la base de nombreux problèmes ou confusions lors de la transposition d'un texte juridique tchèque en anglais. Par exemple, le terme britannique *company*, défini par la loi Companies Act 1985, est identique dans sa signification juridique et aussi dans ses effets juridiques avec le terme *corporation* défini par la loi Revised Model Bussines Corporation Act 1984 comme société commerciale enregistrée. Si l'on prend en considération seulement la caractéristique linguistique et conceptuelle de ces deux termes, on peut conclure qu'il s'agit des synonymes totals. Mais les contextes, dans lesquels ces termes peuvent être correctement utilisés, diffèrent l'un de l'autre, d'où il suit qu'il ne s'agit pas de synonymes fonctionnels. Mais on ne peut confondre ces deux termes ni dans le cadre du droit britannique, ni dans le cadre du droit des Etats-Unis. Le terme *company* dans le droit des Etats-Unis désigne habituellement une entité non enregistrée,[4] le terme *corporation* est un sujet commercial inscrit au registre des sociétés; le terme *corporation* dans les textes britanniques d'origine désigne la société dont le but commercial n'est pas primaire et dont l'équivalent tchèque est *korporace*, tandis que le terme *company* désigne une société commerciale inscrite au registre des sociétés (Companies House).

On peut citer comme exemple aussi le terme britannique *frustration* (mode de la dissolution du contrat) qui a son équivalent américain dans le terme *impossibility*; le concept désigné par le terme britannique *theft* (défini par la loi Theft Act 1967 comme le terme juridique désignant le vol) est désigné comme *larceny* dans les lois des Etats-Unis. En outre, en Grande-Bretagne le mot *jail* est une dénomination populaire de la prison; *jail* en anglais juridique américain désigne la maison d'arrêt ou un local dépendant de la station de police ou de la municipalité locale où les personnes sont gardées à vue, et dont les synonymes sont *police cell* ou *holding cell.* On peut aussi trouver de différentes désignations du terme tchèque *podzákonný právní předpis* : le terme britannique ou canadien *statutory instrument*, */executive/ regulation* utilisé aux Etats-Unis ou le terme australien *legislative instrument.*

On se pose donc la question de savoir lequel des deux ou plusieurs équivalents possibles on peut indiquer comme un équivalent le plus pertinent dans le dictionnaire juridique bilingue et par quel appareil explicatif on doit accompagner les équivalents particuliers. Les réponses dépendront pleinement du contexte linguistique, matériel et social dans lequel l'équivalent respectif doit être utilisé. Non en dernier lieu, la réponse dépendra de la politique de l'éditeur en ce qui concerne la possibilité, et de son éventuelle étendue, d'insérer dans le dictionnaire les instructions pour la traduction des textes juridiques. A notre avis et d'après nos expériences,

---

4 La dernière édition du dictionnaire juridique Black's Law Dictionnary admet que le terme *company* peut être synonyme au terme *corporation*, cependant seulement *corporation* est le terme de la loi régissant les sociétés commerciales enregistrées aux Etas-Unis.

aucun dictionnaire tchèque - langue étrangère ne peut suffisamment instruire son utilisateur sur la façon d'utilisation de l'équivalent respectif. Le choix dépendra toujours du motif qui conduit l'utilisateur à consulter le dictionnaire (par ex., rechercher un équivalent directement applicable lors de la traduction ou de l'interprétation, ou seulement trouver une inspiration qui sera développée par une étude approfondie des dictionnaires de la langue respective ou des autres sources); le choix dépendra aussi des connaissances linguistiques et juridiques de l'utilisateur et, non en dernier lieu, c'est la personne du destinataire du texte d'arrivée qui sera déterminante. Il serait donc très difficile d'élaborer les instructions comment traiter la langue juridique d'arrivée qui seraient, du point de vue de la forme, compatibles avec le dictionnaire. La typologie de genre des textes juridiques et de leurs fonctions est tellement vaste, et sur le plan comparatif tchèque-anglais non élaborée, qu'il n'était possible d'insérer dans le dictionnaire aucune instruction concrète; une étude comparative typologique et de genre des textes juridiques tchèques et anglais fera l'objet d'une future analyse à part.

3. Cadre linguistique

3.1. Langue de spécialité et terminologie

A la différence de la langue tchèque, qui connaît un seul terme pour désigner la variante de la langue utilisée dans les plus différentes branches de la recherche de base ou appliquée et dans les disciplines scientifiques, c'est-à-dire *odborný jazyk* (en français *langue de spécialité*), on peut trouver en langue anglaise plusieurs dénominations : *language for special / specific purposes, sub-language, scientific language, specialized language* (Pearson 1998: 28).

La langue de spécialité est une notion difficile à définir et on peut la considérer sous plusieurs angles. Du point de vue pragmatique, il s'agit d'un sous-système de la langue commune, fondé sur un choix concret, sur une combinatoire et un emploi des unités (éventuellement des formules) morphologiques, lexicales et syntaxiques existantes, qui servent de la façon la plus pertinente aux objectifs stylistiques, communicatifs et de genre du texte respectif dans le domaine spécialisé concret et dans le contexte social concret. La "spécialité" de ce sous-système est une catégorie pragmatique primaire qui reflète les objectifs et les besoins communicatifs de ses utilisateurs, c'est-à-dire des spécialistes en discipline concrète. Du point de vue linguistique, il s'agit d'une analyse des textes spécialisés existants et d'une définition ultérieure des procédés qui ont conduit à leur élaboration, c'est-à-dire la détermination des règles au niveau du lexique, du syntaxe et du texte, qui, étant respectées, conduiront à la production d'un texte spécialisé généralement acceptable. Le profane considère comme langue de spécialité chaque discours qui utilise la terminologie, les constructions syntaxiques plus compliquées et le sujet qui ne fait pas partie de la vie de tous les jours. Bien que Picht et Draskau (1985: 3) définissent la langue de spécialité (LSP) comme "une variante formalisée et codifiée de la langue utilisée dans un but spécial et dans un contexte respectif", nous sommes persuadés qu'une telle définition correspond plutôt à ce qu'ils appellent variante de la langue de spécialité, c'est-à-dire la "langue" d'une discipline concrète, par exemple, le tchèque ou l'anglais juridique, le tchèque ou l'anglais commercial, le tchèque ou l'anglais de constructions mécaniques, etc. On peut supposer qu'il existe une intersection de toutes ces variantes qui puisse être considérée comme une langue de spécialité "matérialisée" en tant que telle, mais, à notre connaissance, il n'existe pour l'instant aucune étude concernant le tchèque ou l'anglais qui compare les "langues" des différentes disciplines et sélectionne tout ce que leur est commun.

Pearson (1988: 31) cite six facteurs qui peuvent aider à délimiter la variante de la langue de spécialité :

(1) une discipline concrète (par ex., le droit);
(2) des restrictions lexicales, sémantiques et syntaxiques (par ex., l'emploi de la terminologie);
(3) des "écarts" grammaticaux (par ex., le caractère dénombrable du substantif normalement non dénombrable *an information* dans le sens de *trestní oznámení*;
(4) une haute fréquence des constructions et structures syntaxiques spécifiques (par ex., les locutions phraséologiques figées dans les textes des lois);
(5) des types de textes spécifiques (par ex., les lois ou les contrats);
(6) des marques et des symboles spécifiques;

Les premiers trois facteurs sont, dans diverse mesure, analysés dans cette étude, le quatrième et le cinquième facteurs dépassent le cadre de cet ouvrage et nécessitent une analyse comparative à part. Nous mentionnons ici le dernier point, c'est-à-dire l'emploi du symbole désignant dans les lois tchèques le paragraphe "§", puisqu'il s'agit, du point de vue de la traduction, d'un problème assez grave. Tandis que les lois tchèques sont divisées en *paragraf* (ce qui correspond à l'article français), *odstavec*, *písmeno*, et *věta* , les lois anglaises ont la même structure, mais la dénomination de leur division structurale est différente, ce qui peut, à la première vue, désorienter les utilisateurs : *section*, *subsection*, *paragraph*, *subparagraph*. Dans les citations tchèques, *paragraf* est indiqué par le symbole "§" suivi d'un chiffre arabe; *odstavec* est abrégé en *odst.* suivi aussi d'un chiffre arabe; *písmeno* est désigné par une abréviation *písm.* ou *lit.* suivie d'une lettre minuscule (dans l'ordre alphabétique); la dernière partie structurale *věta* est laissée sans abréviation et le numéro est exprimé par un adjectif numéral écrit par lettres minuscules. Dans les lois anglo-américaines, le symbole "§" est utilisé pour désigner des *paragraf* (F. articles) particuliers seulement dans les collections des lois (A. *collections of laws*), et cela surtout dans la législation des Etats-Unis; dans les lois particulières, on utilise seulement les chiffres arabes en caractères gras; *subsection* est désigné par un chiffre arabe entre parenthèses; *paragraph* est désigné par lettre minuscule entre parenthèses et *subparagraph* est désigné par chiffres romains minuscules entre parenthèses.

D'où il suit que le renvoi à une disposition de la loi tchèque – § 12, *odst.* 3, *písm.* a, *věta třetí* – sera ainsi transposé en anglais : s. 12 (3) (a) (iii). Le traducteur, qui n'est pas familiarisé avec ce procédé et qui essaye de traduire mot à mot le texte de départ, trouvera la transposition de l'anglais en tchèque encore plus compliquée, car il ne sera pas capable de transcoder le renvoi numérique dans une figure tchèque qui soit compréhensible pour le destinataire. Mais s'il s'efforce de transposer mot à mot en anglais la citation tchèque et s'il emploie les abréviations des différentes parties de "paragraf" (F. *article*), la traduction sera lourde, même si l'information communiquée est compréhensible.

La langue de spécialité est caractérisée surtout par l'emploi de la terminologie, quoique le vocabulaire de la discipline concrète ne se compose pas uniquement des termes de spécialité. Les recherches les plus variées effectuées soit en tchèque (Poštolková 1984: 16–17), soit en anglais (Riley 1995: 73–79) ou bien en russe (Zimová, Koníčková 1989) montrent que la langue juridique comprend une échelle des moyens d'expression beaucoup plus vaste et, en général, on délimite trois catégories :

a) La terminologie juridique "propre", par exemple *aberace* (A. *aberration*), *cedent* (A. *assignor*), *estoppel* (Tch. *překážka uplatnění žalobního nároku*) ou *demurrer* (Tch. *procesní námitka*). Il s'agit d'un groupe assez restreint des termes qui ne sont pas utilisés en dehors du domaine du droit, qui ne sont pas devenus partie de la langue commune et qui sont identifiables aussi en dehors de tout contexte comme des termes juridiques. On peut y ranger aussi le répertoire restreint des termes juridiques latins.[5]

b) Les expressions juridiques, qui sont utilisées dans la langue de tous les jours (mais non comme des termes ayant une définition précise), mais qui ont, dans un contexte juridique concret, une définition juridique précise, par exemple, *pozemek* et *nedbalost* et leurs équivalents anglais *land* et *negligence*; leur emploi, distribution et fonction est identique en tchèque ainsi qu'en anglais. On peut ranger dans ce groupe aussi les expressions dont le sens général est différent de celui juridique. Par exemple, le mot tchèque *titul* a, en tchèque ainsi qu'en anglais de tous les jours, un contenu tout à fait différent de celui délimité pour l'emploi terminologique des expressions *titul* et *title* dans la langue juridique.
c) Certaines expressions de la langue commune peuvent acquérir un contenu juridique concret, si elles sont définies par la loi dans un but précis. Par exemple, pour les besoins de la loi britannique "Welfare of Pigs Act 1998" *pig* (le porc) est uniquement un animal élevé aux fins de l'élevage et de l'engraissement. Au cas où un animal de cette espèce serait élevé individuellement dans un but différent que celui fixé par la loi (par ex., comme un animal de compagnie), il ne s'agit pas d'un *pig* en vertu de cette loi, et cet animal, ainsi que son propriétaire, ne sont pas concernés par les dispositions de la loi citée.

Quoique Newmark (1988: 160) montre que la terminologie présente 5–10% environ du texte spécialisé, la plupart de personnes sans une formation linguistique suffisante (y compris les juristes) la considèrent comme un facteur essentiel et unique et, par conséquent, les expressions "langue de spécialité" et "terminologie" sont perçues comme synonymes. Et, si ces personnes parlent de la langue de spécialité, elles préfèrent l'expression "terminologie".

La définition du terme donnée par Felber (1984: 181–2) peut être appliquée aussi sur les termes juridiques, mais avec certaines réserves. Le terme juridique devrait être précis, pertinent, correct du point de vue linguistique et devrait permettre la dérivation des autres parties du discours. En même temps il devrait être formé par par un seul mot et il devrait être monosémique (univoque, portant un seul sens). Tandis que la précision, la pertinence et la correction linguistique sont les exigences que chaque terme <u>doit</u> remplir, faute de quoi il serait inutilisable dans le système linguistique respectif, les conditions de l'ouverture dérivationnelle, de l'univocité et de sa nature d'un mot simple ne sont réalisables qu'avec difficultés. Et cela à cause du fait que la plupart des termes juridiques sont composés de plusieurs mots ou ce sont des unités syntaxiques. L'estimation approximative du nombre des termes complexes, c'est-à-dire composés de plusieurs mots, et des termes simples, formés d'un seul mot, dans le dictionnaire juridique américain Black's Law Dictionnary nous montre que les termes simples présentent approximativement 33% de la terminologie et les 67% sont des termes complexes.

---

[5] La terminologie juridique latine utilisée en droit tchèque ne correspond pas tout à fait aux expressions latines utilisées en droit anglo-américain. Par exemple, les locutions *de lege lata* (relativement à la loi en vigueur) et *de lege ferenda* (quant à la loi à adopter), que l'on rencontre souvent dans les textes juridiques tchèques sont inconnues dans le droit anglo-américain. Egalement, les termes périphrastiques *obiter dicta* et *ratio dicendi*, en tant que deux notions fondamentales du droit anglo-américain des précédents, ne se trouvent pas dans les textes juridiques tchèques.

L'estimation analogique, réalisée en ce qui concerne la teminologie contenue dans un dictionnaire tchèque[6] dit qu'il y a 26% des termes simples et 74% des termes complexes.[7]

Les termes peuvent être rangés dans différents groupes selon les critères les plus variés; notre critère est basé sur deux aspects, c'est-à-dire sur leur qualité ou fonction descriptive et sur leur caractéristique grammaticale (morphologique, lexicale, éventuellement syntaxique). Nous optons pour la division qualitative et fonctionnelle de Bečka (1992: 73) qui distingue les termes spécialisés (définis d'une manière concrète, précise et univoque), les termes descriptifs (créant la taxinomie des disciplines concrètes ou de leurs subdisciplines) et les termes techniques (technologiques) désignant les phénomènes de l'application pratique de la connaissance scientifique. La terminologie juridique anglaise, ainsi que la terminologie juridique tchèque, contient surtout les deux premiers types des termes et, selon la constatation de Fillmore (1978: 168), la langue juridique contient un grand nombre des énumérations taxinomiques les plus variées, et cite comme exemple le terme anglais *murder* (Tch. *vražda*) qui est ultérieurement divisé selon le type et la gravité de l'homicide volontaire. On ne peut pas supposer que les énumérations similaires soient dans le système juridique tchèque et dans celui anglo-américain compatibles et comparables dans ce sens que ces énumérations puissent fournir des équivalents corrects pour la traduction d'une langue à l'autre. Il est toujours nécessaire d'effectuer une analyse conceptuelle dans les langues respectives (Šarčević 1989: 290) qui montrerait les convergences et les divergences dans le contenu des termes dans les deux langues et ce n'est qu'ultérieurement que l'on peut décider si l'expression de la langue de départ peut servir comme équivalent dans la langue d'arrivée, éventuellement, s'il est nécessaire, et dans quelle mesure, de recourir à l'explication du contenu du terme respectif.

Un autre facteur, mentionné dans notre étude, est le caractère normatif de la terminologie. Galinski (1982: 189) la divise en terminologie descriptive, reflétant son emploi dans une pratique spécialisée courante, et en terminologie normative (A. *prescriptive*), représentant la norme conseillée par une institution responsable. Cette division exprime d'une façon pertinente le processus qui se produit dans le cadre de la terminolgie juridique : une institution responsable, c'est-à-dire un organe législatif, adopte une norme, c'est-à-dire une loi, dans laquelle cette institution définit des termes concrets, et suppose que les termes ainsi définis seront de la même manière appliqués dans la pratique juridique. Mais, selon Tiersma (1999: 109), la terminologie descriptive comprend aussi, outre les termes définis par la loi, le jargon juridique, avec lequel on atteint une certaine mesure de la condensation dans la communication juridique courante. Du point de vue de la traduction, il peut s'y créer un problème du choix d'un équivalent convenable. Par exemple, le code de procédure pénale tchèque utilise un terme complexe *peněžitá záruka* (A. *pecuniary security*) au lieu de l'expression courante *kauce*. *Peněžitá záruka* est donc un terme normatif, mais dans la pratique juridique courante on utilise le mot *kauce* (A. *bail*). Le droit anglo-américain, la loi ainsi que la pratique juridique, utilise le terme *bail*; ce ne sont que les vocabulaires juridiques unilingues qui utilisent, pour les besoins de l'explication, l'expression *pecuniary (monetary, cash) security*. En traduisant le terme tchèque *peněžitá záruka* en anglais, il faut se rendre compte qu'il s'agit d'une caution, et il faut prendre en considération l'usage prépondérante dans le milieu juridique anglo-

---

6 Madar, Zdeněk : Dictionnaire du droit tchèque, (Praha, Linde 1995)

7 Le calcul exprimé en pourcentage a été effectué par l'addition des termes simples et des termes complexes dans les plus vastes lettres de ces dictionnaires : la lettre C dans le dictionnaire juridique de Black, pages 202–388, soit 186 pages au total – 1239 termes simples et 2531 termes complexes; la lettre P dans le dictionnaire tchèque, pages 924–1157, soit 233 pages au total – 565 termes simples et 1596 termes complexes.

américain. On peut constater qu'il sera plus compréhensible, dans tous les contextes imaginables et pour n'importe quel destinataire de la traduction, de traduire le terme légal tchèque par un terme légal anglais , mais non mot à mot, c'est-à-dire *peněžitá záruka = bail.*

La caractéristique grammaticale des termes et des unités terminologiques est divisée selon les traits distinctifs en niveaux morphologique, catégoriel (reflétant les catégories grammaticales), lexical et syntaxique (Hoffmann 1982: 399). Les phénomènes les plus intéressants se produisent sans doute au niveau de la morphologie et de la syntaxe. Le suffixe anglais *-er*, désignant un agent, est remplacé dans plusieurs cas par un suffixe *-or*, les substantifs qui se terminent par le suffixe *-er* conservent leur sens d'origine de la langue commune, et le suffixe *-or* signale, dans la plupart des cas, qu'il s'agit d'un terme juridique. Le contraire de ce suffixe est le suffixe *-ee* qui désigne la personne qui subit une action (datif).[8] Ils sont ainsi créés les termes pairs du type *lessor - lessee*, *assignor - assignee*, *obligor - obligee*, *promisor - promisee*, *grantor - grantee*, *mortgagor - mortgagee*, etc., dont le premier terme est la partie active du rapport, c'est-à-dire la personne qui fait quelque chose au profit ou envers la deuxième personne membre du rapport respectif.

Les phrasèmes terminologiques sont les unités syntaxiques qui ont, dans des contextes juridiques concrets, un sens figé. Fillmore admet (1978: 170) qu'il est nécessaire, dans le domaine du droit, de considérer les expressions terminologiques comprenant plusieurs membres comme les unités lexicales. Par exemple, la construction syntaxique *maliciously damaging the property of another* est un terme complexe désignant aux Etats-Unis un délit consistant dans la destruction ou la détérioration de la propriété d'autrui. La désignation d'une infraction pénale selon le droit tchèque, *vražda dítěte matkou*, est aussi un terme, même s'il ne correspond pas à la caractéristique stricte du terme en vertu de l'ISO.

La polysémie au sein de la terminologie présente un facteur d'une assez grande gravité du point de vue de la traduction. Sa fréquence assez haute exige que le traducteur comprenne la problématique juridique et ne se tienne pas seulement de la surface du texte. Il serait souhaitable que le traducteur possède des connaissances tant de la matière du système juridique de la langue du départ, tant de la langue d'arrivée, et qu'il soit capable de mettre en corrélation les equivalents fonctionnels et reconnaître le degré de leur équivalence conceptuelle et fonctionnelle. On peut citer un exemple assez simple de deux termes juridiques tchèques *právo* et *věc*. *Právo* ha deux sens fondamentaux, c'est-à-dire le droit *objectif* (système des normes juridiques) et le droit *subjectif* (prérogative individuelle). Mais, dans la majorité absolue des cas, les attributs spécificatifs *objektivní* (F. objectif) - *subjektivní* (F. subjectif) ne se trouvent pas dans les textes juridiques tchèques et c'est la tâche du traducteur de reconnaître le vrai sens du polysème *právo* : dans le premier cas, il est possible de traduire le terme tchèque par le substantif non dénombrable anglais *law*, et, dans le second, par le substantif dénombrable *right*, d'où il résulte qu'en anglais il ne s'agit en aucun cas d'un polysème. Un autre exemple de la polysémie terminologique tchèque est le terme *věc*. Dans le contexte du droit judiciaire il s'agit d'une cause, c'est-à-dire d'une affaire qui se plaide, dans ce cas on peut utiliser l'équivalent fonctionnel anglais *case*; dans le domaine des droits réels, ce terme tchèque peut être traduit

---

8 En anglais parlé non formel (et relâché du point de vue linguistique), le suffixe *-ee* (en dépit de différentes recommandations des linguistes et des juristes) est productif, parce qu'il aide à dériver des mots motivés d'une façon différente et ayant aussi une connotation différente (sans désigner la personne avec qui ou pour qui on fait quelque chose, comme il en est dans le sens juridique fondamental de ce suffixe); par exemple, *escapee* (personne en fuite), *standee* (personne debout), *arrivee* (personne qui est arrivée), *asylee* (personne qui demande l'asyle).

par un substantif non dénombrable *property*, éventuellement par un substantif dénombrable *thing*.

La problématique du jargon au sein de la langue juridique (tchèque ou anglaise) est très vaste et par sa complexité dépasse le cadre de cette étude. Toutefois il faut souligner que l'on peut parler du jargon non seulement en relation avec le lexique, mais aussi en relation avec les modalités générales de l'expression éliptique et métaphorique (c'est-à-dire au niveau morphologique, lexical et syntaxique). La décision d'un juriste tchèque de *žalovat vyklizení*, et la constatation au cours d'une procédure judiciaire *the prosecutor rests* sont des exemples typiques du jargon juridique au sens large du mot.

3.2. Linguistique de la traduction

La troisième partie de cette étude est consacrée à la linguistique de la traduction, c'est-à-dire, elle décrit le processus de la traduction du texte juridique et les différents pas qui forment ce processus. L'objectif n'est pas de créer les règles pour une bonne et intelligente traduction d'un texte juridique, mais d'attirer l'attention sur les problèmes qui peuvent surgir et proposer une solution de ces problèmes.

En général, il existe deux écoles de traduction. Trosborg (1997: 153) fait la différence entre la traduction fondée sur une approche linguistique, qui est basée sur l'équivalence. La deuxième approche est fondée sur un principe pragmatique (fonctionnel), c'est-à-dire, la fonction du texte d'arrivée y est primordiale. La première approche se reflète dans les ouvrages classiques de la théorie de la traduction (Catford 1965, Nida 1964, Newmark 1988), l'approche fonctionnelle à la traduction trouve ses adeptes dans les ouvrages récents (Nord 1997, Šarčević 2000, Trosborg 1997). Le modèle pragmatique tient compte du contexte situationnel de l'acte communicationnel et, aussi, prend en considération l'attente et les besoins du destinataire du texte d'arrivée. Toutefois la traduction juridique de qualité doit réunir les deux approches : la problématique de l'équivalence ne concerne pas seulement le niveau du lexique (terminologie), mais aussi des ensembles syntaxiques, des textes entiers et des situations de communication; l'équivalence n'est pas donc une catégorie purement linguistique, mais aussi conceptuelle, matérielle et fonctionnelle. L'équivalence est une catégorie de la description comparative juridico-linguistique des textes juridiques (Gémar 2001: 122).

La traduction des textes juridiques devrait être basée aussi sur l'analyse comparative de genre[9] des textes juridiques pour que l'information juridique concrète puissent être transposée dans la langue d'arrivée d'une manière exacte et en même temps compréhensible pour le destinataire. Par exemple, si l'on doit traduire une loi tchèque en anglais, il est indispensable d'étudier les règles législatives de la construction des lois anglo-américaines, leur structure formelle et leur organisation de fond. Outre la matière régie par cette loi, il faut avoir aussi une idée assez complète en ce qui concerne la langue dont les lois anglo-américaines se servent. Il faut connaître aussi les moyens par lesquels est exprimée la normativité d'un tel texte, etc.

Les théoriciens de la traduction des textes juridiques (Šarčević, 2000: 72, Joseph, 1995: 33–34) disent que l'objectif est de créer un texte dans la langue d'arrivée qui assure la même interprétation et la même application, telle qu'elle est supposée dans le texte de la langue de départ. Le traducteur des textes juridiques en premier lieu interprète le texte de départ et ce

---

9 Nous comprenons le genre comme un acte de communication typique pour un but concret (A. genre), par ex., la loi. Jedlička (1977: 29–34) emploie dans ce contexte le terme traditionnelle de la stylistique tchèque "*stylový typ*".

n'est qu'ultérieurement qu'il transpose le produit d'une telle interprétation en langue d'arrivée. Le destinataire du texte d'arrivée devrait y trouver une information claire, précise et la plus complète possible, contenue dans le texte de départ, complétée par les faits et les informations qui lui facilitent la compréhension du texte de départ dans un milieu linguistique, juridique et culturel tout à fait différent.

Comme nous avons déjà souligné, l'équivalence au sens large du mot reste un principe fondamental de la traduction des textes juridiques. Un rôle important dans ce domaine appartient au dictionnaire bilingue, même si dans le domaine juridique le dictionnaire bilingue devrait servir seulement comme "premiers secours" suivi par une analyse comparative que le traducteur devrait effectuer dans chaque cas particulier.

4. Cadre lexicographique

Dans cette partie de notre étude nous traitons les règles et les principes fondamentaux qui se font valoir lors de la création d'un dictionnaire bilingue spécialisé et que nous avons utilisés lors de l'élaboration du "Dictionnaire juridique tchèque-anglais avec les notes explicatives" (Leda Praha, 2001, 2003). A la différence des dictionnaires unilingues, qui sont classés, du point de vue de la forme, selon le but pour lequel ils ont été créés (alphabétiques, rétrogrades, dictionnaires qui procèdent par regroupement, etc.), les expressions contenues dans les dictionnaires unilingues spécialisés sont toujours classées dans l'ordre alphabétique. Mais il faut noter qu'aucun dictionnaire bilingue ne peut être autant exhaustif qu'il puisse comprendre toutes les situations dans lesquelles son consultant peut se trouver lors de la traduction ou la production d'un texte dans une langue étrangère.

Chaque dictionnaire bilingue est basé sur une étude lexicologique comparative et contrastive (Tomaszczyk, 1983: 45) et dans le cas du dictionnaire juridique encore sur l'étude des systèmes juridiques du pays de la langue respective. Comme nous avons déjà noté, la comparatistique juridique pour les besoins de l'élaboration du dictionnaire bilingue juridique où la langue d'arrivée est l'anglais, devrait comprendre les systèmes juridiques fondamentaux des pays où la langue officielle (et d'origine) est l'anglais, parce que ce sont les écarts intrasystématiques et les différences entre les institutions juridiques des pays respectifs qui contribuent, par exemple, à la formation des chaînes synonymiques des équivalents de traduction possibles. Chaque unité d'une telle chaîne synonymique a toutefois, dans la situation de traduction concrète spécifiée par les facteurs essentiels qui déterminent la traduction juridique, sa place unique, insubstituable, et, dans la majorité absolue des cas, il est possible d'utiliser dans la situation concrète (et puis d'une façon cohérente dans le texte entier) seulement un membre de la chaîne synonymique.

Certes, du point de vue quantitatif, la majeure partie du dictionnaire est formée par la terminologie. Pour qu'il soit possible d'offrir au consultant du dictionnaire un équivalent fonctionnel (c'est-à-dire juridique) le plus précis possible dans la langue d'arrivée, il est indispensable d'effectuer une analyse conceptuelle des équivalents potentiels de la langue de départ et de celle d'arrivée pour fixer le taux de leur équivalence ou de leur différence (Šarčević, 1989a: 278) et pour pouvoir préciser dans le dictionnaire le dépassement conceptuel ou, au contraire, le déficit, à l'aide des explications ou des gloses.

Puis il est nécessaire d'effectuer une analyse conceptuelle là où, à première vue, aucun équivalent n'existe, pour qu'il soit possible de trouver une manière comment transposer compréhensiblement un tel concept de la langue de départ en langue d'arrivée. Citons, par exemple, le terme tchèque *přestupek* qui n'a aucun équivalent juridique dans le système juridique anglo-américain. Toutefois, en analysant le fond matériel et juridique de cette infraction, on peut trouver une manière comment transposer ce terme tchèque en anglais tout en conservant à la fois sa valeur juridique et sa précision linguistique.

L'analyse conceptuelle devrait être effectuée à la base d'un dépouillement parallèle extensif (Tomaszczyk, 1983: 45) ou des corpus comparatifs (Teubert, 1996: 241). Il faut étudier les textes juridiques authentiques dans la langue d'arrivée et les soumettre à une analyse minutieuse pour pouvoir trouver tant les équivalents juridiques des termes tchèques, tant la manière comment exprimer dans la langue d'arrivée le concept ou la notion de la langue de départ inexistant dans le système juridique d'arrivée. Certes, le dictionnaire ne peut contenir qu'une fraction des informations acquises par l'analyse conceptuelle, mais il faut fournir l'information essentielle d'une façon adéquate (cf. article "*rehabilitace*").

Le titre du dictionnaire "Dictionnaire juridique tchèque-anglais avec les notes explicatives" indique que le dictionnaire comprend non seulement les équivalents anglais des termes et des groupes de mots à caractère terminologique juridiques tchèques, mais aussi les informations complémentaries sous forme des notes explicatives qui, dans des cas concrets expliquent la vedette tchèque, mais dans la plupart des cas, ses équivalents anglais et les exemples de son usage mentionnés dans l'exemplification. Nous avons opté pour l'expression "notes explicatives" pour le motif qu'il ne s'agit pas d'une définition autoritaire des termes, mais d'une explication ou d'une spécification du concept représenté par le terme respectif.

Le matériel de dépouillement de base était formé par les lois tchèques avec commentaire et le dictionnaire unilingue du droit tchèque que nous citons dans la bibliographie. Une autre source d'informations importante étaient 3 000 pages environ des textes contenus dans les manuels du droit tchèque, des instruments authentiques du droit privé et aussi des modèles publiés, des décisions judiciaires authentiques ou des procès-verbaux de police. Outre les termes spécialisés, les groupes de mots à caractère terminologique et les phrases entières, on peut trouver dans le dictionnaire aussi les expressions utilisées dans le domaine de la science et du droit dans leurs acceptions générales, et cela à cause du fait que la pratique montre que l'ignorance de ces expressions et de leur contenu entraîne souvent des problèmes au niveau de leur compréhension exacte.

Le corpus servant à l'établissement des équivalents des termes tchèques est composé des lois américaines, britanniques, irlandaises, australiennes et canadiennes, des dictionnaires juridiques unilingues, des manuels de droit et des documents juridiques authentiques.

Le manuscrit du dictionnaire contient 9 200 articles tchèques, 29 000 termes tchèques, groupes de mots à caractère terminologique et ensembles syntaxiques dans l'exemplification et environ 46 000 équivalents anglais.

5. Conclusions

La langue du droit se trouve, pendant des dizaines d'années, au centre de l'attention des juristes et des linguistes. Tandis que les juristes concentrent leur attention sur le problème comment exprimer, et dans le texte identifier, une information juridique pour qu'il soit possible d'appliquer le droit (interprétation juridique du texte), les linguistes s'efforcent de dégager les moyens linguistiques par lesquels l'information juridique est exprimée et les modes de sa compréhension du point de vue linguistique (l'interprétation linguistique du texte est souvent réduite à l'interprétation sémantique). Le troisième groupe des spécialistes qui s'occupent de la langue du droit est représenté par les traducteurs, qui combinent l'approche juridique et l'approche linguistique. Dans la majorité absolue des cas ce sont les linguistes quant à leur formation, mais, en tant que traducteurs des textes juridiques, ils sont obligés à étudier aussi la problématique juridique : ils prennent pour point de départ une complexe analyse linguistique et juridique du texte de départ et cherchent à transposer les informations y contenues dans la langue d'arrivée et dans le système juridique d'arrivée de telle façon que le texte traduit soit compréhensible du point de vue juridique et qu'il puisse remplir la fonction pour laquelle ce texte a été élaboré. La comparatistique juridico-linguistique est d'autant plus compliquée que le système linguistique et juridique du texte de départ est éloigné du système linguistique et juridique du texte d'arrivée.

"Le dictionnaire juridique tchèque-anglais avec les notes explicatives" est l'un des instruments qui aident le traducteur à s'orienter dans le domaine juridico-linguistique du droit tchèque par rapport au domaine juridico-linguistique anglo-américain et permet au juriste tchèque de communiquer la réalité juridique tchèque en anglais d'une manière compréhensible pour le destinataire final de l'information traduite.

Le travail sur le dictionnaire sert de base à une autre recherche qui se concentre, dans sa première phase, à la comparaison des différences entre l'interprétation juridique et l'interprétation sémantique du texte et sur leurs conséquences pour une transposition correcte de l'information juridique entre les langues et les systèmes juridiques. Dans une phase ultérieure nous nous concentrerons sur l'analyse comparative tchèque-anglaise et anglaise-tchèque des types (genres) de style juridiques fréquentes qui aboutira à l'élaboration des règles et des procédés pour la traduction des différents types de textes juridiques. En même temps nous envisageons de rassembler des matériaux qui serviront à l'élaboration d'un grand dictionnaire juridique anglais-tchèque qui aiderait ses consultants, d'une part, à mieux s'orienter dans le système juridique anglo-américain par rapport au système juridique tchèque, et d'autre part, à se rendre compte des différences entre la langue du droit anglo-américain et de l'anglais du droit de l'Union européenne.

VI. Bibliography

Alcaraz, Enrique / Hughes, Brian (2002): *Legal Translation Explained.* – Manchester: St. Jerome Publishing.

Al-Kasimi, Ali M. (1977): *Linguistics and Bilingual Dictionaries.* – Leiden: E. J. Brill.

– (1983): The Interlingual/Translation Dictionary. – In: R. R. K. Hartmann, (ed.): *Lexicography: Principles and Practice*, 153–162. London: Academic Press.

Apresjan, Jurij D. (1993): Systemic Lexicography as a Basis for Dictionary-making. – In: W. S. Chisholm (ed.): *Dictionaries. Journal of the Dictionary Society of North America*, N. 14, 1992/1993, 79–87. Cleveland: Cleveland State University.

Arntz, Reiner (1993): Terminological Equivalence and Translation. – In: H. S. Sonneveld, K. L. Loening (eds.): *Terminology: Applications in Interdisciplinary Communication*, 5–19. Amsterdam: John Benjamins Publishing Company.

Arntz, R., Picht, H. (1989): *Einfurung in die Terminologiearbeit.* – Hildesheim: Georg Olms Verlag.

Atkins, Sue, B. T. (1993): Theoretical Lexicography and Its Relation to Dictionary-making. – In: W. S. Chisholm (ed.): *Dictionaries. Journal of the Dictionary Society of North America*, N. 14, 1992/1993, 4–43. Cleveland: Cleveland State University.

– (ed.) (1998): *Using Dictionaries.* Studies of Dictionary Use by Language Learners and Translators. *Lexicographica Series Maior 88.* – Tubingen: Niemeyer.

Austin, J. L. (1962): *How to do things with words.* – Oxford: Oxford University Press.

Bachrach, J. A. (1982): Terminological Aspects of Translation. – In: W. Nedobity, (ed.): *Terminologies for the Eighties, Infoterm Series 7*, 373–379. Munich: K. G. Saur.

Barnhart, Clarence (1980): What Makes a Dictionary Authoritative. – In: L. Zgusta, (ed.): *Theory and Method in Lexicography: Western and Non-Western Perspectives*, 33–42. Columbia: Hornbeam Press.

Bauer, Laurie (1993): *English Word-formation.* Cambridge Textbooks in Linguistics. – Cambridge: Cambridge University Press.

Bečka, Josef (1992): *Česká stylistika.* – Praha: Academia .

Bělič, J., Kamiš, A., Kučera, K. (1978): *Malý staročeský slovník.* – Praha: SPN.

Bergenholtz, Henning, Tarp, Sven (eds.) (1995): *Manual of Specialised Lexicography.* Benjamins Translation Library, Volume 12. Amsterdam: John Benjamins Publishing Company.

Beyer, Vicki, Conradsen, Keld (1995): Translating Japanese Legal Documents into English: A Short Course. – In: M. Morris, (ed.): *Translation and the Law* (ed.). *American Translators Association Series* Volume VIII, 1995, 145–178. Amsterdam, Philadelphia: John Benjamins Publishing Company.

Bhatia, Vijay, K. (1987): Textual-mapping in English legislative writing. *World Englishes*, Vol. 6, N. 1, 1–10. – London: Pergamon.

– (1993): *Analysing Genre. Language Use in Professional Settings.* – London and New York: Longman.

– (1994a): Dynamics of Genre Manipulation. *CIEFL Bulletin*, Vol. 6, N. 1, June 1994, 25–42.

– (1994b): Cognitive Structuring in Legislative Provisions. – In: J. Gibbons (ed.): *Language and the Law*, 136–156. London and New York: Longman.

– (1996): Methodological Issues in Genre Analysis. *Hermes, Journal of Linguistics* N. 16–1996, 39–59. – Arhus: Handleshojskolen.

– (1997): Translating Legal Genres. – In: A. Trosborg, (ed.): *Text Typology and Translation*, Benjamins Translation Library, Vol. 26, 203–216. Amsterdam, Philadelphia: John Benjamins Publishing Company.

Bix, Brian (1993): *Law, Language and Legal Determinacy.* – Oxford: Clarendon Press.

Boguszak, Jiří, Čapek, Jiří (1997): *Teorie práva.* – Praha: Codex Bohemia.

Bone, Sheila (2001): *Osborn's Concise Law Dictionary*. – London: Sweet&Maxwell Ltd.

Bowers, Frederick (1989): *Linguistic Aspects of Legislative Expression*. – Vancouver: University of British Columbia Press.

Bradney, A., Fisher, V., Masson, J., Neal, A., Newell, D. (1986): *How to Study Law*. – London: Sweet & Maxwell.

Brown, Cornelia (1995): Riding the Waves of Fortune: Translating Legislation of the Successor Soviet Republics. – In: M. Morris, (ed.): *Translation and the Law* (ed.). *American Translators Association Series*, Volume VIII, 1995, 67–84. Amsterdam, Philadelphia: John Benjamins Publishing Company.

Brown, Gillian, Yule, George (1983): *Discourse Analysis*. Cambridge Textbooks and Linguistics. – Cambridge: Cambridge university Press.

Burton, William, C. (1998): *Burton's Legal Thesaurus*. – New York: McGraw-Hill.

Candlin, Christopher, N. (1981): Discoursal patterning and the equalizing of interpretative community. – In: L. Smith, (ed.): *English for Cross-Cultural Communication*, 166–199. London: Macmillan.

Capellas-Espuny, Gemma (1999): The Problems of Terminological Equivalence in International Maritime Law. *Translation Journal*, 3/3. http://accurapid.com/journal/ (accessed November 4, 2003).

Catford, John, C. (1965): *A Linguistic Theory of Translation*. – London: Oxford University Press.

Chromá, Marta (1995): *English-Czech Law Dictionary*. – Praha: Leda.

– (2001, 2003): *Czech-English Law Dictionary with Explanations*. – Praha: Leda.

– (2003a): The Language of Arbitration. From Intent to the Act. – In: V. Bhatia, C. N. Candlin, M. Gotti,(eds.), *Legal Discourse in Multilingual and Multicultural Contexts*, 63– 86. Bern: Peter Lang (Linguistic Insights Series).

– (2003b): The Czech Legal System and Contexts. – In: V. Bhatia, C. N. Candlin, J. Engberg, A. Trosborg, (eds.), *Mutilingual and Multicultural Contexts of Legislation. An International Perspective*, 59–77. Frankfurt: Peter Lang.

– (in print a): Cross-Cultural Traps in Legal Translation. – In: C. N. Candlin, M. Gotti (eds.): *Intercultural Aspects od Specialized Communication*. Bern: Peter Lang.

– (in print b): The Czech-English Law Dictionary with Explanations: A conceptual approach to the dictionary-making. – In: M. Rogers (ed.): *Proceedings from LSP Symposium 2003*. Guildford: University of Surrey.

– (in print c): Translating Terminology in Arbitration Discourse: A Conceptual Approach. – In: V. K. Bhatia, C. N. Candlin, J. Engberg (eds.): *Legal Discourse across Cultures and Systems*. Amsterdam: John Benjamins Publishing Company.

Clear, Jeremy (1996): Technical Implications of Multilingual Corpus Lexicography. *International Journal of Lexicography* 1996, v. 9, N. 3, special issue, 383–389 (ed.) R. Ilson, guest editors J. Sinclair, J. Payne, C. Perez Hernandes. – Oxford: Oxford University Press.

Cohen, M. L., Berring, R. C. (1984): *Finding the Law*. – Minnesota: West Publishing Company.

Coleman, J., Kay, C. J., eds. (1998): *Lexicology, Semantics and Lexicography*. Current Issues in Linguistic Theory. – Amsterdam: John Benjamins Publishing Company.

Coleman, Julie (2000): Strange Linguists: the Cant and Slang Dictionary Tradition. – In: J. Coleman, C. J. Kay, (eds.): *Lexicology, Semantics and Lexicography*, 69–86. Amsterdam: John Benjamins Publishing Company.

Collin, Peter (2000): *Dictionary of Law*. – London: Peter Collin Publishing Ltd.

Cruse, D. A. (1993): On Polylexy. – In: W. S. Chisholm (ed.): *Dictionaries. Journal of the Dictionary Society of North America*, N. 14, 1992/1993, 88–96. Cleveland: Cleveland State University.

Curzon, Lesley B. (2002): *Dictionary of Law*. 6th ed. – Harlow: Pearson Education - Longman.

Čechová, Marie, Chloupek, Jan, Krčmová, Marie, Minářová, Eva (1997): *Stylistika současné češtiny*. – Praha: ISV-nakladatelství.

Čermák, František (1995a): Slovník a jazyková kultura. – In: J. Jančáková, M. Komárek, O. Uličný, (eds.): *Spisovná čeština a jazyková kultura*, 208–211. Praha: FF UK.

– (1995b): Překladová lexikografie. – In: Čermák, F., Blatná, R. (eds.), *Manuál lexikografie*, 230–247. Praha: H+H.

– (1997) *Jazyk a jazykověda*. – Praha: Pražská imaginace.

Čermák, František, Blatná, Renata (eds.) (1995): *Manuál lexikografie*. – Praha: H+H.

Daneš, František 1999. Pojem spisovného jazyka v dnešních společenských podmínkách. – In: *Jazyk a text I*, část 2 Praha: Univerzita Karlova, 289–296.

Daneš, František, Grepl, Miroslav, Hlavsa, Zdeněk (eds.) (1987): *Mluvnice češtiny 3*. – Praha: Academia.

Dollerup, Cay (1998): Making a Basic Dictionary: Practical and Metalexicogprahical Considerations. – In: A. Zettersten, V. H. Pedersen, J. E. Mogensen (eds.): Symposium on Lexicography VIII. *Lexicographica Series Maior* 90, 153–163. Tubingen: Niemeyer.

Dušková, Libuše a kol. (1988): *Mluvnice současné angličtiny na pozadí češtiny*. – Praha: Academia.

Elman, Jiří (1991): Některá úskalí při překládání odborné literatury. – In: *Translatologica Pragensia V*, Acta Universitatis Carolinae Philologica 4–5/1991, 143–147. Praha: Karolinum.

Engberg, Jan (1994a): Communicative Signals in Legal Judgements. – In: M. Brekke, Q. Andersen, T. Dahl and J. Myking (eds.): *Applications and Implications of Current LSP Research*, 598–605. Bergen: Fagbokforlaget.

– (1994b): How Legal Language Works – Modal Expressions in Judgements. *Fackprakoch oversattningsteori*, VAKKI-symposium XIV, Vora 1994 Vasa, 22–43.

Farkas, D., Jacobsen, W. M., Todrys, K. W. (1978): *Papers from the Parasession on the Lexicon*. – Chicago: Chicago Linguistic Society.

Felber, Helmut (1982): The General Theory of Terminology and Terminography. Anticipated Developments in the Eighties. – In: W. Nedobity (ed.): *Terminologies for the Eighties*, Infoterm Series 7, 119–136. Munich: K. G. Saur.

– (1984): *Terminology Manual*. Paris: UNESCO and INFOTERM.

Filipec, Josef, Čermák, František (1985): *Česká lexikologie*. – Praha: Academia (Studie a práce lingvistické).

Fillmore, Charles J. (1978): On the Organization of Semantic Information in the Lexicon. – In: D. Farkas, W. M. Jacobsen, K. W. Todrys (eds.): *Papers from the Parasession on the Lexicon*, 148–173. Chicago: Chicago Linguistic Society.

Fine, Toni, M. (1997): *American Legal Systems: A Resource and Reference Guide*. Cincinnati: Anderson Publishing Co.

Fischer, Andreas (2000): Lexical Gaps, Cognition and Linguistic Change. – In: J. Coleman, C. J. Kay, (eds.): *Lexicology, Semantics and Lexicography*, 1–18. Amsterdam: John Benjamins Publishing Company.

Foxley, Eric, Gwei, Godwin (1989): Synonymy and Contextual Disambiguation of Words. *International Journal of Lexicography* 1989, v. 2, N. 2 (ed.) Robert Ilson. Oxford: Oxford University Press, 111–134.

Gabrovšek, Dušan (1998): Dimensions of falseness in False Friends: Implications for Bilingual Lexicogprahy. – In: A. Zettersten, V. H. Pedersen, J. E. Mogensen (eds.): Symposium on Lexicography VIII. *Lexicographica Series Maior* 90, 165–174. Tubingen: Niemeyer.

Galinski, Christian (1982): Standardization in Terminology –an Overview. – In: W. Nedobity, (ed.): *Terminologies for the Eighties, Infoterm Series 7*, 186–226. Munich: K. G. Saur.

Gallardo, Andres (1980): Dictionaries and the Standardization Process. – In: L. Zgusta, (ed.): *Theory and Method in Lexicography: Western and Non-Western Perspectives*, 59–69. Columbia: Hornbeam Press.

Garner, Bryan (1991): *The Elements of Legal Style*. Oxford, New York: Oxford University Press.

– (1995): *A Dictionary of Modern Legal Usage*. – Oxford, New York: Oxford University Press.

– (1999): *Black's Law Dictionary*. – St. Paul: West Group.

– (2001): *Legal Writing in Plain English*. Chicago, London: The University of Chicago Press.

Gémar, Jean-Claude (2001): Seven Pillars for the Legal Translator: Knowledge, Know-how and Art. – In: S. Šarčević (ed.): *Legal Translation, Preparation for Accession to the European Union*, 111–138. Rijeka: University of Rijeka.

Gibbons, John (ed.) (1994): *Language and the Law*. London and New York: Longman.

Grimes, R., Horgan, P. (1991): *Law in the Republic of Ireland. An Introduction.* Dublin: Wolfhound Press.

Groot, Gérard-René de (1987): Problems of Legal Translation from the Point of View of a Comparative Lawyer. *Cahiers de droit* 28, 813–844.

Hartmann, Reinhard, R. K. (ed.) (1983): *Lexicography: Principles and Practice.* London: Academic Press.

Hartmann, Reinhard, R. K. (1983a): On Theory and Practice. – In: R. R. K. Hartmann, (ed.): *Lexicography: Principles and Practice,* 3–11. London: Academic Press.

– (1983b): On Specifying Context. – In: R. R. K. Hartmann, (ed.): *Lexicography: Principles and Practice,* 109–119. London: Academic Press.

– (1989): Lexicography, Translation and the So-called Language Barrier. – In: M. Snell-Hornby, E. Pöhl, B. Bennani (eds.): *Translation and Lexicography,* 9–20. Amsterdam: John Benjamins Publishing Company.

Havránek, Bohuslav a kol. (1989): *Slovník spisovného jazyka českého.* Praha: Academia.

Hietaranta, Pertti (1995): On the Distinction Between Semantic and Communicative Translation. *Folia Translatologica,* 1995, M. Hrala, I. Čeňková (eds.), 5–12. Praha: Karolinum.

Hoffmann, Lothar (1982): Terminology and LSP. – In: W. Nedobity (ed.): *Terminologies for the Eighties,* Infoterm Series 7, 391–402. Munich: K. G. Saur.

Hohnhold, I. (1982): Principles of and Cooperation in Translation-oriented terminology Work. A critical review. – In: W. Nedobity (ed.): *Terminologies for the Eighties,* Infoterm Series 7, 380–390. Munich: K. G. Saur.

Hrbáček, Josef (1994): *Nárys textové syntaxe.* Praha: Trizonia.

Hutchinson, Tom., Waters, Alan. (1993): *English for Specific Purposes.* Cambridge: Cambridge University Press.

ISO R 1087 (1990): *Terminology and Vocabulary.* Paris: ISO.

Jacobson, Roman (1959/2000): On Linguistic Aspects of Translation. – In: L. Venuti (ed.): *The Translation Studies Reader,* 113–118. London: Routledge.

Jančáková, Jana, Komárek, Miroslav, Uličný, Oldřich (eds.) (1995): *Spisovná čeština a jazyková kultura 1993.* Praha: FF UK.

Jedlička, Alois (1977): Lingvistické předpoklady vědy o překladu. – In: A. Popovič (ed.): *Preklad odborného textu.* Práce I. celoštátnej konferencie o preklade odborného textu na PedF v Nitre v septembri 1972, 25–39. Bratislava: Štátne pedagogické nakladatelstvo.

Joseph, John, E. (1995): Indeterminacy, Translation and the Law. – In: M. Morris, (ed.): *Translation and the Law* (ed.). *American Translators Association Series* Volume VIII, 1995, 13–36. Amsterdam, Philadelphia: John Benjamins Publishing Company.

Kachru, Braj (1980): The New Englishes and Old Dictionaries: Dictionaries in Lexicographical Research on Non-native Varieties of English. – In: L. Zgusta, (ed.): *Theory and Method in Lexicography: Western and Non-Western Perspectives,* 71–101. Columbia: Hornbeam Press.

Klégr, Aleš (1993): Word-class constancy in translation: the noun in Czech and English. *Prague Studies in English* XX, 113–118. Praha: Karolinum.

Klinck, Dennis R. (1992): *The Word of the Law.* Ottawa: Carleton University Press.

Knapp, Viktor (1995): *Teorie práva.* Praha: C.H.Beck.

Knapp, Viktor a kol. (1998): *Tvorba práva a její současné problémy.* Praha: Linde.

Knittlová, Dagmar (1981): K pragmatickému aspektu překladu. *Slavica Pragensia XXIV,* Acta Universitatis Carolinae Philologica 4–5/1981 Problémy překladu a tlumočení, 59–68. Praha: Karolinum.

– (1989): K otázkám lingvistiky překladu. *Translatologica Pragensia III,* Acta Universitatis Carolinae Philologica 2–3/1989, 169–182. Praha: Karolinum.

– (1991): Funkční ekvivalence: Podmínka adekvátnosti překladu. Osersův překlad Čapkovy Války s mloky. – In: *Translatologica Pragensia V,* Acta Universitatis Carolinae Philologica 4–5/1991, 211–222. Praha: Karolinum.

Koller, Werner (1979): *Einfürung in die Übersetzungswissenschaft.* Heidelberg-Wiesbaden: Quelle und Meyer.

Kopeckij, L. V. (1935): O lexikálním plánu hospodářského jazyka. *Slovo a slovesnost I.* Praha: Pražský lingvistický kroužek.

Kořenský, Jan, Cvrček, František, Novák, František (1999): *Juristická a lingvistická analýza právních textů. Právněinformatický přístup.* Praha: Academia.

Kraus, Jiří (1995): Existuje rétorika vědeckého jazyka? – In: J. Jančáková, M. Komárek, O. Uličný, (eds.): *Spisovná čeština a jazyková kultura 1993,* 195–200. Praha: FF UK.

Krieger, S. H., Neumann, R. K., McManus, K. H., Jamar, S. D. (1999): *Essential Lawyering Skills.* New York: Aspen Law&Business

Kuhn, Sherman (1980): The Art of Writing a Definition that Does Not Define. – In: L. Zgusta, (ed.): *Theory and Method in Lexicography: Western and Non-Western Perspectives,* 115–121. Columbia: Hornbeam Press.

Kurzon, Dennis (1986): *It Is Hereby Performed...: Explorations in Legal Speech Acts.* Amsterdam: John Benjamins Publishing Company.

Lambert , José (1993): Translation, Societies and the Shift of Values. *Folia Translatologica* Vol. 2, 27–49. Prague: Charles University Faculty of Arts.

Landau, Sidney I. (1993, 2001): *Dictionaries: The Art and Craft of Lexicography.* Cambridge, England: University Press.

– (1993): Wierzbicka's Theory and the Practice of Lexicography. – In: W. S. Chisholm (ed.): *Dictionaries. Journal of the Dictionary Society of North America,* N. 14, 1992/1993, 113–119. Cleveland: Cleveland State University.

Lavigne, Eric (2001): Translation Tools in the Translation Service of the European Commission. – In: S. Šarčević (ed.):, *Legal Translation. Preparation for Accession to the European Union,* 35–64. Rijeka: University of Rijeka.

Leclercq, H. (1982): What About the Determination of the Term "term". – In: W. Nedobity, (ed.): *Terminologies for the Eighties, Infoterm Series 7,* 137–143. Munich: K. G. Saur.

Legislativní pravidla vlády (The Rules of Legislative Drafting). Resolution of the Government of the Czech Republic N. 596 of 14th June 2000. (in Czech).

Lehrberger, J. (1986): Sublanguage Analysis. – In: R. Grishman, R. Kittredge, R. (eds.), *Analyzing Language in Restricted Domains,* 19–38. Hillsdale, New Jersey: Lawrence Elbaum Associates.

Lewandowska-Tomaszczyk, Barbara (1990): Meaning, Synonymy, and the Dictionary. – In: J. Tomaszczyk, B. Lewandowska-Tomaszczyk (eds.): *Meaning and Lexicography, Linguistic and Literary Studies in Eastern Europe* Vol. 28, 181–208. Amsterdam: John Benjamins Publishing Company.

Lind, Age (1998): Semantic Booby-Traps and Lexicographic Minefields: On the Making of a Norwegian-English Dictionary of Law. – In: A. Zettersten, V. H. Pedersen, J. E. Mogensen (eds.): Symposium on Lexicography VIII. *Lexicographica Series Maior* 90, 209–216. Tubingen: Niemeyer.

Lotko, Edvard (2000): *Slovník lingvistických termínů pro filology.* Olomouc: Univerzita Palackého v Olomouci.

Louisiana Civil Code 1996. St. Paul: West Publishing Co.

Lundquist, Lita, Picht, Heribert, Qvistgaard, Jacques (eds.) (1998): *LSP Identity and Interface Research, Knowledge and Society.* Proceedings of the 11th European Symposium of Language for Special Purposes, Vol. I, II, Copenhagen, August 1997 Copenhagen: Copenhagen Business School.

Mackintosh, Kristen (1998): An Empirical Study of Dictionary Use in L2-L1 Translation. *Lexicographica Series Maior* 88, Using Dictionaries, ed. by B. T. Sue Atkins, 123–149. Tubingen: Niemeyer.

Madar, Zdeněk a kol. (1995): *Slovník českého práva.I, II.* – Praha: Linde.

Makkai, Adam (1980): Theoretical and Practical Aspects of an Associative Lexicon for 20th century English. – In: L. Zgusta, (ed.): *Theory and Method in Lexicography: Western and Non-Western Perspectives,* 125–146. Columbia: Hornbeam Press.

Malkiel, Jakov (1980): The Lexicographer as a Mediator Between Linguistics and Society. – In: L. Zgusta, (ed.): *Theory and Method in Lexicography: Western and Non-Western Perspectives*, 43–58. Columbia: Hornbeam Press.

Marconi, Diego (1997): *Lexical Competence*. Cambridge, Massachusetts: The MIT Press.

Martin, Elizabeth A. (2002): *Dictionary of Law*. – Oxford: Oxford University Press.

Martin, Willy J. R., Al Bernard P. F., Van Sterkenburg, Piet J. G. (1983): On the Processing of a Text Corpus. – In: Hartmann, R. R. K. (ed.), *Lexicography: Principles and Practice*, 77–87. London: Academic Press.

Mellinkoff, David (1992): *Mellinkoff's Dictionary of American Legal Usage*. – St. Paul: West Publishing Co.

Meyer, I., Skuce, D., Kavanagh, J., Davidson, L. (1997) Integrating linguistic and conceptual analysis in a WWW-based tool for terminography. Available:
http://www.cs.queensu.ca/achallc97/papers/p021.html [accessed: August 4, 2003].

Morris, Marshall (ed.) (1995): *Translation and the Law*. American Translators Association. Scholarly Monograph Series, Volume VIII 1995 Amsterdam, Philadelphia: John Benjamins Publishing Company.

Moulin, André (1983): LSP Dictionaries for EFL Learners. – In: Hartmann, R. R. K. (ed.), *Lexicography: Principles and Practice*, 144–152. London: Academic Press.

Mounin, Georges (1999): Teoretické problémy překladu (translated into Czech from French original *Les Problemes théoretique de la traduction*, Editions Gallimard, 1990) Praha: Karolinum.

Munday, Jeremy (2003): *Translation Studies. Theories and Applications*. London: Routledge.

Nedobity, Wolfgang (ed.) (1982): *Terminologies for the Eighties*. Infoterm Series 7 Munich: K. G. Saur.

Newmark, Peter (1981): *Approaches to Translation*. Oxford: Pergamon Press.

– (1988): *A Textbook of Translation*. London: Prentice Hall Int.

– (2003): *A Textbook of Translation*. 7th impression. London: Prentice Hall Int.

Nida, Eugene (1964): *Toward a Science of Translating*. Leiden: E.J.Brill.

– (1975): *Language Structure and Translation*. Stanford: Stanford University Press.

Nord, Christiane (1991): *Text analysis in translation*. Amsterdam / Atlanta: Rodopi.

– (1997): A Functional Typology of Translations. – In: A. Trosborg, (ed.): *Text Typology and Translation*, 43–66. Amsterdam: Benjamins.

– (1999): Translating as a Text-Production Activity. http://www.fut.es/~apym/symp/nord.html (accessed 31 August 2003).

Ooi, Vincent B. Y. (1998): *Computer Corpus Lexicography*. Edinburgh Textbooks in Empirical Linguistics Series, Editors: Tony McEnry, Andrew Wilson. Edinburgh: Edinburgh University Press.

Opitz, Kurt (1983a): On Dictionaries for Special Registers. – In: Hartmann, R. R. K. (ed.), *Lexicography: Principles and Practice*, 53–64. London: Academic Press.

– (1983b): The Terminological/Standardised Dictionary. – In: Hartmann, R. R. K. (ed.), *Lexicography: Principles and Practice*, 163–180. London: Academic Press.

Pearson, Jennifer (1998): *Terms in Context*. Amsterdam: John Benjamins Publishing Company.

Penner, James (2001): *Mozley and Whiteley's Law Dictionary*. – London: Butterworths Tolley.

Picht, H., Draskau, J. (1985): *Terminology. An Introduction*. Guildford: University of Surrey.

Picht, Heribert (1982): Reflexions on Training in Terminology in the 1980s. – In: W. Nedobity, (ed.): *Terminologies for the Eighties, Infoterm Series 7*, 172–185. Munich: K. G. Saur.

Piotrowski, Tadeusz (1990): The Meaning-Text Model of Language and Practical Lexicography. – In: J. Tomaszczyk, B. Lewandowska-Tomaszczyk (eds.): *Meaning and Lexicography, Linguistic and Literary Studies in Eastern Europe* Vol. 28, 277–286. Amsterdam: John Benjamins Publishing Company.

Poštolková, B., Roudný, M., Tejnor, A. (1983): *O české terminologii*, Praha: Academia.

Poštolková, Běla (1984): *Odborná a běžná slovní zásoba současné češtiny*, Studie ČSAV 21–84, Praha: Academia.

Pym, Anthony (1997): *Koller's Äquivalenz Revisited.* On-Line Reviews http://www.fut.es/~apym/on-line/reviews/kollerreview.html. (accessed November 5, 2003). Originally published in *The Translator*, Manchester: St Jerome, 3/1 (1997), 71–79.

Quirk, Randolph, Greenbaum, Sidney, Leech, Geoffrey, Svartvik, Jan (1995): *A Comprehensive Grammar of the English Language.* London: Longman.

Reed, David (1993): Some Terminological Problems of Translating Common Law Concepts from English to French. – In: H. S. Sonneveld, K. L. Loening (eds.): *Terminology: Applications in Interdisciplinary Communication.* 79–86. Amsterdam: John Benjamins Publishing Company.

Riggs, Fred. W. (1982): Descriptive Terminology. Its Relevance for the Social Sciences. – In: W. Nedobity, (ed.): *Terminologies for the Eighties, Infoterm Series 7*, 144–160. Munich: K. G. Saur.

– (1989): Terminology and Lexicography: Their Complementarity. *International Journal of Lexicography* 1989, v. 2, N. 2 (ed.) Robert Ilson, 89 –110. Oxford: Oxford University Press.

– (1993): Social Science Terminology: Basic Problems and Proposed Solutions. – In: H. S. Sonneveld, K. L. Loening (eds.): *Terminology: Applications in Interdisciplinary Communication*, 195–220. Amsterdam: John Benjamins Publishing Company.

Riley, Alison (1995): The Meaning of Words in English Legal Texts: Mastering the Vocabulary of the Law – A Legal Task. *Law Teacher 29–30*, 1995, 68–83. London: Sweet and Maxwell.

Rogers, Margaret (1997): Synonymy and Equivalence of Special-language Texts. In: *Text Typology and Translation,* edited by Anna Trosborg, Benjamins Translation Library, Volume 26, 217–245. Amsterdam: John Benjamins Publishing Company.

Rogers, M., Ahmad, K. (1998): The Translator and the Dictionary: Beyond Words? *Lexicographica Series Maior* 88, Using Dictionaries ed. by B. T. Sue Atkins, 193–204. Tubingen: Niemeyer.

Sager, Juan C. (1981): Approaches to Terminology and the Teaching of Terminology. *Fachsprache*, Vol. 3, 3–4/1981, 98–106. Wien: Wilhelm Braumuller.

– (1990): *A Practical Course in Terminology Processing.* Amsterdam: John Benjamins Publishing Company.

– (1997): Text Types and Translation. – In: A. Trosborg, (ed.): *Text Typology and Translation*, 25–42 . Amsterdam: Benjamins.

Sager, J. C., Dungworth, D., McDonald, P. F. (1980): *English Special Languages: Principles and Practice of Science and Technology.* Wiesbaden: Brandstetter Verlag.

Sekaninová, Ella (1993): *Dvojjazyčná lexikológia v teórii a praxi.* Bratislava: Veda, SAV.

Shvejtser, Alexander (1993): The Cultural Barrier and Translation Strategies. Translation Strategies and Effects in Cross-Cultural Value Transfer and Shifts. Folia Translatologica Vol. 2, 1993, 101–104. Praha: Karolinum.

Schelle, Karel / Schelleova, Ilona (2002): *Rozhodčí řízení.* Praha: Eurolex Bohemia.

Simeoni, Daniel (1993): Lexis, Rhetoric and Institutional Transfer in the Translation of Public Discourse – The Case of Institutional Metaphor. *Translation Strategies and Effects in Cross-Cultural Value Transfer and Shifts. Folia Translatologica* Vol. 2, 1993, 71–86. Praha: Karolinum.

Sinclair, John M. (1995): Introduction. *Collins Cobuild English Dictionary.* London: Harper-Collins.

Sinclair, John et al. (1996): Corpus to Corpus: A Study of Translation Equivalence. *International Journal of Lexicography* 1996, v. 9, N. 3, special issue (ed.) R. Ilson, guest editors J. Sinclair, J. Payne, C. Perez Hernandes, 171–178. Oxford: Oxford University Press.

Sinclair, J. M., Coulthard, R. M. (1975): *Towards an Analysis of Discourse: The English Used by Teachers and Pupils.* London: Oxford University Press.

Smith, Sylvia (1995): Culture Clash: Anglo-American Case Law and German Civil Law in Translation. – In: M. Morris, (ed.): *Translation and the Law* (ed.). *American Translators Association Series* Volume VIII, 1995, 179–200. Amsterdam, Philadelphia: John Benjamins Publishing Company.

Snell-Hornby, M., Pöhl, E., Bennani, B., (eds.) (1989): *Translation and Lexicography.* Amsterdam: John Benjamins Publishing Company.

Snell-Hornby, Mary (1988): *Translation Studies, An Integrated Approach.* Amsterdam: John Benjamins Publishing Company.

– (1990): Dynamics in Meaning as a Problem in Bilingual Lexicography. – In: J. Tomaszczyk, B. Lewandowska-Tomaszczyk (eds.): *Meaning and Lexicography, Linguistic and Literary Studies in Eastern Europe* Vol. 28, 209–226. Amsterdam: John Benjamins Publishing Company.

Solan, Lawrence M. (1993): *The Language of Judges*. Chicago, London: The University of Chicago Press.

Sonneveld, H. S., Loening, K. L. (eds.) (1993): *Terminology: Applications in Interdisciplinary Communication*. Amsterdam: John Benjamins Publishing Company.

Steiner, Roger J. (1989): The Absence of Text: The Bilingual Dictionary as an Index. *International Journal of Lexicography* 1989, v. 2, N. 3 (ed.) Robert Ilson, guest editor Fredric Dolezal, 249–257. Oxford: Oxford University Press.

Straková, Vlasta (1990): K otázkám překladu odborného textu. *Translatologica Pragensia IV*, Acta Universitatis Carolinae Philologica 4/1994, 17–22. Praha: Karolinum.

Superanskaja, A. V., Podolskaja, N. V., Vasileva, N. V. (1989): *Obshtchaja Terminologija: Voprosy teorii*. Moskva: Nauka.

Swales, John (1981): Definitions in Science and Law – Evidence for Subject-Specific Course Components. *Fachsprache*, Vol. 3, 3–4/1981, 106–112. Wien: Wilhelm Braumuller.

– (1990): *Genre Analysis. English in Academic and Research Settings*. Cambridge: Cambridge University Press.

Šarčević, Susan (1989a): Conceptual Dictionaries for Translation in the Field of Law. *International Journal of Lexicography* 2/4, (ed.) Robert Ilson, 277–293. Oxford: Oxford University Press.

– (1989b): Lexicography and Translation Across Cultures. – In: M. Snell-Hornby, E. Pöhl, B. Bennani (eds.): *Translation and Lexicography*, 211–222. Amsterdam: John Benjamins Publishing Company.

– (2000): *New Approach to Legal Translation*. The Hague, London, Boston: Kluwer Law International.

– (2001): Translation Procedures for Legal Translators. – In: S. Šarčević (ed.):, *Legal Translation. Preparation for Accession to the European Union*, 75–110. Rijeka: University of Rijeka.

– (ed.) (2001): *Legal Translation. Preparation for Accession to the European Union*. Rijeka: University of Rijeka.

Teubert, Wolfgang (1996): Comparable or Parallel Corpora? *International Journal of Lexicography* 1996, v. 9, N. 3, special issue (ed.) R. Ilson, guest editors J. Sinclair, J. Payne, C. Perez Hernandes, 238–264. Oxford: Oxford University Press.

Thomas, Patricia (1993): Choosing Headwords from Language-for-Special-Purposes LSP. Collocations for Entry into a Terminology Data Bank. Term Bank. – In: H. S. Sonneveld, K. L. Loening (eds.): *Terminology: Applications in Interdisciplinary Communication*, 43–68. Amsterdam: John Benjamins Publishing Company.

Tiersma, Peter M. (1999): *Legal Language*. Chicago and London: The University of Chicago Press.

Tognini-Bonelli, Elena (1996): Towards Translation Equivalence from a Corpus Linguistics Perspective. *International Journal of Lexicography* 1996, v. 9, N. 3, special issue (ed.) R. Ilson, guest editors J. Sinclair, J. Payne, C. Perez Hernandes, 179–196. Oxford: Oxford University Press.

Tomaszczyk, Jerzy (1983): On Bilingual Dictionaries. – In: Hartmann, R. R. K. (ed.), *Lexicography: Principles and Practice*, 41–51. London: Academic Press.

Tomaszczyk, J., Lewandowska-Tomaszczyk, B., (eds.) (1990): *Meaning and Lexicography*. Linguistic and Literary Studies in Eastern Europe Vol. 28, Amsterdam: John Benjamins Publishing Company.

Tomášek, Michal (1990):. K vybraným problémům překladu právního jazyka. *Translatologica Pragensia IV*, Acta Universitatis Carolinae Philologica 4/1994, 113–120. Praha: Karolinum.

– (1991): Právo – interpretace a překlad. – In: *Translatologica Pragensia V*, Acta Universitatis Carolinae Philologica 4–5/1991, 147–157. Praha: Karolinum.

– (1998): *Překlad v právní praxi*. Praha: Linde.

Toury, Gideon (1990): Translation-specific Lexical Items and Their Representation in the Dictionary. – In: J. Tomaszczyk, B. Lewandowska-Tomaszczyk (eds.): *Meaning and Lexicography, Linguistic and Literary Studies in Eastern Europe* Vol. 28, 287–300. Amsterdam: John Benjamins Publishing Company.

Trimble, Louis (1985): *English for Science and Technology: A Discourse Approach.* Cambridge: Cambridge University Press.

Trosborg, Anna (ed.) (1997a): *Text Typology and Translation.* Benjamins Translation Library, Volume 26. Amsterdam: John Benjamins Publishing Company.

– (1997b): *Rhetorical Strategies in Legal Language. Discourse Analysis of Statutes and Contracts.* Tubingen: Gunter Narr Verlag.

Van der Meer, Geart (1998): How to Find the Correct Target Language Equivalent. – In: A. Zettersten, V. H. Pedersen, J. E. Mogensen (eds.): Symposium on Lexicography VIII. *Lexicographica Series Maior* 90, 217–228. Tubingen: Niemeyer.

Vančura, Zdeněk (1934): *Hospodářská linguistika: Pokus o její teorii.* Praha.

Varantola, Krista (1998): Translators and their Use of Dictionaries. *Lexicographica Series Maior* 88, Using Dictionaries ed. by B. T. Sue Atkins, 179–192. Tubingen: Niemeyer.

Vermeer, Hans J. (1978): Ein rahmen für eine allgemeine translationstheorie. Reprinted in Hans J. Vermeer (ed.) 1983. *Aufsätze zur Translationstheorie*, 48–61. Heidelberg: Vermeer.

Weinreich, U., Labov, W., Weinreich, B. S. (eds.) (1980): *On Semantics.* University of Pennsylvania Press.

White, James Boyd (1990): *Justice as Translation: An Essay in Cultural and Legal Criticism.* Chicago and London: The University of Chicago Press.

Widdowson, Henry G. (1979a): *Explorations in Applied Linguistics.* Oxford: Oxford University Press.

– (1979b): Rules and procedures in discourse analysis. – In: T. Myers (ed.): *The Development of Conversation and Discourse,* 61–71. Edinburgh: Edinburgh University Press.

Wierzbicka, Anna (1993): What Are the Uses of Theoretical Lexicography? – In: W. S. Chisholm (ed.): *Dictionaries. Journal of the Dictionary Society of North America,* N. 14, 1992/1993, 44–78. Cleveland: Cleveland State University.

Zettersten, A., Pedersen, V. H., Mogensen, J. E. (eds.) (1998): *Symposium on Lexicography VIII Lexicographica Series Maior* 90, Tubingen: Niemeyer.

Zgusta, Ladislav (1971): *Manual of Lexicography.* Praha: Academia, The Hague: Mouton.

– (ed.) (1980): *Theory and Method in Lexicography: Western and Non-Western Perspectives.* Columbia: Hornbeam Press.

– (1980): Some Remarks on the Context of Lexicography. – In: L. Zgusta, (ed.): *Theory and Method in Lexicography: Western and Non-Western Perspectives*, 3–29. Columbia: Hornbeam Press.

– (1993): Lexicography, Its Theory and Linguistics. – In: W. S. Chisholm (ed.): *Dictionaries. Journal of the Dictionary Society of North America,* N. 14, 1992/1993, 130–138. Cleveland: Cleveland State University.

Zimová, J., Koníčková, N. (1989): Příruční rusko-český slovník obecné, obecněvědní a obecněprávní slovní zásoby v právnických textech I, II. Praha: SPN.

Žemlička, Milan (1995): K vývojovým předpokladům současné odborné terminologie. – In: J. Jančáková, M. Komárek, O. Uličný, (eds.): *Spisovná čeština a jazyková kultura 1993*, 201–203. Praha: FF UK.

Law Dictionaries

A Dictionary of Modern Legal Usage. (1995). B. Garner. – Oxford, New York: Oxford University Press.

Black's Law Dictionary. (1999). B. Garner (ed.). – St. Paul: West Group.

Burton's Legal Thesaurus. (1998). W. Burton. – New York: McGraw-Hill.

Czech-English Law Dictionary with Explanations. (2001, 2003). M. Chromá. – Praha: Leda.

Dictionary of Law. (2000). P. Collin (ed.). – London: Peter Collin Publishing Ltd.

Dictionary of Law. 6th ed. (2002). L. Curzon (ed.). – Harlow: Pearson Education - Longman.

Dictionary of Law. (2002).E. A. Martin (ed.). – Oxford: Oxford University Press.

English-Czech Law Dictionary. (1995). M. Chromá. – Praha: Leda.

Mellinkoff's Dictionary of American Legal Usage. (1992). D. Mellinkoff. – St. Paul: West Publishing Co.
Mozley and Whiteley's Law Dictionary. (2001). J. Penner (ed.). – London: Butterworths Tolley.
Osborn's Concise Law Dictionary. (2001). S. Bone (ed.). – London: Sweet&Maxwell Ltd.
Slovník českého práva.I, II. (1995). Z. Madar (ed.). – Praha: Linde.

English language dictionaries

Collins Cobuild English Dictionary (1995). – London: HarperCollins Publishers.
Longman Dictionary of English Languages and Culture (1992). – Longman Group UK Limited.
Oxford English Dictionary (2002). CD ed. – Oxford: OUP.
Webster's New World Dictionary. Student ed. (1981). – New York: Simon&Schuster.

Czech language dictionaries

Slovník spisovného jazyka českého (1989). B. Havránek (ed.). Praha: Academia
Malý staročeský slovník. (1978). J. Bělič, A. Kamiš, K. Kučera (eds.). Praha: SPN.
Slovník lingvistických termínů pro filology. (2000). E. Lotko. Olomouc: Univerzita Palackého v Olomouci.

Bei Fragen zur Produktsicherheit wenden Sie sich bitte an:
If you have any questions regarding product safety,
please contact:

Walter de Gruyter GmbH
Genthiner Straße 13
10785 Berlin
productsafety@degruyterbrill.com